KINSHIP
IN AN
URBAN SETTING

KINSHIP
IN AN
URBAN SETTING

Bert N. Adams

UNIVERSITY OF
WISCONSIN

MARKHAM PUBLISHING COMPANY
CHICAGO

To Diane

Preface

For many years sociologists living and working in an urban-industrial society virtually ignored kinship relations as a topic for serious research investigation. The 1950's and 1960's, however, have seen the appearance of many brief discussions of urban social interaction, kin functioning, and parent-adult offspring mutual aid, as well as lengthier treatises on various aspects of kinship in the Western World. The result has been some contradictory conclusions, several tentative ideas, a few established findings, and some terminological confusion. Despite this state of affairs interest in the phenomena of urban kinship continues unabated.

The purpose of the present work is three-fold: to *synthesize* as much of the relevant literature as seems feasible; to *characterize* kin networks and relations in one urban place according to their subjective and objective dimensions; and to *focus* many issues which cannot be resolved by means of a broad-scale or extensive research design carried out in one city. Characterization includes such problematic features of the extant literature as the effects of the economic-occupational values of urban society upon kin relations, and the roles of adult siblings, cousins, and other kin in the life of the city dweller. Yet quite obviously, in the process of summarizing and answering certain questions, others will merely be posed—thus, the three-fold nature of our purpose.

It is an extremely rewarding experience to investigate an aspect of social experience or existence upon which we all perceive ourselves to be expert. For each individual brings first-hand knowledge of kinship into the interview setting. Nevertheless, the author must continually remind himself that he, too, has kin whom he treats, and about whom he feels, one way or another. Perhaps some comfort may be found in the fact that in the course of the present study, which is exploratory at many points, the author's presuppositions (even his nascent hypotheses) are found as often as not to be incorrect. The very commonness of kin involvements, we must add, and the respondents' openness to discuss them, must be given much of the credit for any insights contained in this volume.

One difficulty in an attempt to synthesize concerns terminology. Authors and researchers frequently utilize different phrases or terms with a single referent. For example, the extended family, the wider kin group, the kin network, and the kindred, have been used at various times to indicate the same social category. Likewise contacting, seeing, visiting, and interacting all pertain to the behavior of two individuals *vis-à-vis* each other. Because of such difficulties, we have included in Appendix B a glossary of the more fundamental or basic terms employed in this study.

Books are corporate endeavors; their authors draw upon many experiences and the ideas of others in the course of their completion. Only a few intellectual debts can even be acknowledged, much less repaid. Acknowledgement seldom can or should go beyond those who have had a relatively direct hand in the accomplishment of the task; and so it is in the present work. The author wishes particularly to express appreciation to the National Institute of Mental Health, whose Public Health Service Fellowship (MH-15,571) made possible the collecting and processing of the data contained herein. Invaluable assistance, in the form of encouragement in the early stages of the research and critical suggestions concerning certain aspects of the manuscript, was received from Charles E. Bowerman and Richard Simpson. Other valuable ideas were offered by Michael T. Aiken, Anthony Costonis, and Howard E. Freeman, in their reading of certain portions of the material. It was John Gulick who aroused the desire to learn about urban kinship which eventuated in the present project.

The incisive, enthusiastic, and accurate work of interviewers Joan Munger, Richard Knapp, Gwendolyn and Blake Tharin, Don Campbell, and Donald Ploch contributed greatly to the accomplishment of our task. The Institute for Research in Social Science, University of North Carolina, and Computer Center, University of Wisconsin, made their research facilities available so that the data could be analyzed. Finally, the editorial staff of Markham Publishing Company made suggestions which contributed greatly to the readability of the manuscript.

Bert Newton Adams
August 10, 1967

Table of Contents

List of Tables

Chapter I

AN INTRODUCTION
TO URBAN KINSHIP

The changing world of the mid-twentieth century has as a key
dimension the trend toward urbanization. This trend is both demo-
graphic and social; that is, the proportion of the world's population
living in urban places is ever increasing, and the influence of urban
ways is a pervasive phenomenon. In keeping with the trend, materials describing numerous aspects of urban existence now abound.

Cities are those agglomerations of people and activities where
the major functions of the industrial society are carried out. Cities
are economic and political foci, whose interconnections and influence over their surrounding regions are unquestionable. Movement
of people from urban place to urban place in search of economic
and/or professional opportunity is an accepted aspect of urban life.
So is the fact that the social networks of urban dwellers are not en-
compassed within the communities in which they live. Not only are
many of their immediate social contacts of a segmental and impersonal nature, but the means of communication and transportation
make possible the continuing viability of relationships despite residential separation. Thus, economic motivations, specialization, seg-
mentalization, and social network scatter are generally recognized
concomitants of urban residence.

There are, however, features of city life which too infrequently
have been subjected to intensive analysis. One of these is kinship
relations. Despite the emphasis given to kinship in anthropological
studies of exotic peoples, such a concern has been peripheral to sociological studies of Western urbanism.[1] In the 1920's, '30's, and

1

'40's, kinship was ignored by urban sociologists as relatively unimportant, while in the 1950's and '60's its acknowledged significance appears to have been overshadowed by its complexity. The
result has been several sociological studies of specific aspects of
urban kinship, as well as a few key monographs by anthropologists
on the subject, as they have turned their attention to Western society.

The kinship system has adapted to urban, industrial society.[2] For
some this has meant residential separation and utilization of the
means of communication for keeping in touch with kin. For many
it has meant an alteration in the kinds of activities engaged in with
kin. For all it has meant reconciling the economic-achievement motives of modern society with the particularistic obligations and ex-
pectations inherent in kinship relations. This monograph is about
kinship relations in one middle-sized city. It seeks to answer many
of the questions concerning the functioning of the kin network in
such a setting. While exploratory at many points, there has also
been considerable groundwork laid in previous studies. Thus, we
begin with a discussion of what is known about urban kin relations
in Western society.

What Is Known?

(1) *Western urban kinship is bilateral in nature.* Except for
tracing surnames through the male line there is normative equality
in relations with the two sets of kindred. Of course, practical devia-
tions from bilaterality in kin involvements are dictated by the volitional or "choice" character of the kin relations of any specific individual or couple.[3]

(2) *Urban man has primary relationships, among them certain
kin,* as well as the impersonal and segmental relations often perceived as characteristic of urban life. That the urbanite lacked such
relations is an inference drawn from the "classical urban theory" of
the Chicago school of sociology by certain of its critics. This viewpoint, in terms of kin relations, may be briefly summarized as
follows.[4] According to Louis Wirth, urbanites may be best characterized by secondary rather than intimate or primary relationships.
Other institutions than the family and kin group care for health,

help in hardships, and provide for education, recreation, and cultural advancement. The fact is, Wirth asserts, that "the family as a unit of social life is emancipated from the larger kinship group characteristic of the country, and the individual members pursue their own diverging interests in their vocational, educational, religious, recreational, and political life."[5] The customary residential pattern is neolocal, newly married couples ordinarily settling apart from both sets of parents. At marriage, then, the individual is drastically segregated, in comparison with other societies, from his parents and siblings. Such an isolated, open, kinship system seems most functional for or well adapted to our occupational system and urban living.[6]

While the proponents of this point of view were in fact writing comparatively and historically, the supposed notion that urbanites are isolated from primary relations has since been dispelled again and again in studies of the friendship and kinship contacts of urbanites. These observations invariably "call into question those propositions of urban sociology which suggest that the city . . . denies its residents the opportunities for the kind of intimate social relations that contribute to social integration."[7] The great difference between urban and rural dwellers is not in the lesser amount of "primary" social interaction among the former, but in the greater amount of secondary, or impersonal and segmental, contact among them. The urbanite has primary social relationships, some of which are provided by the kin network.[8]

(3) Besides furnishing primary relationships, *urban kindred function* in several other ways. A body of literature has arisen refuting the idea that economic and other needs formerly met within the kin network are now being served solely by non-kin agencies. Mutual aid, especially between parents and their adult children, is a safeguard against the impersonality and competitiveness of city life. Furthermore, the kin network often plays a positive role in residential migration, one individual or family establishing an economic and residential "foothold" in a community, to be followed there later by other kin.[9]

(4) *Degree of kin relationship influences greatly the degree of actual interpersonal involvement in bilateral systems.* Parents are

almost uniformly intimate or primary kin, with siblings next in importance, and other kin, such as aunts, uncles, and cousins, on the whole, of lesser importance.[10]

(5) Working-class people are less likely to be residentially mobile in search of occupational opportunities than are middle-class people. The result is that *working-class kin networks are generally less scattered* geographically, *and* are therefore *available for more frequent interaction.*[11]

(6) *Females are more involved in kin affairs* than are males. They bear the major burden of the general obligation to keep in touch with kin, and mother-daughter and sister relationships are ordinarily found to be subjectively or attitudinally closer than are the other sibling and parent-child relationships according to the individual's sex.[12]

While other characteristics of urban kin relations have been discussed in various works, the foregoing are especially well substantiated. In summary, it is known that Western urban kinship relations are normatively bilateral, and provide primary relationships, mutual aid, and other services for urban dwellers. Comparatively, parent–adult-offspring relations are the closest both subjectively and objectively, or interactionally, while working-class kin networks are closer objectively and female kin closer subjectively than their categorical alternatives.

Open Questions

What is known or established regarding urban kinship is easily balanced by the problematic, the tentatively concluded, and the uninvestigated. Among the open questions are the following: (1) *What are the occasions for and kinds of interaction between kin, and what is their significance?* The sources affirming the existence of primary relationships in urban places have used as their principal, and in some cases their sole, criterion frequency of interaction. Whether this is an adequate indicator of relationship significance remains to be demonstrated. Although several studies discuss mutual aid, and a few report kin interaction on special occasions, such as holidays, there is still relatively little information on the occasions for and kinds of interaction between kin in an urban setting. Recreational activity, visiting in the home, working or shopping together, belonging to the same religious or other organization—all these are possible circumstances under which kin interaction might occur.[13] Each of these is, in turn, likely to have its peculiar rationale, whether enjoyment, assistance, or the reinforcing of kin bonds.

(2) *What are the subjective or attitudinal dimensions of urban kinship?* Affectional ties to one's parents are assumed to be close, but the conditions for variation in affection toward parents and other kin have not been spelled out. A second subjective aspect of urban kin relations is their role as a comparative reference group. Tamotsu Shibutani defines this as "a standard or check point which an actor uses in forming his estimate of the situation, particularly his own position within it."[14] Although any aggregate, group, or individual may be utilized as such a reference or comparison point, one's kindred are immediately and perpetually available for this purpose. "How am I doing?" is readily answerable with reference to one's parents, brothers, and sisters. While noted in a few studies, research on the process and extent of identification and comparison within the kin network has been negligible.[15]

A third important subjective aspect of social relations, including those between kin, concerns values and interests. That values, affection, and interaction are related is a general postulate of interaction theory. However, the extent or significance of value consensus within the kin network has been ignored. The fourth subjective factor—kin obligation—is not simply based on the "social responsibility norm," that is, on the receipt of past help.[16] Rather it is based on the fact that the relationship exists. It tends to be reciprocal, so that each party has both rights and duties, as exemplified in relations between adult offspring and their aging parents.[17] What is not known, however, is the effect of obligation upon the relationship. To the economic-achievement oriented person, kin obligation, while a major feature of urban kinship, is barbaric and anachronistic.[18] To the adjustment oriented person, selective obligation to kin is one method the family uses to adapt to industrialism and the urban environment.[19] The question regarding kinship obligation is thus two-fold: how does kin obligation vary with degree of relationship, and is strong obligation, when present, an alienative element?

(3) *What is the characteristic relationship between adult siblings or more genealogically distant kin in urban society?* Most studies of Western kinship focus upon young-adult–parent relations, with siblings, cousins, grandparents, and other kin treated tangentially. Thus, much additional information, both subjective and objective, is needed on these other kin in order to explicate the basic notion that a fundamental determinant of kin involvement is degree of relationship.[20] Since neolocality, or living in a residence separate from parents and siblings after marriage, is normative in our family system, it is expectable that parent-child and sibling relations will be more intense in adulthood than will relations with other kin, except under extenuating circumstances, such as being raised by an aunt or grandparents. However, the character of the various relationships has not been defined.

(4) *How does the kin network articulate with other societal systems?* The neighborhood, economic-occupational sphere, and voluntary associations are some of the systems in modern urban society which have assumed functions performed by kin in many traditional land-based societies. While certain authors have begun to investigate the complex interplay in the Western world between kinship and other community systems, much remains to be done.[21] The present study focusses primarily upon relations *within* the kin network, but reference will be made from time to time to this articulation.

(5) *What are the dimensions of the kin network?* This is the first of two issues which has not been ignored, but rather is problematic. Consideration of the questions *how many* and *where,* or the size and distribution of kin networks, has yielded extremely varied results.[22] Part of the problem has been one of definition, of whom to include in the enumeration. In addition, generalizations regarding residential movement and kin distribution diverge drastically. A. O. Haller, for example, comments that many, or most, urbanites are now second and third generation residents of the same city, with a kin web already present. Earlier Talcott Parsons had stated

that in a very large proportion of cases the geographical separation of adult children and their parents is considerable.[23] Understanding the dimensions of urban kin networks better, and reconciling such antithetical statements, would seem to be of help in relating the occupational and kin values of urbanites.

We have chosen to use the term kin network rather than kin group for a specific reason. To the lay reader the notion of group signifies a well-defined and usually localized body of persons-in-relationship. On two counts this does not quite fit the attributes of urban kin networks. For one thing, the urban kin network is seldom entirely localized; in fact, it is often greatly scattered, being held together by the telephone, the mails, and periodic visits. Furthermore, one can never definitively draw the boundaries between kin networks as mutually exclusive groups. Both because of in-laws and perceptions of kin, every person's kin network differs in some degree from every other person's.[24] Thus, we have chosen to speak of kin networks rather than kin groups, with the term "kindred" used from time to time as a comprehensive designation.

(6) *What is the effect of occupational mobility upon kin relations?* Here the problem of occupational-achievement values versus kin values is confronted directly. Certain authors have explicitly stated that "upward mobile persons keep only shallow ties with members of their kindred if they keep them at all; downward mobile persons may be neglected by their kindred."[25] This viewpoint is based upon two assumptions regarding urban life: first, occupational disparity, or difference in status, bespeaks divergent systems of life values, and different values make satisfactory social relationships difficult; and second, the social demands upon the mobile are such that they must sever former ties and establish relationships within their current occupational milieu in order to validate their social roles.

That these assumptions do not hold for kin relations in general has been argued by several authors, who conclude with Michael Young and Peter Willmott that "social mobility appears to have no marked independent influence except as it promotes geographic mobility."[26]

Partial reconciliation of these two positions regarding mobility effects is found in sex differences and degrees of relationship. Willmott and Young report that contacts between a son and his father are detrimentally affected by upward or downward mobility, but not those between the other offspring-parent combinations. Occupation is more salient in the daily life and consciousness of the male.[27] Therefore, it seems probable that a disparity between the occupational positions of two males, be they son and father, brothers, or cousins, has a greater weakening effect upon their relationship than a similar divergence between the occupational levels of two female kin, according to their husbands' occupations. Elizabeth Bott adds that mobility does not break parental ties, for the parents are considered to share in the achievement of their offspring. Rather, the more distant the relative, the more objective status differences receive consideration and determine interaction.[28]

The economic-achievement values of urban, industrial society, in their impingement upon kinship, are very likely related in too complex a fashion to be explained simply by individual occupational mobility or stability. The complexity of this, as well as the previous four questions, is well expressed in a quotation from William J. Goode on mobility and kinship. While kin networks have been found to be alive, it has not been proved that mobility does not affect family or kin patterns.

> It seems necessary to look at differing and changing patterns of communication, the frequency of interaction among kin under conditions of mobility, and the comparative size of kin networks when some siblings or relatives have been mobile and others not. In addition, it seems necessary to find out which kinds of activities are engaged in with mobile kin as against nonmobile kin; and which areas of social interaction remain, in which relatives attempt to maintain control over one another and to express family sentiment.[29]

Understanding urban kinship involves analyzing the manner in which various characteristics of urban life—residential mobility, transportation, communication, and economic-achievement values

—are related to kin interaction and attitudes. Such is the concern of this volume.

The Methodological Approach

The Setting

Greensboro, North Carolina, was selected as the location for a quasi-exploratory investigation of urban kinship. The city is more than 150 years old and includes several established or "Old South" families, in which one might expect kin ties to be relatively strong. Furthermore, Greensboro has exhibited rapid industrial growth and in-migration, as evidenced in the doubling of population between 1950 and 1964. The city is an educational and insurance center, Jefferson Standard and Pilot Life having their headquarters there, and is also the site of large-scale industries, among them hosiery and textiles, cigarettes, terra-cotta pipe, and fertilizer. Thus, while the study of one middle-sized city does not permit generalization to all urban places, Greensboro does incorporate within it a valuable cross-section of the geographically mobile and stable, migrants from the nearby farm and from the Northeastern metropolis, white collar and blue collar families.

The Sample

During the summers of 1963 and 1964 interviews were administered to 799 individuals in Greensboro. The sample was drawn by means of a block sampling procedure, and several restrictions were placed upon inclusion. All of the respondents were to be white, married, married only once, and for twenty years or less. It was felt that, within the operating budget of the study, it would be impossible to sample adequately all age or racial groups, or various marital statuses. The limiting of investigation to young-to-middle-aged, white, marrieds, was believed to guarantee maximum extension of the kin network, since a large proportion of the respondents' parents were still living and few of their own children had left home.

The respondents included 467 females and 332 males. The median age of the husbands was 34.5 years, the wives 32.3 years, and their median length of marriage was ten years and ten months. Outright refusals numbered seventy-three, or 8.8 per cent of the total number of persons approached.

If the husband was at home, he was ordinarily interviewed in preference to the wife. Approximately once in every four cases the wife was interviewed in the evening even though the husband was available, in order not to underrepresent working wives. All interviews were conducted in private, i.e., the spouse was not present as the questions were asked. The predominance of females is explained by the greater likelihood of their being home.

Kinship is not a difficult subject on which to interview. Once the individual was convinced that the interview did not pertain to intimate aspects of his personal life, a frequently overt reaction went something like this: "Well, what are relatives for if you can't talk about them?" Another part of the interviewers' impression was that the great majority of young married Greensboroites, regardless of positive or negative feelings toward specific kin, considered themselves experts on such matters. This "expertise" and the accompanying frankness of response was noted by each of the six interviewers as a definite asset to the study.

Factors Affecting Kinship

Three key factors which affect kin relations in urban, industrial society, according to the sources already available, include the sex of the individual, his or her occupational status or level, and residential history. Besides noting the sex of the respondent, the sex of each relative they discussed, such as cousins, was also ascertained.

A result of sampling which at first puzzled the author is the distribution of respondents according to occupational strata. The sample includes, according to the husband's occupation, 197 top professional and high managerial persons (25 per cent), 289 lesser managerial, sales, and clerical (37 per cent), 174 skilled craftsmen and foremen (22 per cent), and 128 semi-skilled and unskilled (16 per cent). The 62 per cent white collar diverges considerably from the proportion of male heads-of-households in Greensboro reported to be white collar in the 1960 census, which is 46.5 per cent.[30] However, upon further inspection it is evident that two restrictions placed upon sample inclusion, i.e., whites only and married but once, account for virtually the total discrepancy between the sample and the city in stratum proportions. Almost 25 per cent of Greensboro's population is non-white, and of the non-whites 71 per cent are in semi- or unskilled positions. When the non-whites are omitted, the percentages of white male heads-of-households in the four occupational categories are: 22 per cent professional and high managerial, 34 per cent lesser managerial, sales, and clerical, 20 per cent skilled craftsmen and foremen, and 24 per cent semi-skilled and unskilled. While the lower blue-collar category is still underrepresented by some 8 per cent in the sample, this discrepancy is accounted for by the greater prevalence of broken homes at the lower occupational levels.[31]

The basic white-collar, blue-collar distinction forms the foundation for our investigation of the relation between generational occupational mobility and kinship. By our definition, the upwardly mobile are those whose fathers are, or were before retirement or death, employed in a blue-collar occupation, but who themselves are in a white-collar position. The downwardly mobile are those blue-collar persons whose fathers are or were white-collar. The stable white and blue collar are those of the same general occupational category as their parents. Within the sample there are ninety-three upwardly mobile males and 115 females, twenty-six downwardly mobile males and thirty-eight females, 111 stable white-collar males and 160 females, and eighty-six stable blue-collar males and 139 females. Thirty-one individuals are either students or did not adequately describe their own, or more often their father's, occupation, making it impossible to determine intergenerational similarity or disparity of occupational level.

Length of residence in Greensboro and migratory patterns comprise a third factor related to kinship, i.e., residential history. The respondents who have lived their whole lives in Greensboro number 207, or 26 per cent of the sample. The same percentage, in actuality 211 respondents, have been Greensboro residents for more than ten years, but not their entire lives. The percentages having resided in their present city from three to nine years, and for two or less years, are 27 and 21, respectively. Thus, there is an approximately equal division between those who have resided in Greensboro ten or more years and less than ten years.

Among the 592 who have moved to Greensboro from elsewhere, the distance from which they come is important. More than 70 per cent of the immigrants (over 50 per cent of the total sample) resided previously in North Carolina, South Carolina, or Virginia, i.e., within a radius of about 250 miles of Greensboro, with 41 per cent of the mobile having lived less than 100 miles from their present location. Eleven per cent moved from a Southern state beyond the three-state area, while 13 per cent (seventy-six respondents) migrated from the northeastern United States. The other 4 per cent (twenty-five persons) came from the Midwest, Far West, or abroad.

Kin Categories

A fundamental determinant of kin involvement, in conjunction with the above factors, is genealogical distance or degree of relationship. Three kin categories were employed throughout the present study: *parents* and *siblings*, who together are referred to from time to time as the kin of orientation (those from the same family of orientation), and *secondary* kin. The latter category includes all other kin: grandparents, aunts, uncles, cousins, and so on.

Both the parents of 444 respondents were living, and living together. Another 184 had a widowed mother, fifty-seven had a widower father, and the parents of thirty-nine individuals were divorced or separated. In addition, seventy-five respondents had neither parent living. The investigation of relations with parents centers about the 444 with parents living together, the other circumstances being brought into the discussion briefly and comparatively.

To maximize knowledge of siblings while holding constant neither the factors affecting kin involvement nor the characteristics of relations, the respondents were questioned in detail about the sibling closest to them in age. Among the 697 who had at least one living sibling, 170 were males discussing their brother. Another 324 cross-sex relationships were included, either a male referring to his sister, or a female to her brother. The investigation likewise incorporated 203 sister relationships, the female respondents discussing their age-near sisters. Of these sibling pairs, 76 per cent were within four years of age. Relations with other siblings are introduced following the discussion of the age-near sibling, in order to complete the picture.

Discussion of secondary kin focuses on the cousin whom the respondent knew best, maximizing the possibility of cousin involvement, as well as providing indirect information on aunts and uncles. There were 685 respondents who knew at least one cousin well enough to discuss him or her. In addition, all respondents answered a few basic questions on interaction with and attitudes toward secondary kin in general.

Relationship Characteristics

The investigation utilizes measures of both objective and subjective aspects of kinship. The objective, or interactional, characteristics include size and distribution of kin networks, frequency of interaction and kinds of or occasions for interaction with specific kin. Also included are telephoning and letter writing, or the non-face-to-face means of keeping in touch. To avoid estimation, frequency is based upon the actual number of times the respondent reports having contacted a relative, not on a hypothetical average. That is, the interview question is stated thus: "In the past two years how often have you seen (telephoned, written) your . . . ?" The responses include four or more categories of frequency, as can be seen in Appendix A.

The young Greensboro adults were asked to state how frequently within the past two years they had engaged in any of a long list of activities, occasions for interaction, and various forms of mutual aid.[32] These were then combined to form eight "contact types," as follows: (1) *home visiting* is the interaction which occurs at one home or the other, including either simple conversation visits or types of home recreation, such as card playing or picnics. (2) *Social activities* are those pursuits which take the participants away from home, combining commercial recreations, or those demanding an immediate cash outlay, such as bowling, golf, or movies, outdoor recreation, such as hunting or camping, and shopping. (3) *Voluntary organizations* are churches, unions, or clubs, although in the case of parents the primary activity of this kind which is shared is religious attendance.

Another possible aspect of life which may be shared with kin is (4) *working together* at the same occupation and location. The diverse occasions which may draw kin together are combined into (5) *rituals,* or ceremonial occasions. These include holidays, birthdays, anniversaries, and large family reunions, any or all of which may perpetuate family traditions and ties. (6) *Communication* is operationally defined as keeping in touch by mail or telephone. While this is not a measure of relational intimacy, it is nevertheless an indicator of the continuing interest of two persons or families in each other.

Finally, there are the reciprocal aspects of mutual aid. Thus, from the standpoint of the young adult respondent, there is (7) *aid received* from a specific relative, and (8) *aid given* to that relative. Exchange of aid may be in the form of tangible aid or services. Tangible aid is either the direct provision of cash or a loan, or more often the less direct method of gift-giving, over and above the ritual exchange of items on birthdays and Christmas. Services include help in emergencies or sickness, baby-sitting or child care, and sewing, yard work, or other manual work.

These, then, are the kinds of and occasions for contact between two kin. In the ensuing analysis, the occurrence of any one of the sub-activities, e.g., shopping or baby-sitting, with a given frequency, e.g., monthly or more, is used to signify the presence of that type of contact with the designated frequency.

The foregoing objective characteristics are but one aspect of kin relations. There are also the subjective elements, involving such characteristics as affectional closeness, value consensus, identification, and obligation. Determination of affectional closeness is in answer to the question: "How close would you say you feel to your . . . ?" Responses of "quite close" and "extremely close" are combined and designated as strong feelings of closeness. Value consensus is ascertained by the following question: "Do you and your . . . agree in your ideas and opinions about the things *you* consider really important in life?" Answers of "yes, completely," and "yes, to a great extent" appear to indicate substantial value consensus, as distinct from value divergence. Idealization of or identification with the relative is determined by responses to this question: "Would you like to be the kind of person your . . . is?" Close identification is based upon the responses "yes, completely," and "in most ways." Feelings of obligation are ascertained in the present study by asking the young adults how important certain reasons for keeping in touch are in relation to a particular relative. Reasons include: "Because they need your help in some way," and "because you feel you ought to, or have a duty to, keep in touch." The former appears to elicit expressions of specific or material obligation, while the latter signifies a general obligation to maintain contact. A final subjective characteristic of kin relations concerns the overall perception on the respondent's part of the importance of relatives in his total scheme of things. They may be very important, somewhat important, or unimportant, and this may be related to his involvements with specific kin within the network.

By utilizing both objective and subjective measures of kin involvement, it is hoped that a general characterization of kin relations in one urban place may be forthcoming. To summarize, the factors affecting kin relations, employed in this study, include: one's sex, occupational or social status, and residential history, and the degree of kin relationship. Relationship characteristics include the dimensions of the kin network, the objective attributes of a specific relation, including frequency of, kinds of, and occasions for contact, and the subjective attributes of closeness, value consensus, identification, obligation, and kin importance.

The Plan of the Book

Much of the study of urban kinship is necessarily exploratory in nature, keeping direct hypothesis testing to a minimum. For this and other reasons we have chosen to present our findings in tabular form, utilizing percentages and omitting tests of significance.[33] The general plan of the work is to present the dimensions and overall importance of the kin network in Chapter II. By dimensions we mean the numbers and dispersion of the young adult Greensboroites' kin. Chapters III through V are devoted to the objective and subjective relations between the respondents and the major kin categories: parents, siblings, and secondary kin, in that order. In each of these four chapters the important findings of other kinship studies are reviewed so that our results might be placed within the total perspective of present knowledge of urban kinship. In the concluding Chapter the results are summarized and interrelated, in order to provide a characterization of the involvement of urbanites in kin affairs, and to lay the groundwork for further intensive studies of such phenomena.

Chapter II

THE DIMENSIONS
AND IMPORTANCE OF
URBAN KIN RELATIONS

Relatives are to a great extent "givens" in the individual's social milieu. He does not choose them, he *has* them. They may be numerous or few, scattered or clustered, remote or proximate, depending upon the fertility, migration, and interpersonal history of previous generations. It is the kin network as a whole, its dimensions and perceived importance, which commands our attention in the present chapter.

Not all kin are treated alike. Some may be allowed into the hidden recesses of the individual's life, others may be objects of occasional contact, and still others may be known of but not known. Raymond Firth draws this valuable distinction between types of kin relations labelling them intimate, effective, and nominal kin.[1] Intimate kin comprise the core of one's kin network, and are likely to include parents, one or more siblings, and perhaps a grandparent or other intense secondary kin relationship. The effective kin are those with whom regular contact is maintained, but with neither great intensity nor involvement. The individual may have few or many kin of whom he is aware, but whom he has never seen and is little concerned about, or with whom he has at one time been in contact but is no longer. These are his nominal kin.

The determination of kin network dimensions was made as facile as possible for the Greensboro respondents by asking them to enumerate those kin whom they would recognize if they passed them on the street. According to Firth's three-fold classification, such a method of identification will incorporate the intimate and effective kin, as well as a few of the nominal kin with whom the respondent is no longer in touch, but who have been seen recently enough that recognition is deemed possible. Nevertheless our recognizable kin, henceforth designated as the individual's kin *acquaintances,* and Firth's first two kin categories are roughly equivalent. Kin acquaintances, let it be noted, include not only one's blood relatives but their affines or spouses as well. A cousin's wife and an aunt's husband are considered to be part of the individual's kin network. Below are described the dimensions of the kin networks of young adult Greensboroites.

Section One: Number and Dispersion of Kin

Number of Kin Acquaintances

Various researchers have sought to ascertain the numbers of consanguineal or blood kin. Yet a lack of correspondence in sampling and in the specification of kin to be enumerated prevents a ready comparison of the findings. Definitional problems which are seldom answered in studies reporting numbers of kin, include the following: Are the respondent's own spouse and children counted or not? Does the total include all known kin or does it stop with a particular category, such as first or second cousins? Are the affines of one's consanguineal kin included, as in the present study, or not? Finally, and most crucial, does the size of the kin network signify both blood kin and in-laws, or does it comprehend only the blood or consanguineal kin? Our enumeration does not include in-laws, omits the respondent's family of procreation, i.e., spouse and children, as well as those he would not recognize, is inclusive with respect to degree of relationship, and considers affines as kin.

The numbers of kin reported in other studies range from a mean of thirteen kin down through first cousins,[2] tabulated by 161 college students and middle-class Boston adults, to a mean of 215 kin in a sample of fifty-two Montreal French Canadians.[3] The most carefully defined tabulation of kin is found in Firth's study of ninety middle-class north London households, in which he distinguishes effective from nominal kin. The mean number of nominal kin is 40, of effective (including intimate) or contacted kin is 20.5, and the numbers of effective kin range in his sample as high as 120.[4]

Besides the aforementioned definitional difficulties in several of the studies, we are still faced with a glaring discrepancy between Paul Reiss' and Philip Garigue's results in Boston and Montreal, respectively. Of course, Garigue's enumeration does not stop with first cousins as does Reiss'. A second partial explanation for the large numbers of kin found by Garigue is the characteristically Roman Catholic and working-class background of his sample.[5] While these factors would not appear to account for the entire difference between means of 13 and 215, they nevertheless introduce the possibility of occupational stratum differences in numbers of kin acquaintances.

The 799 young Greensboroites under investigation listed a total of 31,021 kin acquaintances—a mean of 38.8 whom the respondent felt he would recognize "if he passed them on the street." Many respondents indicated that they had had no face-to-face contact with certain of these kin for as long as fifteen years, but were positive that they could still identify them. Thus, as we expected, some of Firth's nominal kin were included in the enumeration. Ranging from two to 585 kin acquaintances, the sample manifests a sizeable skew toward the upper extreme, with forty-one respondents (about 5 per cent) tabulating 100 or more kin. The median number of kin per respondent is 27.6, and since this statistic is not sensitive to the skewness of the distribution it will be utilized more than the mean throughout this chapter.

One concern of the interviewers was to avoid simple estimation on the part of the respondents. This was accomplished by requesting the residential location of kin acquaintances. While in a few instances the numbers were so large that approximation was allowed, the lack of extensive clustering at such round figures as ten, twenty-five, or fifty indicates that sheer conjecture was minimal. The modal category was twenty-two kin, but only twenty-six respondents stated that this was the number they would recognize. In fact, every number from eight to twenty-four kin was represented by fourteen to twenty-six young adult respondents.

At no point in the literature has the sex of the individual been related to numbers of kin acquaintances. Nevertheless, the central role of the female in kin affairs is a widely accepted fact. That greater female involvement includes more widespread as well as more intense contacts is affirmed by the Greensboro results. The young married females recorded a median of 29.7 kin acquaintances, as compared with a median of 26.2 for the males.

Regardless of the young adult's sex, parents play a key role in the maintenance of a wide range of kin contacts. Young and Willmott note in their London study that the mother's death often results in a loss of contact between her children and her siblings, i.e., between nephews and nieces and their aunts and uncles.[6] The mother, primarily, has linked these and other kin in a communication and contactual network. The authors specify further that the death of an aunt or uncle may cause loss of contact with cousins. The association between kin acquaintances thus revolves about certain "significant others" among them. This is demonstrated in the present study when we note the effects of the death of one or both parents upon the size of the kin network. Young adults both of whose parents are still living have a median of 30.8 kin acquaintances, those with either mother or father deceased have a median of 22.7, and those with neither parent living reported a median of twenty.

A third factor, besides sex and significant kin, which may affect the size of the kin network is the occupational position of the young adult, and the comparison between his position and that of his parents. There are indications in the literature that occupational stratum and mobility may have an independent influence upon the kin network, although the evidence that mobility means a shrunken network in size is meagre. David M. Schneider and George C. Homans comment that the upwardly mobile keep shallow ties with their kin, if they keep them at all, and the downwardly mobile may be neglected by their kindred. Similarly, in Garigue's study the upwardly mobile urban French Canadians report the greatest loss of contact with their lateral, or same generation, kin.[7] As for simple stratum comparisons, numerous authors have pointed out the intense involvement of the working classes in kin affairs. Nowhere, however, has direct reference been made to stratum differences in *extensive* kin knowledge.

In Table II-1 the downwardly mobile, as expected, report fewer kin acquaintances than do the occupationally stable, both among

TABLE II-1

Median numbers of kin acquaintances, according to the sex and occupational stratum and mobility of the young married adults*

Sex	Occupational Stratum and Mobility	Number of Respondents	Median Number of Kin
Males	Upward White Collar	(93)	29.7
	Stable White Collar	(111)	24.7
	Stable Blue Collar	(86)	26.3
	Downward Blue Collar	(26)	18.8
Females	Upward White Collar	(115)	35
	Stable White Collar	(160)	30.3
	Stable Blue Collar	(139)	24.9
	Downward Blue Collar	(38)	21.8

* This table omits those respondents who either are students, or who did not identify their father's occupation adequately so that intergenerational comparisons could be made.

males and females. Whether this is due to neglect by their relatives or to a purposeful withdrawal on their part is impossible to ascertain from such a table. The upwardly mobile, in contrast, not only do not exhibit a shrunken kin network, but actually enumerate a larger number of kin acquaintances than any of the other three stratum-mobility groupings. While this does not necessarily imply intense kin involvement among the upwardly mobile, it is nevertheless somewhat unexpected that they should record the largest numbers of recognizable kin. Perhaps Litwak's concept of status gain and deference may account in part for this finding. His viewpoint may be interpreted as the utilization of the kin network as a comparative reference group. That is, one maintains contact, however tenuously, with lower status kin in order to receive their deference and to gain status comparatively by such contacts.[8] Such an explanatory device must remain conjectural until the delineation of the specific kin relationships of the upwardly mobile has been completed. It is apparent in Table II-1 that the two categories of occupationally stable young adults are between the two mobility categories in numbers of kin acquaintances.

In summary, those likely to have larger numbers of recognizable kin include females, those with both parents still living, and the upwardly mobile occupationally. The size of the kin-acquaintance network, on the other hand, is quite limited among the downwardly mobile in this study.

Dispersion of Kin Acquaintances

The purported isolation of the urban nuclear family from kin has been disputed on numerous occasions. Isolation or propinquity should be apparent in observing the dispersion or distribution of the kin of our urban sample. A previous study, that of Paul Reiss, records the location of the kin, down through first cousins, of 161 middle-class Bostonians. Among those listed, 12 per cent live in Boston, 37 per cent are in the metropolitan area or county, 22 per cent live elsewhere in New England, 21 per cent are outside New England but east of the Mississippi River, and the other 8 per cent are elsewhere.[9] A general equivalence to Reiss' five spatial categories is achieved in our study by dividing kin into those living in Greensboro, those within 100 miles, those living elsewhere within the three-state area of North Carolina, South Carolina, and Virginia, those elsewhere in the South or Northeast (including Louisiana, Arkansas, Kentucky, West Virginia, and Pennsylvania, and states northward), and those living outside the South and East. Categories two and three, i.e., the 100-mile radius and the three-state area, are larger than Reiss' corresponding categories, but have a lower population density.

Employing the five-fold division, the 31,021 kin acquaintances of the young adult Greensboroites are distributed as follows: 16.6 per cent in Greensboro, 32 per cent within 100 miles, 28.4 per cent within the three-state area but more than 100 miles from Greensboro, 17.3 per cent elsewhere in the South and East, and 5.8 per cent elsewhere. These results are quite similar to those of the Boston study. Reiss' modal category, for example, is the Boston metropolitan area, while ours is a radius of 100 miles from Greensboro —about two to two and a half hours' driving time. Almost 50 per cent of the kin acquaintances, or 15,000 of them, are within 100 miles of the respondents.

Turning to the factors which influence the dispersion of kin, the primary association is with the migratory or residential mobility history of the individual, which is, in turn, closely linked to his occupational position and family background. Those who have never lived outside Greensboro since marriage are most likely to have their kin living close by. In fact, almost half (49 per cent) of the kin of the 204 residentially stable respondents also live in Greensboro. However, those 261 respondents who have made one or two moves of fifty or more miles since marriage have but 36 per cent of their kin within 100 miles of them, and the 115 who have moved three or more times are within 100 miles of but 23 per cent of their kin acquaintances.

One's occupational position, we have said, is closely associated with his geographic mobility. Sixty-six per cent of the blue-collar individuals have never lived more than fifty miles from Greensboro, regardless of whether their parents are white or blue collar. By comparison, only 46 per cent of the white-collar Greensboroites have never lived further than fifty miles from their present location. There are differences not only in amount of mobility by occupational status but in the primary reason for mobility when it occurs. In the course of the interviews the blue-collar respondents frequently made such comments as: "My brothers and I never did get along so I finally just moved over here to Greensboro," or "My wife and I got tired of having to see my parents every Friday and Saturday night so I got a job at . . . and we came to the city." A much more usual comment from a white-collar respondent was: "I wish I could see my folks more often but my work keeps me moving around." What these respondents are expressing is the following: since industrial working classes can find semi- or unskilled work in one modern city about as well as in another, their migration tends to be related most directly to social group, especially kin, relations. Satisfactory relations make movement unlikely; unsatisfactory relations at times result in movement for the sake of escape, not because of greater opportunity elsewhere. The exception to this is, of course, the movement of ruralites into urban blue-collar opportunities. The modern middle or white-collar class, on the other hand, tend to move primarily in response to career demands with less direct concern for the location of kin. Thus, among blue-collar respondents the tendency is for relationships to take precedence over opportunity in residential mobility or stability, while among the white-collar opportunity takes precedence over relationships. Of course, this is only a modal tendency, and the high blue collar and lower white collar shade into each other gradually in this regard.

There are actually two dimensions to the distribution of the kin network. The first concerns distance from *ego,* or the respondent, and the second concerns density or clustering, i.e., the distance that kin live from each other. The former dimension, as already indicated, is determined to a great extent, although not entirely, by the migratory history of the respondent. This is, in turn, closely associated with his personal occupational history, as indicated above. But the dispersion of his kin from each other is a function not of *ego's* migration but of the character of the various kin in their occupational and migratory histories. Therefore, the stable middle class and downwardly mobile, whose family backgrounds and kin networks are predominantly middle class, tend to be similar in kin dispersion, as are the upwardly mobile and stable working class. Our primary interest, however, is not in the simple clustering or dispersion of kin; we are concerned about the proximity or distance of kin from a specific individual within the network—the young adult respondent. In Table II-2 we investigate the proximity of the respondent's kin utilizing the two factors of personal migratory history and family (or father's) occupational position simultaneously. The results are hardly unanticipated: the less residentially mobile the individual has been, the more determinative of kin proximity is his father's occupational position (Table II-2).

Another important issue in the dispersion and clustering of kin networks concerns rural versus urban differences in background.

TABLE II-2

**Clustering of kin acquaintances within 100 miles of Greensboro,
according to the occupational stratum and mobility and
migratory history of the young adults**

Respondents' Geographic Movement Since Marriage	Occupational Stratum and Mobility	Number of Respondents	Per cent having most of their kin within 100 miles
Always in Greensboro	Upward White Collar	(40)	70
	Stable White Collar	(53)	49
	Stable Blue Collar	(86)	63
	Downward Blue Collar	(18)	39
Always —50 Miles	Upward White Collar	(61)	44
	Stable White Collar	(67)	27
	Stable Blue Collar	(60)	58
	Downward Blue Collar	(24)	38
One or more moves of 50 or more Miles	Upward White Collar	(107)	22
	Stable White Collar	(151)	15
	Stable Blue Collar	(79)	34
	Downward Blue Collar	(22)	32

Seymour Martin Lipset and Reinhard Bendix assert that migrants
from rural areas to cities tend to take over lower-status positions
upon arrival.[10] In addition, rural-urban migration tends to cover
shorter distances than urban-urban migration in Western industrial
societies. The present study manifests several interesting results in
terms of these phenomena. First, the majority of the young Greensboro adults who are from rural areas are now in blue-collar occupations. Furthermore, almost half of the ex-farm offspring have
their parent(s) still living within 100 miles of them—an indication
that their migration patterns have ordinarily been simply from a
farm to a nearby city, in this case Greensboro, in search of urban
opportunity. Finally, there are more ex-farm females than males,
almost two-to-one, more than the numbers of female and male respondents would lead one to expect. In fact, blue-collar males are
predominantly Greensboro natives, while the females have often
come from surrounding small towns and farms, where their kin
networks are still clustered. It is possible that male farm out-mi-
grants tend to go to the smaller towns, whereas the females jump

directly to the larger cities. In any case, one factor accounting for both the clustering and the nearness of the kin networks of those respondents with blue-collar parents is rural-urban migration.

In summary, an important factor in one's distance from his kin is, as expected, his personal occupational position and migratory history. The current white-collar individual, regardless of his parents' occupational status, tends to move more often and across greater distances than does the young blue-collar adult. This movement tends to be in the pursuit of opportunity, while blue-collar movement, when it occurs, is more often due to relationship difficulties. Not the respondent's but his father's occupational stratum is more closely associated with the dispersion, as opposed to the clustering, of recognizable kin. Thus, among the non-migratory, the upwardly mobile and stable working class resemble each other in kin scatter, as do the downwardly mobile and stable middle class. One aspect of parental background which seems to be related both to greater clustering and proximity of kin is rurality, with ex-farm Greensboroites usually having come from within 100, and often less, miles of the city. The manner in which the two factors—personal occupational stratum and father's occupational stratum—articulate with other characteristics of kin relations remains to be investigated.

Section Two: How Important Are Kin?

Having delineated the general dimensions of the kin networks of young adult Greensboroites, we turn to a question which may give some conception of kinship in the lives of the respondents. Every individual in the sample reported at least two consanguineal or blood kin that he would recognize if he passed them on the street. But how important, we asked, are relatives in the total life situation of these persons? In closing the interview, the respondent was asked just that.[11] Although inadvertently omitted from some of the earlier interview schedules, this question was answered by 604 respondents. Among these, 292 (48 per cent) feel that relatives are very important in their lives, almost as many—248 (41 per cent)

—perceive their relatives as somewhat important to them, and sixty-four (11 per cent) state that kin are unimportant.

The greater involvement of females in kin relations, noted throughout the literature, appears once again in the wide divergence between the sexes in expressions of kin importance. The modal response of the young married females is that relatives are one of the most important aspects of their lives, while among the males kin are considered modally as "somewhat important." The percentages for the 339 females who answered the question are: 58 per cent feel that kin are very important, 35 per cent somewhat important, and 8 per cent unimportant. The comparable percentages for the 265 responding males are 37, 49, and 14.

An immediately anticipated explanation for differences in the perceived centrality of kin in one's life would be numbers and proximity. However, when the sex of the respondent is controlled, differences in the professed importance of kin according to numbers of kin acquaintances or residential location of the majority of kin are negligible. Those with few kin and those whose kin are remote were as likely to say that they are important as were the young adults with many kin clustered in Greensboro. A partial explanation for this finding is the concept of significant relatives. The interviewers frequently recorded such comments as the following: "Outside of my parents, relatives aren't the least bit important to me." Or even more pointedly: "I just don't see any sense in keeping in touch with a flock of people just because they're relatives unless you really like them. My parents, sister, grandparents, a couple of aunts and uncles and one cousin are very important to me. As for the others . . . phooey!" It was noted earlier in the present chapter that the death of certain key relatives, particularly parents, may result in loss of contact with others. These same significant kin may be of central importance as well in the determination of the perceived importance of "kin in general." That parents do play such a role to some extent among the males is apparent when 30 per cent of those with neither parent living stated that kin are very important, while 26 per cent said they are unimportant. This is compared with percentages of 38 and 14, respectively, among those males with one or both parents living. The role of parents was much more pronounced in the females' perception of kin importance, with 62 per cent of those with both parents living, 51 per cent with one parent living, and 42 per cent with neither parent living stating that kin were very important to them. Neither among the males nor the females is the discrepancy due to parents great enough to alter the modal response category, but the role of these significant kin is nevertheless apparent. Nor is it surprising that those who are most likely to be intensely involved in kin affairs—the females—were more sensitive to the importance of such key persons as their parents in their perception of kin importance.

A second reason for the non-association between network dimensions and expressed importance may derive from the respondents' interpretation of the question. Emotional attachment to and concern for specific persons, including kin, does not require proximity. Parents are intimate kin, comments Bott, even when they are not physically accessible.[12] The young married adults evidently interpreted the question to mean: "Are relatives of importance to you?" not "Are relatives an important aspect of your daily activities?" Thus, the variable is more subjective or social psychological than it is objective, being virtually unrelated to the accessibility or proximity of large numbers of kin.

Observation of the downwardly mobile has thus far resulted in the discovery of a limited kinship network relative to the other three stratum and mobility groupings. We now find in Table II-3 that they are also least likely, regardless of sex, to state that kin are a very important part of their lives. The differences between downwardly mobile females and the other three categories are particularly striking. It thus appears that a definite alienation has occurred between the downwardly mobile and their kin. Further analysis of relations with specific kin should help to clarify the nature of the rift. Other significant features of Table II-3 include the slightly lesser importance of relatives expressed by the upwardly mobile wives. These females, it will be recalled, identified the largest network of kin acquaintances of any single sex-stratum category. Yet they are less likely than either category of occupationally stable females to state that kin are a very important factor in their lives.

Perhaps their knowledge of large numbers of kin signifies that these kin are initiating continued contacts with them, due to the status gain which accrues from the contact, rather than that these young adults are themselves fostering extensive kin ties. The upward mobile males, on the other hand, demonstrate no less positive response to their kin with respect to importance than do the stable middle class. Hypothetically, they may see their upward mobility as

TABLE II-3

The importance of kin in the young adults' "total scheme of things," according to their sex and occupational stratum and mobility

Sex	Occupational Stratum and Mobility	Number of Respondents	Importance of Kin, in Per Cent			
			Very Impt.	Some-what Impor-tant	Rela-tively Unimpor-tant	Total Pct.
Males	Upward White Collar	(75)	39	52	9	100
	Stable White Collar	(98)	34	52	14	100
	Stable Blue Collar	(60)	45	40	15	100
	Downward Blue Collar	(22)	27	50	23	100
Females	Upward White Collar	(85)	52	36	12	100
	Stable White Collar	(122)	64	33	3	100
	Stable Blue Collar	(94)	60	32	8	100
	Downward Blue Collar	(26)	31	54	15	100

more directly a product of family factors, such as the inculcation by one or both parents of mobility aspirations and kin encouragement, than do the upwardly mobile females, who gained their higher status by marriage. Finally, it is noteworthy that the only category of males who perceive relatives modally as very important is the stable blue-collar males, who are also the most likely among the eight sex-stratum categories to have the majority of their relatives in general, and their parents specifically, located in Greensboro.

How can we summarize the findings concerning the importance of kin? First, the more *intensive* involvement of females in kinship is observed to complement the earlier finding of more *extensive* knowledge. The downwardly mobile are not apt to include kin among the central aspects of their lives. On the other hand, the occupationally stable females overwhelmingly indicate that their kin are very important to them. Small numbers or residential distance from the bulk of one's kin do not necessarily result in kin being considered unimportant, since significant relatives may be considered intimate and a vital part of the individual's life regardless of their location.

Summary

Young adult Greensboroites are involved in kinship networks ranging from two persons remote from the respondent to 585 kin acquaintances with whom contact is maintained by periodic family reunions and other contacts of various sorts. Between these extremes the median number of recognizable kin is 27.6. The majority, about 60 per cent, of the enumerated kin reside outside Greensboro but within the three-state area of North Carolina, South Carolina, and Virginia—a radius of some 250 miles. Many of the respondents or their parents migrated to Greensboro from somewhere in this three state region.

Kin are considered one of the primary aspects of life by almost 50 per cent of the respondents. The females, who have been found by numerous authors to be more active in and to supply continuity to kin affairs, not only are more likely than the males to consider their kin important, but are also able to identify more kin acquaintances.

The kin relations of the stable middle classes are ordinarily characterized by considerable spatial dispersion, but a large number are recalled and kin are frequently considered an important aspect of their lives. Upward mobility has thus far manifested none of the alienating effects postulated by Schneider and Homans, at least in terms of network dimensions. The major differences between the upwardly mobile and the stable middle classes are the slightly greater proximity of the kin networks of the upwardly mobile, a function of their working class background, and the tendency for them to enumerate even *more* kin acquaintances than the stable middle classes. Only among the upwardly mobile females is there some indication that kin are of less importance than they are to the non-mobile middle class females. These three differences, however, are minor at best. Generally speaking, the dimensions and over-all significance of the kin networks of the upwardly mobile are quite similar to their non-mobile sex-stratum counterparts.

The kin networks of the occupationally stable working class, in contrast to the stable middle class, are summarized in the word "proximate." Clustered close around, the dominance of kin in blue collar men's and women's lives may be observed in various ways. These are the only males who modally consider kin a very important part of their lives. In addition, these are the only respondents who are likely to spend, and to desire to spend, their leisure with kin rather than with non-kin. In short, we find that, as a whole, kin are considered almost equally important subjectively by the stable blue-collar and white-collar individuals in our sample, but in all probability they are objectively more central to working class life. Once again, the significance of these findings should become more explicit and complete as we investigate specific kin.

What, finally, are the outlines of the kin networks of the downwardly mobile? For whatever reasons, they seem characterized by some form of alienation. Regardless of sex, these young adults claim the smallest numbers of kin acquaintances, and are least likely—dramatically so in the case of females—to feel that kin are very important to them.

One further word needs to be said about occupational mobility and the network. A basic difficulty in the discussions of mobility effects found in the literature is the inexplicit nature of the comparison group. Are the upwardly mobile, for example, to be compared with stable blue-collar or stable white-collar individuals in their kin relations? In other words, are they to be viewed in relation to those who are similar in status to their parents, or those similar to their current status? Since the upwardly mobile present something of a mid-point between the stable middle class and stable working class in dispersion of kin, it is obvious that divergent results will occur depending upon the point of comparison. Compared to the stratum from which they have come, or into which they were born, i.e., the working class, they will appear to have weaker kin ties, since the likelihood of their greater residential mobility will cause them to have fewer kin accessible for interaction. But compared to the stratum of which they are now a part, i.e., the middle class, they present a picture of substantial kin involvement, since they are more likely than the second generation members of their new stratum to have kin living close by. We may observe over and over in the chapters which follow that the upwardly mobile do in fact form basically a median category between the stable middle and working classes in their kin relations.

Several other features of the kin network according to sex and occupational stratum will continue to be salient in the ensuing investigation of specific kindred. In what ways are the kin relations of the upwardly mobile merely a mid-point between the two stable categories, and in what ways do they closely resemble either the stable middle class or stable working class respondents, or diverge entirely? How viable are the kin relations of the stable middle class in the face of network dispersion? What is the effect of the proximity and therefore frequent contact of young blue-collar adults with their kin upon certain key relationships? Furthermore, of what nature is the implied alienation between the downwardly mobile and their kin? Does it include infrequent interaction as well as subjective non-importance?

In conclusion, the relevant dimensions of the kin network depict a large number of known kin, only a fraction of whom are proximate enough for daily or even weekly interaction. We observe great variation not only in numbers and location of kin, but in the perceived importance of these kin to the individual. A recurrent problem throughout this chapter has been the role of key individuals within the network. The issue has been highlighted in noting that the death of one or both parents results in a diminution in the number of kin acquaintances and in a less intense feeling of kin importance. We therefore turn in Chapter Three to parents as a prime focal point of the kinship network.

Chapter III

YOUNG ADULTS
AND THEIR PARENTS

The unique kinship tie between young adults and their parents in modern urban society is exemplified in the fact that for many persons the term "family" includes not only their own spouse and children, but their parents as well. Neolocality and the key role of the parents in the socialization process are both temporal and causal antecedents of this uniqueness. The parent is not simply "just another relative," and the importance of this intergenerational tie has already been inferred in Chapter Two. However, the objective and subjective aspects of young adult—parent relations are yet to be delineated. These form the subject matter of this Chapter.

Discussion of parental relations is confined to the 444 young adults both of whose parents are still alive and living together. Those with a widow or widower parent or from a broken home are analyzed briefly and separately at the close of the chapter.

Section One: Frequency of Young Adult-Parent Contact[1]

Interaction is a fundamental attribute of the social relationship, so much so that its frequency has often been used essentially as an index of intimate interpersonal involvement.[2] While social relations do not *require* face-to-face contact to remain viable, the sorts of contact which are possible over long distances are severely limited. Thus, although frequency of interaction by no means fully characterizes the social relationship, including that between young adults and their parents, its utilization in previous studies of interpersonal

33

association and its indirect indication of the day-to-day salience of two individuals to each other make it a logical beginning point.

The two fundamental determinants of interaction frequency with kin, says Paul Reiss, are "the degree of kin relationship and the distance of residence," with distance invariably overriding degree of relationship in governing frequency of face-to-face contact.[3] Distance is the prime limiting condition upon interaction, not deciding who will, but who *may* interact. As Bott puts it: "Proximity is a quasi-necessary, but not a sufficient condition of intimacy. . . ."[4] The importance of residential distance to interaction frequency with parents is apparent when we note that in the present sample all those whose parents live in Greensboro, 155 of them, stated that they see their parents at least monthly, and better than five out of six see their proximate parents weekly. Sixty-one per cent of the 113 respondents whose parents live within 100 miles of Greensboro see them more than once a month. However, at the other extreme, none of the 176 whose parents live more than 100 miles away see them weekly, and less than 25 per cent of them see their parents as often as once a month.

The residential distance separating parents from their married children is clearly a function of the residential mobility of one or both of them. Yet it does not follow that each move the individual makes takes him further from his parents. Although the more mobile are less likely to be currently living near their parents, there are numerous cases in which the last move has brought the young adult back to the community where the parents are located, or else his parents have followed him to Greensboro.[5] Therefore, a word of caution is in order concerning the use of individual geographic mobility as a relational variable. While this may be appropriately used in conjunction with personal factors, such as education or occupational history, it is less than adequate for interpersonal comparisons. Both in relation to specific kin, such as parents, and to location of the kin network *in toto* (Chapter II), the concomitant migration of the other party or parties must be taken into consideration. A more accurate comparative variable, which accounts for and is based upon the geographic mobility or stability of the two parties, is simply present residential distance.

Sex, Occupational Stratum and Mobility, and Frequency of Interaction with Parents

A general asymmetry in kinship relations according to the sex of the individual became evident in Chapter II. That the young adult female is closer to her parents, as well as to kin in general, than is the young male to his parents has been postulated by several authors.[6] Does a differential feeling of closeness manifest itself in differential interaction frequency? This question must of course be approached through the intervening variable residential distance from parents. Several pertinent comments appear in the kinship literature regarding the comparative residential proximity of parents according to the sex of the offspring. The sources dealing with the working class or blue-collar family are in general agreement that the tendency is for a young couple, when they have a choice, to live near the wife's parents in preference to the husband's.

At variance with these working class findings is a study, with occupational position undefined, in which 490 Pennsylvania families are found to be almost equally likely to live near or with the husband's or the wife's parents. William Smith's discovery of no difference by sex in residential separation from parents is given more general expression by Reiss, who feels that residential "mobility has a random effect upon the distance of residence of specific kin."[8] This statement assumes that relations with particular kin have little or no influence upon residential location, and while it may hold for the upper-middle class occupation or career-oriented family, it is hardly an accurate characterization of the population, at least with respect to intimate kin such as parents.

Thus, we have two views regarding residential separation from the two sets of parents. The first, drawn from working-class research, asserts that proximity to the young wife's parents tends to be greater. The second is simply a null hypothesis of no difference in distance from parents by sex. Interestingly, our findings diverge from both of these viewpoints: 39 per cent of the husbands' parents live in Greensboro and only 32 per cent of the wives'.[9] The young married females, however, are more likely to have their parents outside of Greensboro but within 100 miles, and beyond 100 miles the differences are negligible. Furthermore, the blue-collar disparity by sex is even greater than the white-collar: 5 per cent more of the parents of white-collar males are in Greensboro, as compared with 11 per cent more of the working-class males' parents.

The direct contrast of our results to those reported elsewhere may be interpreted partially by the difference in definition of distance categories. In each of the blue-collar studies the great majority of parents lived in the same community with their adult offspring; for example, 68 per cent of the parents in Komarovsky's study were immediately available, and 93 per cent were within a two-hour drive.[10] The distinction which actually is made in these studies is between the wife's parents in the same block and the husband's three blocks away, or across town. This is apparent in Young and Willmott's claim that *among those whose parents are in the same borough* the tendency is toward "matrilocality."[11] These authors have but a few cases of cross-country migration with which to deal, and it is precisely this extra-community movement which is revealed in our results, not relative location within the same city. As the findings indicate, there are more natives of Greensboro among the males, and more short distance migrants from farms and nearby towns and cities among the females.

It is now possible to discuss frequency of interaction realizing that, at least in Greensboro, the tendency is for the parents of the male to be slightly more proximate. Except in the study by Lee M. Robins and Miroda Tomanec, which reports no differences by sex, the trend in the research is to see a greater feeling of closeness between females and their parents resulting in more frequent interaction between them.[12] Perhaps the greatest insight into sex differences in parental interaction has been afforded by Young and Willmott. Their social network analysis includes not only individuals living in a London borough but also former residents who have moved to a residential suburb. Within the city borough daughter-parent interaction predominates. "Over half the married women," the authors comment, "saw their mothers within the previous twenty-four hours and 90 per cent of them within the previous week. This was more than they saw their fathers or the married men saw either of their parents."[13] However, the situation is altered among those who have moved to the suburbs. Kinship visiting in the suburb is about one-fifth what it used to be. More important, the husbands now see their parents and siblings more than their wives see theirs.

Young and Willmott's findings may be explained in the following manner. When the parents live close by, the young husband is able to see them once or twice a week. His work ordinarily prevents frequent face-to-face contact during the week. The non-working wife is more flexible in her visiting pattern. She and her parents, especially her mother, eat meals and visit together during weekdays. Thus, if "weekly or more" is used as a category of interaction frequency, sex differences will not be appreciable. But if the category is divided into "more than once a week" and "weekly" the wife's contact is seen to be more frequent. When the distance separating young adult and parents is moderate, the control of family resources such as the automobile by the working class male results in his greater ability to get around. As the authors note, very often the ex-borough (Bethnal Green) male will stop by to see his parents on the way home from work in London. The wife, on the other hand, must make a special trip or persuade her husband to take her and the children to see her parents. Whether such variations in the visiting patterns of Londoners and ex-Londoners are relevant to the parental interaction of Greensboroites may be observed in Table III-1.

Had we simply employed "weekly or more" as a frequency classification, sex differences in interaction with parents living in the same city would be imperceptible. Yet a decidedly greater number of females are in contact with their parents face-to-face more than once a week. At the other extreme, our findings bear out somewhat the greater maneuverability of the young husbands; i.e., the males are likely to interact with their parents more frequently when they are separated by 100 miles or more. A provocative aspect of Table III-1 is the widely divergent frequencies of contact with parents who live outside Greensboro but within 100 miles. While Young and Willmott's finding of more frequent male interaction with non-local parents is substantiated when residential distance is greater than 100 miles, it is not supported under conditions of moderate residential separation. It almost seems that living in the same city

TABLE III-1

Frequency of interaction with parents, by the sex of the young adult, controlling residential distance

Where do Parents Live?	Sex of Young Adults	Number of Respondents	Frequency of Interaction, in Per Cent					
			Over Once a Week	Weekly	Monthly-Weekly	Several Times Yearly	Yearly or Less	Total Pct.
Greensboro	Males	(79)	48	33	19	—	—	100
	Females	(76)	72	16	12	—	—	100
—100 Miles	Males	(36)	6	8	58	25	3	100
	Females	(77)	4	16	62	17	1	100
NC-SC-Va.	Males	(39)	—	—	39	51	10	100
	Females	(54)	—	—	32	61	7	100
Elsewhere	Males	(33)	—	—	18	42	39	99*
	Females	(50)	—	—	4	48	48	100

* Percentages in this or other tables which differ from 100 are due to rounding.

with one's parents makes frequent interaction imperative, living over 100 miles apart makes frequent interaction impossible, while living in different communities but within 100 miles leaves room for a modicum of personal choice. The validity of this generalization must, of course, be examined in other contexts.

The slightly greater proximity of the males and somewhat more frequent interaction of the proximate females virtually neutralize each other, with the result that actual interaction frequency with parents by sex is approximately equal.

When we turn from sex to occupational status we recall that in Chapter Two the kin networks of the young adults from a middle-class background were found to be more dispersed than those from a working-class background. Several authors assert that this is true for parents as well as for relatives in general, i.e., working-class people by and large live closer to their parents than do middle class people.[14] An obvious explanation is that the demands of the job market in a modern society are such that the blue-collar individual can ordinarily find work in one community as well as in another, while the white-collar individual may very well have to "pursue his career" from place to place.

The question of residential distance from parents becomes even more intriguing and problematic when two polar positions are noted. Migration is, according to Parsons, an ubiquitous character-istic of the middle-class element of our society. He proposes, in his treatise on kinship, that "the typical conjugal family lives in a home segregated from those of both parents. . . . In a very large proportion of cases the geographical separation is considerable."[15] Opposing this view, A. O. Haller feels that geographic mobility has been stressed out of proportion to its frequency of occurrence. In fact, he says, many, if not most, urbanites are now second or third generation residents of the same city.[16] The day may even be upon us, he feels, when middle-class persons will be able to be educated and find positions within their original city of residence.

How do the Greensboro results stack up against these polar opin-ions, as well as the accepted findings of greater proximity between blue collar parents and offspring? First, 15 per cent more of the working class respondents have their parents living in Greensboro.

However, with regard to Parsons' idea, we find that over half of the middle class and two-thirds of the working class adults' parents live within 100 miles of Greensboro. Furthermore, there are numerous young adults whose parents live at a distance but whose parents-in-law are close by. The striking result is therefore that 45 per cent of the middle class and 60 per cent of the working class have either their own or their spouse's parents residing in Greensboro. Although it is of course impossible to determine exactly what Parsons meant by the term "considerable," these data do not seem to support his contention that in most cases urban middle class adults are "considerably" separated from both sets of parents.[17]

As for Haller's hypothesis, we have already noted in Chapter One that only 26 per cent of the respondents are second generation Greensboroites, having spent their entire lives there. Another 26 per cent have lived there over ten years. In other words, only half of the young adults have been in Greensboro as long as ten years. Haller's hypothesis, however, was not derived from a city such as the one we are investigating. It arose from observation of the megalopolis, such as Chicago or New York. The residential stability of a city's population is a function of population growth or decline, a stable New England city and a fast-growing California community being widely divergent in this regard. With respect to Greensboro, and very likely a large number of middle-sized cities, the evidence concerning parental location lies somewhere between the views of Parsons and Haller: the majority live within 100 miles of one or both sets of parents, half have one set in Greensboro, but only about one in four has lived his entire life in this city.

Upward mobility has meant for many young adults movement from one North Carolina community to another. Regardless of sex, the upwardly mobile are less likely to have their parents living in Greensboro, but are more likely to have them within 100 miles than are the non-mobile middle class. The downwardly mobile, while generally from a middle-class-dominated kin network, manifest little sign of personal residential migration. Therefore, their kin are dispersed similarly to the stable white collar, but their parents tend to be living in closer proximity to them than in any of the other three stratum-mobility groupings.

Proximity is the key to frequent interaction, and stratum differences, apart from differential migration or distance patterns, have not been apparent in several studies.[18] However, the association between occupational mobility and interaction frequency may not be a simple effect of distance. Numerous researchers have noted the role of parents in arousing high aspirations in their children. The *mobile* family, says Carson McGuire, is moving up by adherence to middle-class ideas and practices, or, more often, "mother and father are encouraging their child to achieve an education and move upward."[19] The style of life of such mobile families may in fact resemble quite closely that of the middle classes. Another type of parental influence on mobility involves an achievement-oriented mother or father, who desires his or her child to "do better" despite the complacency or even opposition of the marriage partner. This McGuire calls the *divergent* family.[20]

The dissociative consequences of differential mobility, i.e., one or more of the children mobile and other children non-mobile, for family relationships have also been reported in studies of aspirations among high school and college students. Families with differentially mobile siblings interact less, have divergent values, and are ambivalent toward each other.[21]

The inconsistency of these findings with the positive role of parents in mobility aspirations attested to in the other studies reported above emphasizes the multiple problems in studying occupational mobility among students. First, the hypothetical aspiration level of the student is not synonymous with the actual achievement of that level. In fact, one interpretation of aspiration assertions might be that the young person who is rejecting an unsatisfactory home background in general manifests this rejection by answering a question concerning the kind of work he hopes to do in such a way as to reject his father's type of work as well. Nor is it at all certain that the parental attitudes expressed by college respondents will extend into settled adulthood. Some of the aspirers may not succeed, but the ones who do are apt to demonstrate their gratitude to their parents. In any case, student aspirations and achievement motivations are not a completely satisfactory indicator of the relation between mobility and adult kin relationships.

More significant evidence of the disruptive effect of mobility upon kin ties is contained in Robert P. Stuckert's study of 266 young couples in Milwaukee, Wisconsin. His mobile respondents are less likely to express a desire for a location which would facilitate kin interaction, nor are they as likely to use their kin as a reference group. More important, the socially mobile have much less contact with relatives than do the socially stable.[22] Nowhere does Stuckert specifically single out and analyze parental relations; he is interested in the network. This fact, plus the difficulties inherent in student samples, leaves us with extremely tentative evidence for the lessening of parent—married offspring interaction among the upwardly mobile.

An opposing viewpoint states that social or occupational mobility does not necessarily weaken kin ties, particularly with parents. A chief proponent of this position, Litwak, notes in several articles that kin interaction may be an end in itself, not predicated upon either economics or authority structures. Visits with relatives and friends are not an either-or proposition; they may be separate, the individual gaining status by friendly associations with his new stratum and deference from his kin. Litwak, and other researchers, have found no differences in kin interaction between the mobile and the non-mobile.[23]

Perhaps the most pointed statement regarding mobility and parental relations comes from Bott. Mobility, she asserts, does not break parental ties, for the parents are considered to share in the achievement. The more distant the relatives, the more objective status differences receive consideration, and determine interaction. Here, then, is a first hint that much of the disagreement between those who say that mobility does or does not affect kin relations adversely may be due to the broadness of the generalizations. Certain relationships may be neglected or weakened while others, such as parental ties, may if anything be stronger than between young working class adults and their parents. A crucial question is whether the dominance of middle class success values in this urban, industrial society is great enough to strengthen ties between the "successful" offspring and their parents, including both the stable middle class and upwardly mobile, while the ties of young blue collar adults to their parents are weakened by their lack of success by societal standards.

With this lengthy introduction we are prepared to examine the relation of occupational status and mobility to frequency of interaction. Over 50 per cent of *every* category stated that they see their parents monthly or more (see Table III-2). As we would expect, the greater proximity of working-class respondents and their parents makes for more frequent interaction between them. The location-interaction comparisons in the last two columns of the Table are of interest regarding the downwardly mobile females. They are the *only* sex-stratum category which has a lower percentage interacting monthly with parents than living within 100 miles of them. In contrast, the upwardly mobile interact with parents more frequently than, and utilize proximity as effectively as, do the non-mobile middle classes. At least with respect to interaction frequency, the data strongly support the view of Litwak and Bott that upward mobility does not affect relations between these primary relatives. Judgment on the effect of downward mobility will still be suspended pending further evidence.

Communication: The Question of Non-Face-to-Face Contact

The conception among urban sociologists of the "isolated nuclear family," while often inaccurately represented by its critics, seems to have been predicated upon two ideas: (1) the ubiquity of residential migration in urban society, and (2) the view that one's social network consists of those significant other persons with whom he interacts frequently. However, as we have already seen, residential migration, while frequent, is clearly not a universal characteristic of urbanites. Yet even more important is the fact that separation does not necessarily mean isolation, for the same forces which have increased the likelihood of migration have developed means for keeping in touch across the miles. A lack of interaction may not signify either a loss of contact or a lack of interpersonal influence; the mails and the telephone, as well as high-speed transportation facilities, are available to the separated to help them avoid losing contact. Thus, while it is not claimed that a letter or telephone conversation is equivalent to a visit, it nevertheless ap-

TABLE III-2

Frequency of interaction with parents, and a comparison of proximity and interaction frequency, according to the sex and occupational stratum and mobility of the young adults

Sex	Occupational Stratum and Mobility	Number of Respondents	Frequency of Interaction, in Pct.				Comparison	
			Weekly or More	Monthly-Weekly	Less Than Monthly	Total Pct.	Parents −100 Miles	Monthly or More
Males	Upward White Collar	(52)	31	40	29	100	67	71
	Stable White Collar	(66)	27	29	44	100	47	56
	Stable Blue Collar	(53)	49	25	26	100	68	74
	Downward Blue Collar	(10)	60	30	10	100	90	90
Females	Upward White Collar	(72)	26	35	39	100	57	61
	Stable White Collar	(90)	30	26	44	100	52	56
	Stable Blue Collar	(72)	42	29	29	100	68	71
	Downward Blue Collar	(19)	26	26	47	99	68	53

pears that a primary reason for the "isolation" view is simply that migration theory outran communications theory.

Several authors have stated that the means of communication make possible contact between the remote.[24] Yet they have presented little supporting data, and the actual frequency of their utilization thus remains problematic. Litwak, for example, indirectly denies that there are important differences in non-face-to-face communication by status groups. He says in defense of his predominantly middle class sample that "if it can be shown that his (Parsons') hypothesis does not hold for this group, then it is unlikely to hold for any division of society."[25] The paucity of empirical evidence regarding the use of the telephone and letters obliges us to explore its extent in the present study.

A most satisfactory departure for generalizations concerning the use of the communications media would seem to be young adult-parent relationships. The expected intimacy and strength of this kinship bond is as likely to result in frequent telephoning and letter writing as is any single social relationship. In the Greensboro sample, we find, not unexpectedly, that frequency of letter writing varies directly with the distance of the parents from Greensboro. Thus, the percentages writing yearly or less are 99 among those whose parents are in Greensboro, 56 per cent when the parents are within 100 miles, 28 per cent if the parents live elsewhere in North and South Carolina or Virginia, and only 7 per cent if the parents are outside the three-state area. The prevalence of letter-writing between the separated is best seen when we note that over two-thirds of those whose parents live over 100 miles away write them at least once a month.

As for telephoning, of course the greatest frequency is when both parents and adult offspring live in Greensboro, in which case 70 per cent talk to each other weekly or more. But the noteworthy aspect of telephone utilization is that 156, or *54 per cent*, of those 289 respondents whose parents live outside Greensboro have a long-distance conversation with them at least once a month.[26]

Earlier in the chapter, differences between the sexes in interaction with parents were found to be small, and occupational stratum differences were found to be determined by the distance factor, with the working classes living closer to their parents and seeing them more frequently. In relating sex and occupational status to telephoning and letter writing, the greater verbal and financial resources of the middle class are seen in Table III-3 to influence considerably the utilization of these communication means. The stable white-collar respondents and their parents use the telephone with markedly greater frequency when proximate and the mails when remote. Despite the small number of downwardly mobile, it is apparent that they resemble the stable white-collar, which indicates that the parents' occupational status is as important as that of the offspring in such two-way communication. Once again the upwardly mobile are in general a median category between the stable middle and working classes.

The widespread adoption of the telephone, and the utilization of it as well as the mails for keeping in touch have been postulated by Marvin B. Sussman and Lee Burchinal, and other researchers. Despite the less frequent use of long-distance telephoning by the non-mobile working-class adults, only 22 per cent of the 283 young adults whose parents live outside Greensboro talk to them as infrequently as once a year. A further insight into the manner in which communication keeps residentially separated parents and children in touch may be afforded by simply observing the frequency of the most frequent form of contact between the young adult and his parents, whether this be face-to-face, by mail, or by telephone, and noting the extent to which residential distance reduces the frequency of *any* form of contact. Although, as we have said, it is not argued that a telephone call or letter is equivalent to a visit, many, if not most, individuals consider them the next best thing. Table III-4 shows the frequency of any form of contact according to the residential distance of the parents.

The young adults whose parents live outside Greensboro can be seen to be customarily in monthly, with almost one-third in weekly, touch by letter or telephone. Such contacts help to maintain this intimate kin tie between periodic visits. In fact, only 23 persons, less than 8 per cent of the residentially separated and 5 per cent of the total sample, are in contact with their parents less than once a month. These 23 include one downwardly mobile, four stable mid-

TABLE III-3

Frequency of communication between young adults and their parents, by sex, occupational stratum and mobility, and residential distance

Sex	Occupational Stratum and Mobility	Number of Respondents with Non-Local Parents	Per cent Writing Non-local Parents Monthly+	Pct. Telephoning Non-local Parents Monthly+	Number of Respondents with Local Parents	Pct. Telephoning Local Parents Monthly+
Males	Upward White Col.	(35)	34	57	(17)	88
	Stable White Col.	(43)	79	54	(23)	96
	Stable Blue Col.	(24)	33	42	(29)	66
	Downward Blue Col.	(3)	(2)*	(2)*	(7)	86
Females	Upward White Col.	(57)	51	56	(15)	60
	Stable White Col.	(64)	70	67	(26)	96
	Stable Blue Col.	(45)	49	36	(27)	70
	Downward Blue Col.	(12)	75	67	(7)	100

* These are N's; percentages were not figured on such small numbers.

TABLE III-4

Frequency of the most frequent form of contact—whether face-to-face, by mail, or by telephone—between young adults and their parents, by residential distance

Location of Parents	Number of Respondents	Frequency of Most Frequent Contact, in Pct.				
		Weekly or More	Monthly-Weekly	Several Times Yearly	Yearly or Less	Total Pct.
Greensboro	(155)	93	7	—	—	100
−100 Miles	(113)	35	58	5	2	100
Beyond 100 Mi. in NC, SC, or Va.	(93)	27	60	10	3	100
Elsewhere	(83)	30	66	4	—	100

dle class, seven upwardly mobile, and eleven stable working class respondents. Separation does tend to reduce contact from weekly to monthly, but our data support the viewpoint that in urban, industrial society the social network is simply not a spatially restricted phenomenon. Separation does not mean isolation, and occupational mobility does not seem to result in substantially less contact between the young adult and his parents.

To conclude that interaction and communication occur is not to characterize the contact between these intergenerational kin of orientation, though many studies of the social relations of urbanites have stopped at this point. The preceding findings, while valuable, are but skeletal; they leave unanswered such "meaty" questions as: what are the sorts of situations which bring young adults and their parents together, and in what types of activities do they engage? These questions, and the relation of sex and occupational position to them, are the subjects of Section Two.

Section Two: Kinds of Contact Between Young Adults and Their Parents

There have been few detailed investigations of the patterns of contact between various kin, or specifically between parents and their adult offspring, but several authors have referred in general terms to such activities. In a paradigm for the study of kinship in urban society, Alan D. Coult and Robert W. Habenstein hypothesize that kin ties are functional for economic support, emotional support, marriage, birth, death, career, travel, residence, and succession to societal positions.[27] They do not elaborate, but the major focus of the list is upon tangible and intangible aid, with lesser foci upon ceremonies and visiting for its own sake. Even though separate nuclear family residence is preferred, adds Donald McKinley, it is nevertheless "considered desirable that ties with closer relatives be maintained through visits, favors, and letters."[28] In his insightful discussion of kin interaction, Bernard Farber summarizes three types of activities. Kin interaction, he says, includes: (1) participation in rituals and ceremonies, in which equal opportunity for those in the same kin relationship is stressed; (2) promotion of the welfare of family members, with aid based upon greater resources and upon trust between individuals; and (3) open communication between and concerning relatives, which is necessary for intimacy, trust, and the other characteristics of primariness.[29] Farber is aware that kin networks differ in the extent to which they fulfill these functions; however, his distinctions between ritual occasions, aid, and primary communication between kin are valuable.

A few authors have reduced the list of kin activities to a two-fold division. Rueben Hill, J. Joel Moss, and Claudine G. Wirths, for example, indicate that, in the Southern town they studied, kinfolk are the focal point of visiting and are also most often turned to with problems or in emergencies.[30] An explicit statement of this categorization of kin activities is that by Sussman and Burchinal: "The major activities linking the network are mutual aid and social activities. . . ." Similarly, Axelrod states that "relatives continue to be an important source of companionship and mutual support. . . ."[31]

Not all authors are satisfied with stating the dual nature of kin interaction. In a brief article on relations between young parents and grandparents, Ruth Albrecht reports that most of their involvement with each other is visits, not obligations. Litwak likewise observes in his research on occupational mobility and kin that in a bureaucratized society relations between relatives are commonly an end in themselves. Sometimes they entail the giving and receiving of aid, but more often they simply offer primary relations to the urban individual.[32] Goode expresses summarily the viewpoint that kin are less instrumental and more sentimental than formerly. Presently, he asserts, help to and from kin is less frequent than is simple visiting.[33]

The documentation of young adult-parent contact, beyond these sketchy characterizations of kin relations in general, is quite meagre, being limited to isolated comments in various sources. According to Alvin Schorr's discussion of filial responsibility to aging parents, the dominant pattern of young adult-aged parent interaction involves helping "each other with chores, visiting, and showing concern."[34] Young and Willmott observe that where parents and children live in close proximity the rendezvous for the daughters is the "Mum's" or mother's home. Here the daughters and their children are likely to eat their noon meals almost every day. Important occasions for sustaining this relationship, Peter Townsend notes, are the ceremonial and holiday occasions during the year.[35] These include national holidays such as Christmas and, in the United States, Labor Day and Independence Day, as well as family birthdays and anniversaries. Sussman finds among eighty Cleveland families that 74 per cent of the working-class and 81 per cent of the middle-class families have large gatherings at least once a year, ordinarily on a national holiday or other ceremonial occasion.[36]

No other single aspect of urban kinship has received more attention than has the mutual aid which flows between relatives. The work of Sussman in particular has brought to light the help pattern which exists primarily between parents and their married children. In his doctoral research, Sussman discovered that 154 out of 195 middle-aged, middle-class parents were undertaking to help their married children establish themselves. Such aid, the parents felt, was necessary in order to assure that the child would not fall below his parents in socio-economic status.[37] In a subsequent study, Sussman found in a small Cleveland sample a similar amount of aid in both occupational strata, white- and blue-collar. Within the month previous to his data collection, the most widespread form of aid from children to their parents had been help during illness, while from the parents to children financial assistance and help during illness were equally distributed. The middle classes were found to give significantly more financial aid, child care, advice, and valuable gifts than the working classes. Help in sickness and the direction of flow of aid is similar in the two strata.[38] Harry Sharp and Morris Axelrod, in the Detroit Area Study, also discovered widespread aid among various kin, chiefly between parents and children.[39]

The flow of aid between parents and their married children is chiefly from the parents, and includes a variety of tangible items, intangibles, and services. Direct financial aid is relatively infrequent, but is most commonly received by the young married couple during the early years of marriage. The aging parents seldom take regular care of their grandchildren while the parents work, but when they live close by, the mother is likely to do "occasional baby-sitting" for her daughter. Perhaps the most significant form of continuing mutual aid is in emergencies, such as sickness, child-birth, or a death in the family. For example, Townsend notes among his aged London respondents that the exchange of services, including baby-sitting and the emergencies mentioned above, is a primary connecting link between the generations. Such intangibles as advice and emotional support have received less attention than have tangible aid and services, but a considerable quantity of advice-giving has been noted by Sussman and Gordon F. Streib. One form of parental aid which seems to have virtually disappeared from the scene is the procurement of a job by the father for his son. Sussman finds among his New Haven respondents several cases of such nepotism, but in a later summarizing article reports that job procurement occurs but seldom.[40]

The scattered references to kinds of and occasions for contact, and the more detailed investigations of parent-married child mutual aid, provide a general basis for organizing our exploration. The primary aim is to determine those types of contact by which this inter-generational kin relationship operates. As indicated in Chapter I, the respondents were asked how often within the past two years they and their parents had participated in any of a long list of occasions, activities, or mutual aids. These were then combined to form *eight contact types:* (1) home visiting; (2) social activities; (3) voluntary organizations; (4) working together occupationally; (5) rituals; (6) communication, i.e., telephoning or letter writing; (7) aid received; and (8) aid given. In much of the ensuing discussion, aid given or received will be further divided into tangible aid and services, but this is for the purpose of understanding differences according to sex and occupational stratum, not because there is any particular distinction with respect to the comparative importance of these two types of aid. In Table III-5 the occurrence of the types of contact between young adults and their parents is delineated.

To the extent that it can be determined by kinds of contact, the relations of young adults and their parents are focused in the various methods of and occasions for keeping in touch. Frequent communication, home visiting, and the sharing of ritual occasions dominate contact between these kin. Thus, simple visiting, as Goode asserts, is more frequent than the exchange of aid between parents and adult offspring. Nevertheless, the receipt of aid by the young adult is second only in frequency to visiting and communication. Less widespread and frequent are the giving of aid to parents, the sharing of social activities, and organizational involvement. The infrequent participation in extra-home or social activities is particularly significant in view of the large number of activities subsumed therein. In terms of outdoor or commercial recreations, or even

TABLE III-5

Frequency of occurrence of the contact types in young adult-parent relations during the past two years (N=444)

Contact Types	Frequency of Occurrence, in Per Cent				
	Monthly or More	Several Times Yearly	Once or Twice a Year	Never	Total Pct.
Home Visits	52	27	14	7	100
Social Activities	12	27	21	40	100
Voluntary Organizations	13	14	11	62	100
Working Together	2	—	1	97	100
Ritual Occasions	9	43	28	21	101
Communication	82	6	5	7	100
Aid Received by Young Adult	22	37	20	21	100
Aid Given to Parents	13	27	19	41	100

shopping, parents are simply not utilized as companions by the majority of young married adults. Common employment is virtually non-existent, there being only seven respondents who work regularly with their parent or parents. Five respondents indicate that on their vacation they work on the family farm, thus sharing the parental occupation once a year; this, however, was not the intent of the question. The seven instances of working together are mentioned only in passing in the remainder of this chapter, the assumption being that this possible area of young adult-parent contact occurs with insignificant frequency in the present sample. We shall, however, return briefly to consider occupation and kinship in Chapter IV on sibling relations.

Contact Patterns: A Tentative Approach to the Role of Parents in the Life of the Young Adult

The distribution of occurrences of contact types within the past two years has been recapitulated in Table III-5. Much of the work on mutual aid refers to the "help pattern" which exists, after determining that a form of aid has occurred but once. It is our conviction that the word "pattern" must be reserved for recurrent activity. A reference to the rendering of services by parents may be used to exemplify the problem. A summer vacation visit may include an evening of grandparental baby-sitting while the young couple go out. The term "help pattern" hardly seems appropriate as a description of this single event. Or an adult daughter and her mother may go shopping together once for a gift for the daughter's husband. To label this a significant pattern of social activities would seem to border on hyperbole.

What, then, may be employed as a guide to patterning? We may observe recurrence within the types of contact, utilizing a given frequency of occurrence as an indication of patterning. Furthermore, when a given contact type is patterned among a large number of young adults and their parents, it may then be considered a significant aspect of this relationship. An immediate problem involves the non-equivalence of types of contact: who, for instance, would claim that receiving a letter four times a year is analogous to receiving a check for $200 that often? Yet the incorporation of several different forms of aid or social activities into one contact type means that all but one of the sub-categories may be completely absent from the relationship and it will still appear with the required frequency. Thus, the ease with which certain areas can achieve "patterning," due to the number of specific activities subsumed, offsets to a degree the relative incongruity between them.

A second factor in determining contact patterns concerns the frequency most suitable to indicate recurrence or a pattern. Clearly, an event occurring once in the past two years is not discernibly patterned, and our intent is to discover as far as possible those ways in which parents play an important role in the lives of their adult offspring. Contact as often as monthly by letter or telephone demonstrates a substantial interest in keeping in touch. On the other hand, the ritual occasions do not occur in most families that often. Thus, while it over-emphasizes the regularity and dispersion of patterned communication, *involvement in some sub-activity of a contact type three or more times a year for the past two years appears to be* a reasonable enough—though necessarily arbitrary—requirement for it to be deemed *a contact pattern* between the young adult and his parents. Despite the aforementioned dissimilarities in contact types, we will utilize occurrence several times a year throughout the discussion of patterning in this and subsequent chapters in order to achieve a basis for comparison.

An important distinction is between those forms of contact which demand interaction and those which do not. Home visiting, ritual interaction, all forms of shared activity, and the exchange of services necessitate face-to-face contact. Only communication and tangible aid can recur across the miles. Therefore, it is not surprising that 98 per cent of those whose parents live in Greensboro engage in a pattern of home visits, and 51 per cent in patterned social activities, while only 35 per cent of those whose parents live more than 250 miles away have a pattern of home visits and 20 per cent have a pattern of social activity. The opportunity for recurrence despite distance is seen in the fact that patterned communication actually increases from 81 per cent of the proximate to 99 per cent of those separated by 250 or more miles. Likewise, the giving of tangible aid to parents in a patterned manner varies only from 22 per cent of the proximate to 18 per cent of those whose parents are 250 or more miles away.

To summarize, the patterning of young adult-parent contact when they are in the same city is focussed in home visiting, with most of the young adults also keeping in touch with their parents by telephone, attending ritual get-togethers when they arise, and receiving various sorts of services, particularly baby-sitting, from their parents. Much smaller numbers of the proximate exchange other forms of aid or are involved in various social activities or organizations with their parents. The means of communication are employed almost unanimously as a substitute for interaction by the residentally separated, although those young adults who have parents fairly close by continue to visit with them regularly and to see them on ritual occasions in a patterned manner. Among the re-mote, the significance of this kin tie is apparently restricted to showing concern by keeping in touch, with but scattered instances of involvement in any of the other contact types in a patterned way.

The kinship literature affords little basis for anticipating differ-ences by sex or occupational stratum in most of the types of con-tact. While there may be differences in certain of the sub-activities, e.g., daughters and their mothers are more likely to shop together, it is far from certain that these differences will be manifested in the contact patterns. However, a few studies have found sex and occu-pational stratum differences with respect to mutual aid. Sussman's study of a small Cleveland sample reported a few significant social class differences, the major types of aid, with the exception of help in sickness, being more frequent among the middle classes.[41] The young adult's sex has been found by two authors to be associated with the help pattern. Ethel Shanas finds in her NORC study of 2,567 old people that daughters are more often turned to in crisis than are sons. The same conclusion is reached by Townsend, who relates that daughters are the chief source not only of emergency help but of other aid for their mothers as well.[42]

Differential occupational mobility, contends E. E. LeMasters, re-sults in less frequent interaction, differing values, and ambivalent feelings between family members. Although differences in interac-tion frequency according to mobility or stability were not found apart from considerations of residential distance, it is possible that differing values and interests may result in a more restricted distri-bution of contact patterns among the mobile. However, the evi-dence is sparse enough to warrant exploring sex and stratum-mo-bility variations without specific hypotheses. Aid is subdivided into tangibles and services for clarification (see Table III-6).

Over-all sex differences are minor except in the exchange of mu-tual aid. While the females are more likely to shop regularly with their mothers, the young males offset this by a more frequent en-gagement with their fathers and/or mothers in the various forms of extra-home (commercial and outdoor) recreation. Home visits and ritual occasions demonstrate little divergence by sex for the sample as a whole, except among the downwardly mobile where numbers

TABLE III-6

The patterned engagement of young adults and their parents in the contact types during the past two years, according to the sex and occupational stratum and mobility of the young adults

Sex, Occupational Stratum, and Mobility		Number of Respondents	Occurrence Several Times Yearly or More, in Per Cent								
			Home Visits	Activities	Organizations	Rituals	Communication	Tangibles Rec'd	Services Rec'd	Tangibles Given	Services Given
Males	White Collar Upward	(52)	83	44	29	52	92	29	52	33*	37
	Stable	(66)	77	41	29	52	96	33	36	14	24
	Blue Collar Stable	(53)	79	11—	21	49	66—	21	40	15	32
	Downward	(10)	90	30	20	80*	90	40	60*	20	20—
Females	White Collar Upward	(72)	76	42	29	54	90	32	50	18	28
	Stable	(90)	76	52*	29	49	98	43*	47	12	27
	Blue Collar Stable	(72)	79	39	28	53	81	35	63*	24	40*
	Downward	(19)	79	47	21	37—	95	26	37	11	16—

* Indicates a percentage which is important for its magnitude; — indicates a percentage which stands out due to its smallness.

are small. However, sex differences in the giving and receiving of aid are in evidence, and are consistent with the literature on independence training in our society. Komarovsky, in her classic discussion of sex roles, comments that during college "women do not become emancipated from their families to the same degree or in the same manner as men do."[43] The young married male has been taught greater independence from his family than has the young married female. Urie Bronfenbrenner states it thus: "the qualities of independence, initiative, and self-sufficiency . . . are especially valued for boys in our culture."[44] The results of this differential independence training, and the lesser responsibility of the male for the day-to-day care of his own children, are seen in the 64 per cent of the young married females who report having received a pattern of aid from their parents during the past two years, in comparison to 53 per cent of the males, and the 43 per cent of the males who have given patterned aid to their parents, as compared to 37 per cent of the females. Much of the aid given by the males is either in direct financies, i.e., cash or loans, or involves helping the parents in their home. The aid received by the females is largely baby-sitting or child care help from her mother, or may be in the form of sizable gifts. The wife's parents are ordinarily careful not to offer direct sums of money, in order not to usurp the young son-in-law's position as family provider.[45]

A brief discussion of the contact patterns of the various sex and stratum-mobility categories may shed some light upon relationships with parents. Differences between the upwardly mobile males and their stable middle class counterparts are negligible except in the area of mutual aid. Litwak mentions in his mobility research the possibility of aid crossing class lines, and explains that the downwardly mobile individual is likely to be the recipient.[46] These upwardly mobile Greensboro males are, in fact, the most likely of any of the eight categories to give tangible aid to their parents, who are working class. This is not, however, a one-direction relationship, for the parents, particularly the mother, are apt to sew or baby-sit or aid the upwardly mobile son and his family in some way as well. Of course, the greater proximity of upwardly mobile adults to their parents accounts for a portion of the difference between them and the non-mobile middle class. Nevertheless, proximity merely permits, it does not demand, greater involvement in contact patterns. The only reasonable conclusion one can draw is that upwardly mobile males manifest no sign of a restricted activity pattern with their parents; rather, they have a broader base of mutual aid which is consonant with a close tie and is in keeping with theirs and their parents' needs.

Upwardly mobile females are likewise quite similar to their non-mobile counterparts, but they are not as likely to receive tangible aid or to engage in social activities. The receipt of financial aid or gifts by stable middle-class males and females is basically a manifestation of their parents' greater financial resources. When the white collar mother and daughter live close to each other they are frequently shopping or movie companions. Once again, it is their financial resources which make possible the regular shopping trips or recreational activities.

The similarity in contact patterns of the upwardly mobile and the stable white collar exemplifies a rather intriguing variation on the theme of anticipatory socialization. By anticipatory socialization is usually meant the assumption, on the part of the young person who is changing his social status, of a network of friends and a style of life which resembles that of the status into which he is moving, rather than the status from which he has come. Hilde Himmelweit is reported by Ralph Turner to have found that "the parents of a group of upwardly mobile boys from working-class backgrounds in London exhibited more consistently middle-class attitudes than even a comparable group of middle-class parents."[47] The phenomenon we are observing among young upwardly mobile Greensboroites and their parents may very well be the previous assumption by their parents of a middle-class style of life, which carries over into adult contact patterns between the generations. Only in the case of mutual aid, where need and opportunity are determinative, are there substantial differences between the two categories of currently middle-class males, and the female disparity in engagement in social activities would hardly be indicative of disinvolvement between mobile adults and their parents.

Stable blue-collar position and downward mobility are quite distinctive in their effects upon relations with parents. The down-wardly mobile males, about whom generalization is tenuous due to the small numbers, are likely to receive patterned aid from their parents, but are unlikely to give any form of patterned aid (only two of ten do). Thus, like the upwardly mobile males, the down-ward seem to correspond to Litwak's postulate regarding the giving and receiving of aid across social status lines. The close proximity of these downwardly mobile males and their parents is evidenced in the patterning of drop-in visits and the frequent sharing of ritual occasions. The downwardly mobile females, on the other hand, as Schneider and Homans hypothesize, show definite signs of neglect by or alienation from their parents. Despite a tendency to live close, they are not apt to share in family rituals regularly, and they are the least likely to give or receive any forms of aid on a regular basis. This is antithetical to Litwak's position regarding the down-wardly mobile, and may mean that their parents are actually slight-ing them, due to their having married "below their station."

Working-class mothers and daughters have a close and appar-ently economically necessary bond in the face of their husbands' less secure occupational positions. The division of labor in blue-collar families is such that kin relations tend to be the domain of the female.[48] Young working-class females in Greensboro demon-strate a specific obligational tie with their parents, especially their mothers, by being most likely to have an extensive pattern of ex-changed services and of aid in general. Outside of simply keeping in touch, i.e., visiting and telephoning, mutual aid is the key attri-bute of the stable working-class female's relationship with her par-ents. The working-class male whose parents are working class, in contrast, is extremely unlikely to engage in any patterned social ac-tivity with his parents when they are proximate, or to keep in regu-lar touch by letter or telephone when residentially separated. This lack of patterned involvement is especially striking when it is re-called that the working-class males are modally in much closer proximity to their parents than any of the other sex-stratum group-ings.

The lack of patterned involvement of the downwardly mobile females and stable working-class males in a wide range of contact types is underscored if we simply add the number of contact patterns and divide by the number of respondents. With eight possible contact types, the mean number of patterns in young adult-parent relations is just under four. Six of the eight sex and stratum-mobility groupings range from a mean of 3.8 to 4.2 contact patterns. The downwardly mobile females and stable blue-collar males, however, are represented by 3.4 and 3.2 patterned contact types, respectively. Also remarkable is the manner in which middle-class children of middle-class parents make use of parental availability. What I mean is this: these young adults are frequently separated by at least some distance from their parents. A few of the separated bridge the gap by frequent trips, as well as by communication and tangible aid sent through the mails. This, however, does not account for the widespread patterning of types of contact between them and their parents. It is the few who do live close to their parents who almost unanimously engage in a broad range of patterned contacts, including social activities, telephoning, visiting, and often mutual aid and organizational attendance as well. Thus, the stable middle-class and their parents have a mean of four contact patterns —very close to the mean for the entire sample.

Haller has been quoted as saying that it is now possible for the young adult male to make his occupational choice without leaving his home community. This is more true for the working-class man, but it is questionable when applied to the company representative or the college teacher. It is therefore at least possible that the geographic mobility of the working-class male, when it occurs, should be viewed as movement *from* a situation more than *to* it. We may in this sample be observing a few blue-collar males who have escaped an unhappy kinship situation and a great many others who are proximate to their kin, but not necessarily by choice, while the occupationally-oriented migration of many middle-class persons may be despite a relatively close parental tie. Such social psychological or subjective factors, when analyzed, should provide further understanding of variations by sex and occupational stratum and mobility in the relations of young adults and their parents.

Summary of Young Adult-Parent Contact

The over-all pattern of young adult-parent contact is one of extremely frequent interaction and/or communication. Residential distance places a considerable limitation on all forms of contact except non-face-to-face communication by letter or telephone. Among the proximate, the bond with parents varies by sex and occupational stratum as follows: currently white-collar males share a wide range of types of patterned contact, with the upwardly mobile more likely to manifest patterns of mutual aid, especially tangible help given and services received. Neither the upwardly mobile males nor females appear to have the restricted range of contacts with their parents that might be expected if there were much ambivalence or alienation between them. The stable middle-class females frequently have their mothers as social companions, and are also apt to receive tangible aid regularly. Blue-collar males with blue-collar parents are radically different from their female equivalents in the objective significance of their relations with their parents. Dropping in when they live close and, more often than not, corresponding when separated are the predominant features of these males' parental contacts. The females, on the other hand, exhibit a genuine obligational tie with respect to helping and receiving help from their parents, and are generally similar to the middle class females in the other types of contact. Downwardly mobile males in our sample live close to their parents, which is apparent by their frequent home visits and ritual get-togethers. They also modally receive help from their parents regularly, which may be a strengthening factor in the relationship. Either neglect by the parents, or a mutual parting of the ways, seems to characterize the downwardly mobile females. A severe instance of such sundered relations is the daughter of an insurance salesman who is married to a warehouse foreman, formerly a truck driver. Her parents live just outside Greensboro, but she and her husband have not seen or communicated with them for two years. She explains the problem thus: "My parents rejected my husband when we got married. For a time I tried to continue seeing them, but I finally had to choose between them and my husband. I decided to drop my parents entirely—at least until their feelings changed." While this is an extreme case, it may be illustrative of the difficulties inherent in the situation of the downwardly mobile female.

Any particular nuclear family persists through the lifetime of its members, although in Western societies they cease to live together. Thus, the family of orientation is transformed by marriage and neolocal residence into the kin of orientation. The significance of young adult-parent relations appears to be basically an extension of activity patterns formed during the years before the launching or marriage of the offspring. Intimacy and mutual concern are ordinarily characteristic of early relationships. Since economic interdependence and authority are for the most part no longer key attributes of our kinship system,[49] it is possible for the developing patterns to continue into adulthood in the form of patterned visiting and communication, with help when needed. Though interests may diverge, this divergence is not likely to alter the concern which children and parents have for each other. Nor does the marriage of the young adult usually destroy the intimacy of the parental tie or reduce the desire of the parents to help when the occasion or need for it arises. Thus, the contact patterns present a picture of continuing contact, of regular help as needed, of ritual reunions to renew old traditions and bonds, and of infrequent sharing of activities and organizational commitments between these age-differentiated adult kin.

The roles which parents play in the life of the young adult are thus built upon ongoing relationships. The primary change is that, with the independent adulthood of the offspring, what was once a one-way sense of responsibility has become a reciprocal obligation. The relationship between this obligation and affection for parents, as well as the other subjective aspects of this kin tie, is delineated in the next section.

Section Three: Subjective Aspects of Young Adult-Parent Relations

Similarity of attitudes, strong emotional attachment, and frequent interaction have been assumed by Homans and other interaction theorists to be closely associated. If, however, two individuals are not free to dissolve a social relationship because of location or obligatory necessity, the association between consensus, affection, and interaction no longer holds.[50] Emotional closeness or affection, similarity of values and interests, and obligatory necessity: these are therefore some of the key subjective aspects of a social relationship. Their variation, in relations between young adults and their parents, according to sex and occupational position, their interrelations, and their association with interaction or contact form the subject matter of the present section.

Herbert Blumer has warned of the pitfalls in studying attitudes. Attitudes are often used synonymously with motives as drives to action. Yet as explanations of behavior, most attitudinal or subjective variables are less exact than the action patterns they purport to explain. Instead of as predictors of behavior, attitudes may be studied in their own right, yet the result is an infinite number of "attitudes," not generic concepts.[51]

A second difficulty with subjective analyses of social relations originates in what Reinhard Bendix and Bennett Berger have called the perspective of "dual tendencies."[52] Interpersonal relations, these authors assert, are both intimate and impersonal, primary and secondary simultaneously, incorporating features of both attributes. If social concepts involve such dual tendencies, then each social fact should be searched "for what it hides as much as for what it reveals."[53] This viewpoint is especially applicable to the verbal replies to subjective questions regarding kinship relations.

Aware of the haziness of most subjective variables and alert to the hidden meanings in attitudinal responses, we approach young adult—parent relations with both caution and confidence that the subjective aspects of this kin tie can in some measure be described and are of value in understanding—even if not in explaining—the objective findings which have preceded. Affection and value consensus are the first foci of attention.

Affection and Value Consensus in Young Adult-Parent Relations

Similar attitudes about salient issues is a key factor predisposing two individuals to mutual attraction. The correlation between affectional closeness or emotional attachment and consensus in values and interests, asserted by several authors, is determined in the present study by single questions seeking to ascertain affectional closeness and value consensus.[54] Henceforth we shall refer to affectional closeness or distance and to value consensus or divergence.

More young Greensoboroites indicate that they have a close affectional tie to their parent (65 per cent) than that they and their parent share the same values (54 per cent). However, the association between closeness and consensus is such that 69 per cent of those who are close to one of their parents also perceive a substantial value consensus with that parent, while 74 per cent of those who are affectionally distant from their mother or father are similarly characterized by a perceived value divergence from that parent.

There are very likely to be variations in affectional closeness and value consensus which depend upon the sex and occupational stratum of both the young adult and his parent. The earlier discussion of interaction frequency according to the sex of the young adult was introduced by the statement that females are generally believed to be closer to their parents and other kin than are males. This is considered to be subjectively true, even though we did not find it manifested objectively.[55]

Value consensus according to the sex of the parent or offspring has received little attention *per se*. Theodore Newcomb and George Svehla reported several years ago in a study of attitudes in 558 Cleveland families that daughters are influenced more by their mothers, and more by both parents than are sons.[56] However, attitudes toward the church, war, and communism, investigated in the Cleveland study, are not necessarily analogous to the life values incorporated in a question regarding value consensus. It is, however, likely that the role of mother in adulthood does signify that daughters and their mothers will manifest a substantial convergence of values in adulthood.

The question of occupational status differences in affection for parents is introduced well by Mirra Komarovksy's research. Among her blue-collar couples she finds that the better educated are closer in affection to both parents.[57] If this trend holds throughout levels of education, we might expect young middle-class adults to have a closer affectional tie to their parents than do working-class adults. The issues involved are, however, more complex than simply the educational or occupational attainment of the offspring. Differential socialization, including the role of each parent by occupational level, is very likely to be reflected in adulthood both in affectional and consensual variations in relations to parents. In fact, a principle upon which we are working is that early socialization, adolescent aspirations, young adult occupational choice, and later relations with one's aging parents are of a piece. Thus, in order to understand adult relationships with the kin of orientation we may profitably draw upon the literature regarding socialization in modern urban society, as well as the less plentiful material upon adult relationships *per se*.

What insight can be gained from viewing the socialization literature? Melvin L. Kohn and Eleanor E. Carroll, in a study of parental responsibility allocation, find that middle-class fathers seek to be as supportive of their sons as are their mothers.

> *They (middle-class fathers) do not appear as supportive of daughters; apparently they feel this to be more properly the mother's domain. Working-class fathers seem to play neither the directive role their wives would have them play, nor a more highly supportive role. Rather, they seem to see child rearing as more completely their wives' responsibility.*[58]

Donald McKinley has recently summarized the relation of social status to parental roles in socialization thus:

> *1. Parents tend to be more severe and hostile socializers at the lower levels of society. 2. Fathers at the lower levels, and possibility mothers at the upper levels, tend to be somewhat more severe than their spouses. 3. These two factors are explained as a consequence of the distribution of rewards in the society by class and by sex (of parent) within classes.*[59]

Therefore, says McKinley, the father has greater authority and receives greater affection in higher status, and less in lower status, families than the mother.

The roles of the father and mother in mobility aspirations, and the consequences thereof, have been distinguished by other authors. Joseph A. Kahl found the father's attitude toward achievement a basic determinant of the working-class son's aspirations, and later Robert A. Ellis and W. Clayton Lane reported that a mother who outranks her husband educationally and/or occupationally is a primary factor in the upward mobility of her child.[60] These latter authors indicate that the lower the class, the less likely is the father to have a major influence in the decision to go to college. This is of course consistent with the blue-collar father's generally less significant role in socialization affirmed by Kohn and Carroll.

Divergent viewpoints regarding the effects of mobility upon affectional and consensual ties with parents have already been presented in Chapter One. Young and Willmott's attempt to reconcile the view that mobility alienates with the position that it has little independent effect is based upon the sex of the individual. Mobility, they claim, causes interaction to be less frequent between a son and his father, but does not affect adversely any of the other parent-child sex combinations.[61] While such differences, if present in Greensboro, were obscured in the objective data by considering contact with either parent as simply parental contact, they may be manifested in the sensitive area of feelings. That is, if Willmott and Young's findings are verified, upwardly and downwardly mobile males should feel less close to their fathers than do the occupationally stable males. The same authors comment upon a basic value distinction between males and females. Women ordinarily have the same occupations in adulthood, i.e., being housewives and mothers. Thus, it is averred, they are little affected by status differences between the occupations of their husbands and fathers.[62] This might be rephrased, in the light of other research reviewed above, to state that adult mothers and daughters are likely to share the same values and interests to the extent that these are focussed in home and children. This, however, would not necessarily override the effects of earlier socialization upon affectional ties.

The attempt must be made to incorporate these data into a coherent framework. Ours is a society in which middle-class values dominate, in the school system, the mass media, and elsewhere.

They may be accepted or rejected by the individual, but they are ever-present for comparison or for incorporation as part of the individual's value system. The growing young person, male or female, looks to his father as a symbol of success or failure in terms of society's economic-occupational values. The young person likewise responds to variations in socialization according to the roles and methods of the socializing agents, in this case the parents. The blue-collar father is neither an occupational example to which to aspire nor does he seem frequently to play a key role in the socialization process. In those cases where the blue-collar father is admired, it is his character, not his attainments, which is appreciated.[63] The middle-class father is generally admired and respected by his children as one who incorporates the society's dominant values. Thus, the first portion of our hypothesis or expectation is that (1) regardless of the sex or occupational position of the offspring, affection for and value consensus with a *middle-class father* will tend to be greater than when the father is working-class. Stating the same thing in terms of our stratum and mobility categories, stable white-collar and downwardly mobile young adults— or those with middle-class fathers—will tend to feel closer and hold values more similar to their fathers than do upwardly mobile and stable blue-collar young adults.

How can this be true of the downwardly mobile; did not their fathers fail them? The answer lies in the differing roles of the mother and father in socialization. The mother, regardless of the family's status, ordinarily bears the major day-to-day burden of the child rearing process. Although the middle-class father is a role model and may take more of a hand in socializing the son, the mother is nevertheless in a position to receive the major credit for her children's success, or more particularly to take the blame for their failure. The second part of our hypothetical synthesis of the three strands of data is that (2) the *present* occupational position of the young adult is integrally associated with his feelings toward his mother. If he or she has "made it," in terms of the middle-class success orientation of urban, industrial society, he is grateful primarily to his mother for her encouragement and help throughout the socialization process. If he remains working class or moves from a middle-class family into a working-class position, the mother is likely to be regarded as bearing the major responsibility. As for value consensus with the mother, (3) the young adult males likelihood of consensus rather than divergence is related in the same way as affection. The adult female, however, may express consensus in values and interests with her mother despite a lesser affectional tie to a blue-collar mother. The full hypothesis, in its simplest terms, is that the *parents'* high occupational status is closely related to strong affection for and value consensus with the *father*, the high occupational status of the *young adult* is associated with strong affection for and value consensus with the mother, while the daughter is likely to be similar in values and interests with her mother regardless of either her's or her mother's status. Finally, daughters are closer affectionally and in terms of consensus to their mothers than to their fathers, and to both parents than are sons. Table III-7 presents the results.

Affection and value consensus generally follow the hypothesis, but there are a few key divergences which deserve comment. First, the subjective relations of daughters and mothers do appear closest, as can be observed in the "totals" rows. Second, the daughter's affection for and perception of consensus with her father are associated primarily with the father's occupational position, while the son's relation with his mother is to some extent associated with the son's status. Third, daughters do seem to relate to their mothers affectionally in terms of their own present status, but value consensus of daughters and mothers varies little according to the status of either.

The upwardly mobile females, both affectionally and in values, appear to demonstrate the findings of Ellis and Lane—albeit inferentially—that the mother is instrumental in their upward movement, perhaps as she subtly uses the father as an example of what *not* to look for in a husband. The downwardly mobile male is quite apparently subjectively alienated from his mother. Of course, the relation may not be one of cause and effect; rather, affectional distance and downward mobility may in fact be coincident results of the progressive divergence of values between son and mother during the socialization process. Upwardly mobile males are affection-

TABLE III-7

Expression of affectional closeness to or value consensus with parents, according to the sex and occupational stratum and mobility of the young adult

Sex	Occupational Stratum and Mobility	Number of Respondents	Affectionally Close, in Per Cent		Value Consensus, in Per Cent	
			To Father	To Mother	To Father	To Mother
Males:	Total	(181)	54	59	52	51
Males	Upward White Collar	(52)	54	60	52	52
	Stable White Collar	(66)	65	62	68	58
	Stable Blue Collar	(53)	42	57	34	45
	Downward Blue Collar	(10)	50	40	50	30
Females	Upward White Collar	(72)	58	83	39	65
	Stable White Collar	(90)	71	83	58	64
	Stable Blue Collar	(72)	61	72	44	63
	Downward Blue Collar	(19)	68	68	58	63
Females:	Total	(253)	64	79	49	64

ally and consensually closer to their fathers than hypothesized, being quite similar in subjective relations with both parents. A reasonable explanation for this might be that they have been influenced toward mobility by their father, as Kahl claims, or by their mother, as Ellis and Lane assert, or in some cases by both parents.

The bringing together of research on socialization, aspirations, and adult relationships has shed some light on the subjective aspects of parent-adult offspring relations. While much of the reasoning has been indirectly inferred from responses to questions on values and affectional closeness, the argument has been consistent with the literature and to a great extent with the tabular results. A final mention needs to be made of Willmott and Young's reported lessening of interaction between upwardly mobile sons and their fathers. First, there is no sign in the present subjective data of father-son avoidance or alienation. Secondly, daughters do, in comparison to sons, express a greater similarity of values with their mothers, regardless of occupational status, which is very likely a product not only of early socialization, but of the role convergence which comes with marriage and motherhood on the part of the daughter.

Similarity of Values, Affection, and Contact with Parents

The foregoing analysis leaves as yet unanswered the important question of association between affection, value consensus, and contact between young adults and their parents. Talcott Parsons has implied that sentiment has virtually free reign in determining interaction between kin in American society.[64] Alvin L. Schorr emphasizes, in general agreement with Parsons, the spontaneous nature of filial relations, and Robert M. Dinkel explains difficulties between parents and their adult children with the comment that "only rarely can people who differ in fundamental views continue a satisfactory personal relation."[65]

Yet despite these statements it seems unlikely that such direct association between affection and/or consensus and contact is fully true of any kin relationship, but particularly that between parents and their children. Numerous authors have noted the general obligatory aspects of this kin tie. Elaine Cumming and David M.

Schneider, for example, assert plainly that relations with parents are based on dissimilarity, help, and obligation. Garigue, Hollingshead, Reiss, and Muir and Weinstein also indicate the substantial feelings of obligation which characterize relations between these kin of orientation.[66] The two views, i.e., spontaneity, based on feelings and attitudes, and obligation, are not mutually exclusive, however. Spontaneity is stressed, for example, with regard to specific acts of helpfulness, while obligation is ordinarily treated as a general responsibility to keep in touch.

The complexities of spontaneity and obligation make us uncertain as to what, if any, relation a simple expression of closeness to or value consensus with parents has to interaction frequency. In the Greensboro sample the answer is negative; there is no association between either affection or consensus and simple frequency of interaction. Thus, 35 per cent of those young adults who are close to both parents see them weekly or more, 33 per cent of those affectionally close to one parent see them that often, as do 34 per cent of the respondents who indicate that they are affectionally distant from both parents. Similar comparisons hold for other frequencies of interaction according to affection, as well as for value consensus.

This finding of no difference is a bit deceiving, however. When distance is held constant, the relation between closeness and interaction frequency is clarified considerably (see Table III-8). When young adults and their parents live in the same city, interaction and expressions of closeness continue to demonstrate no association. Likewise, when a distance of 250 or more miles separates the young adult from his parents, the association is negligible. However, when the parents are outside Greensboro but within the surrounding three-state area a certain amount of interaction choice, based upon emotional attachment, seems to exist. Such variations must not be thought of in a causal framework. It may not be that less closeness causes less frequent interaction, or vice versa; more probably both closeness and interaction frequency at a moderate distance are related to family relationships as they have developed over the years.

Early in the present Chapter the proximate were found to be uniformly frequent in interaction with parents and the remote were

TABLE III-8

Expression of closeness to and frequency of interaction with parents, according to the parents' residential location

Location of Parents	Closeness to Either or Both Parents	Number of Respondents	Frequency of Interaction, in Per Cent				
			Weekly or More	Monthly to Weekly	Several Times Yearly	Yearly or Less	Total Pct.
Greensboro	Close to Both	(74)	85	15	—	—	100
	Close to One	(47)	87	13	—	—	100
	Close to Neither	(34)	79	21	—	—	100
−100 Miles	Close to Both	(63)	21	62	18	—	101
	Close to One	(33)	15	70	15	—	100
	Close to Neither	(17)	12	41	35	12	100
NC, SC, Va.	Close to Both	(41)	—	47	51	2	100
	Close to One	(33)	—	33	64	3	100
	Close to Neither	(19)	—	10	58	32	100
Elsewhere	Close to Both	(41)	—	10	42	49	101
	Close to One	(27)	—	11	48	41	100
	Close to Neither	(15)	—	7	53	40	100

uniformly infrequent, while the young adults whose parents were outside Greensboro but fairly close by exhibited a wide range of interaction frequencies. At that point it was postulated that the proximate are constrained to interact frequently, the remote to interact infrequently, but those whose parents are at a moderate distance seemed to have a modicum of choice. The choice now appears to involve subjective differences, and moderate distance appears to be the ideal arrangement for exercising that choice.

While the figures in Table III-8 are suggestive, they are not altogether convincing. The association between closeness and the contact of the residentially separated requires further evidence. Referring to Table III-4 in Section One of this Chapter we note that, when letter writing and telephoning are included with face-to-face interaction as forms of contact, differences in contact frequency with parents living outside Greensboro are negligible by residential distance. Utilizing once again the frequency of the most frequent form of contact, we may for the moment disregard distance and combine all those whose parents live outside Greensboro. However, the possibility that either the sex or occupational stratum of the respondent may be a contaminating factor causes us to divide the sample accordingly. Stratum differences by sex are non-existent in these data. Therefore, in Table III-9 the association between affectional closeness and contact, and between value consensus and contact, are investigated according to the sex of the young adult, when the parents live outside Greensboro.

Affection and contact are highly associated among the males, with 80 per cent of those who feel close to both parents being in touch monthly or more, as compared to only one-third of the young husbands who are close to neither parent. Although weekly contact is more likely when the daughter feels close to both parents, the young married females show little sign of less frequent communication with their parents on the basis of a lesser emotional attachment to them. Causality is once again unspecified, but the seemingly greater choice of young husbands is in complete agreement with the assertion of Muir and Weinstein and the findings of Robins and Tomanec that "women tend to act as the representatives of the nuclear family in fulfilling obligations to relatives."[67]

TABLE III-9

Expressions of affectional closeness, and value consensus, and frequency of the most frequent form of contact—face-to-face, telephone, or letter—with parents who live outside Greensboro, according to the sex of the young adult

Sex	Closeness to Either or Both Parents	Number of Respondents	Frequency of Contact, in Per Cent					
			Weekly or More	Several Times Monthly	Monthly	Several Times Yearly	Yearly or Less	Total Pct.
Males	Close to Both	(46)	26	54	17	2	—	99
	Close to One	(31)	19	45	29	7	—	100
	Close to Neither	(31)	7	26	39	16	13	101
Females	Close to Both	(99)	43	38	14	4	—	99
	Close to One	(62)	32	44	16	8	—	100
	Close to Neither	(20)	35	30	25	5	5	100
	Value Consensus with Either or Both Parents							
Males	Both	(44)	30	54	14	2	—	100
	One	(37)	14	49	32	5	—	100
	Neither	(27)	7	19	41	19	15	101
Females	Both	(68)	40	41	15	4	—	100
	One	(73)	32	42	21	5	—	100
	Neither	(40)	50	30	10	8	3	101

While married males are in touch with their parents almost as frequently as are married females with theirs, the former are able to follow with somewhat greater freedom the dictates of their feelings, provided the parents do not live extremely close by.

Sex differences in relations with parents are highlighted by the lower half of Table III-9. Value consensus has an even closer relationship with contact frequency between males and their parents than does affection. Dinkel's statement that divergent views on basic issues damage personal relations seems to hold to a degree for young males and their parents. They are not linked by as strong an obligatory tie, it seems, and are thus objectively related to their parents in some measure according to the similarity of their values, as well as feelings of affection.

But what of the females? First, there are many less who are high in value consensus than who feel close to their parents. Furthermore, those who express a basic value divergence from both parents tend to be in as frequent, if nor more frequent, contact with them. This seems contradictory to the hypothesized relation between affection, consensus, and interaction, but in fact it illustates an important feature of interpersonal relations. Consensus, affection, and interaction are not a simple causal chain. Maria Rogers, in her critique of Homans' book *The Human Group,* comments that "frequency of interaction increases members *understanding* of one another's temperament, attitudes, etc., and this is as likely to result in decrease of liking as the reverse. . . ."[68] We might state another alternative as follows: intimacy of relationship, including frequency of contact, leads to an understanding of each other and often to the realization of a relatively low degree of value consensus; but if the relationship is characterized by feelings of obligation and concern for each other's welfare, affectional ties may remain strong. Thus, a part of the results of Table III-9 pertains to accuracy of perception, one of the social facts which Bendix and Berger warned us might be hidden under overt responses. We are left once again with an indirect indication of the more intense involvement of females in kin affairs, and their obligatory or concerned tie with their parents.

Males, it was stated above, have considerable freedom to follow the dictates of their feelings, provided the parents do not live extremely near. The final clause of this sentence reminds us that in Table III-8 virtually no relation was found between subjective closeness and frequency of interaction when the parents live in the same city as their adult progeny. Leaving value consensus for the moment, we might expect that, since affectional closeness has little effect upon actual interaction frequency between the proximate, variations based upon feelings will emerge in other aspects of relations with parents. A consequence of the inability to avoid frequent contact is likely to be in the realm of wishful thinking, i.e., in admission of a desire for less frequent contact. An objective manner in which variations in closeness might be related to interaction concerns its initiation. When the young adult feels close to his parents and lives near them he is more apt to initiate frequent interaction with them than if he does not feel close. Thus, we are suggesting that *desires* regarding interaction, and *initiation* of it, are two facets of young adult-parent relations which may be affected by emotional distance or attachment, when proximity minimizes choice.

Investigation of expression of desires for more, less, or the present amount of interaction with parents must be preceded by a word of caution. In a relationship where obligation is presumably strong, such as that under consideration, the obligation covers verbal as well as other forms of behavior. Therefore, when differences are evident regarding affection or desires for interaction, they are likely to represent divergences which are greater than those observed. It is difficult for the individual in contemporary American society, no matter how strong his feelings, to admit that he or she would really like to see less of his parents than he does. Thus, although differences are small according to affection, and over 75 per cent of the proximate sub-sample say they desire the current amount of interaction, it is noteworthy that 19 per cent of those who are close to both parents want to see them more, as compared to 11 per cent of those close to one parent, and 3 per cent (one of thirty-four) of those close to neither parent. Conversely, the percentages expressing a desire for less frequent interaction are 5, 15, and 15 among those close to both, one, and neither parent, respectively. Parenthetically, it should be mentioned that the one individual who is not now close to either parent but who desires more contact with them is a young adult who was raised by grandparents while his parents travelled. Now they have settled down in the same city, and she is anxious to "make up for lost time," to really get to know them.

In this section we are asserting that interaction is an unavoidable consequence of close proximity: if the young adult does not go to see his parents, they will come to see him. Family tradition may demand a visiting or activity pattern despite a lack of enthusiasm on the part of the offspring. The answers of the respondents to a question on the initiation of interaction are most enlightening. Sixty-five per cent of the seventy-four persons who are close to both parents, and whose parents live in Greensboro, state that they initiate most of the interaction, or that they and their parents are equally likely to do so. The percentages of those close to one parent or to neither parent are 52 and 45, respectively. Interaction with parents among this latter group is predominantly due to either tradition or to initiation by the parents, or even the young adult's spouse.

As for the residentially separated, 81 per cent of this sub-sample state that they initiate at least half of the interaction with their parents, and almost half of these 81 per cent almost always originate the contact. This, of course, demonstrates their greater maneuverability and, in some cases, vitality than their parents.[69]

Obligation: An Important Link in Relations with Parents

Hitherto, filial obligation has been assumed and referred to, but has not been focussed upon in the present study. The literature on kin obligation at times clarifies and at times obscures two important dichotomies. First, there is obligation and there are obligations. That is, as affirmed above, there is the general obligation to keep in touch and there are the reciprocal obligations to help each other as needs arise. Cumming and Schneider hint at this distinction when they state that relations with parents are based upon dissimilarity, help, and obligation. According to Reiss, the necessity of keeping in touch with kin is accepted almost universally. The specific obligation to help, on the other hand, is considered by authors such as Dinkel, Koller, and Sussman and Burchinal to be a more spontaneous or voluntary response to the exigencies of a particular situation, an outgrowth of concern for and interest in each other.[70]

The second dichotomy in kin obligation is between close relatives and all others. Garigue notes that his French Canadian respondents make a distinction between obligation to meet close relatives and obligation to meet other kin of ascending generations. Infrequent reunion with many secondary kin satisfies obligation to them; in many instances contact once a year is often enough.[71] This dichotomy between, perhaps, the kin of orientation and secondary kin in obligation may be elucidated by referring to general and specific obligation once again. Specific obligation, i.e., the patterning of aid between kin, is much more common with parents and perhaps siblings than with kin outside the family of orientation. General obligation, i.e., the necessity of showing concern by keeping in touch, requires a greater frequency of contact the closer the genealogical relationship, as Garigue indicates.

Obligation to parents, as indicated in Chapter One, is determined by two questions: one asks if the respondents feel they ought to keep in touch; the other seeks to ascertain whether keeping in touch is based on parental need for help. A final question in this section of the interview asks if their motive for continuing contact is simply that they enjoy their parents and want to keep in touch. This quesion was asked last in order to avoid any tendency on the part of the young adults to express enjoyment first and thus to ignore the obligatory components of the relationship.[72] Nevertheless, direct questioning regarding feelings of obligation contains certain pitfalls which should be made explicit. Young adults are generally aware of the extent to which obligations, or exchanges of help, are a motive for contact with their parents. However, the general feeling of obligation to maintain contact is more difficult to express. If the young adult does not particularly enjoy interacting with his parents, he may communicate a feeling of obligation to keep in touch. But when the relationship is characterized by enjoyment, the young adult may ignore or be unaware of the obligation or concern which undergirds the relationship as well. For him, contact is pleasant, and the attempt to discover whether he would keep in touch out of concern or duty, were his enjoyment to lessen, results in hypothetical fancy. Here we have another example of Bendix and Berger's problem, i.e., the tendency of the social fact to hide as well as to reveal. Enjoyment, we are saying, may in actuality mask a latent sense of obligation. The overt expression of general obligation which is tapped in the present study distinguishes between concern for and interest in parents, which demands contact, and simple enjoyment of such contact as is maintained (even when infrequent).

How many of our respondents perceive obligation as an important aspect of relations with their parents? Despite the hidden dimension of obligation referred to above, only 15 per cent of the young adults express neither general nor specific obligation toward their parents. Fifty-four per cent view either specific or general obligation, or both, as very important in this relationship, and another 31 per cent feel that some form of obligation is somewhat important. General or contact obligation is by far the more prevalent; almost three times as many respondents consider that they have a duty to keep in touch than feel that they must keep in touch because their parents need their help.

Some years ago Hollingshead expressed the belief that there is a stronger obligatory kin attachment in the working class than in the middle class, and he interpreted the more frequent sheltering or caring for relatives as one illustration of this.[73] More recently Muir and Weinstein have explicated what they feel to be the class differences in the meaning of obligation. Those in the lower socio-economic strata, while cognizant of an underlying obligation, are careful to help when able, and expect their kin to do the same. With the economic and other uncertainties of urban working-class life, straight reciprocity is foreign to their thinking. The middle class, on the other hand, are mindful in their occupational lives of repayment demands, and this sort of thinking causes kin relations frequently to resemble a financial transaction. Thus, middle-class help springs in fact from a sense of specific or material obligation, while working-class help is a necessity based upon the more general kinship bond.[74] Although there is a danger of exaggerating the value of expressed differences in the present sample, the white-collar—blue-collar comparisons do lend some support to the views of Hollingshead and Donal Muir and Eugene Weinstein. First, 76 per cent of the working-class and only 66 per cent of the currently middle-class respondents indicate overtly a feeling of general obligation to keep in touch with their parents, which is consistent with Muir and Weinstein's idea. Second, 90 per cent of the working class see some form of obligation as at least somewhat important, as compared with some 82 per cent of the middle class. Finally, the white-collar or middle-class young adults are a little more likely to feel that specific obligations are one reason they keep in touch with their parents, though support for this aspect of Muir and Weinstein's formulation is extremely tentative.

One further component of the problem of motives for contact with parents concerns the relation between expressions of enjoyment and/or obligations and feelings of closeness to parents. A straight-forward probability is that those who are affectionally close to their parents will be most apt to express enjoyment as a reason for keeping in touch. Feelings of obligation, however, are not antithetical to affection, for, as we inferred above, such concern may be as important an element of affectional closeness as is similarity of values and interests.[75] In fact, this is precisely where Dinkel misses the point in his discussion of parent-child conflict. He hypothesizes that it is rare for those with fundamentally differing viewpoints to maintain a satisfactory relationship.[76] However, after marriage and the achievement of independence from parents in urban society, an emotional tie based upon mutual concern may be realized despite divergent ideas or values. The relation between enjoyment and affection, postulated above, should appear more clearly when the parents live in Greensboro than when they live elsewhere. This is due to the minimal choice possible under conditions of proximity. The separated have more control over contact frequency, and thus an expression of enjoyment may simply mean that they enjoy the small amount of contact that they do have. The relation of closeness to enjoyment and obligation, according to the parents' residential location, is presented in Table III-10.

When the parents live in Greensboro, the percentages showing that enjoyment is at least one important reason for keeping in touch are 96, 70, and 36, for those who feel close to both parents,

TABLE III-10

Expressions of closeness to parents in relation to enjoyment of and obligation to them, as important reasons for keeping in touch with them, according to whether the parents live in Greensboro or elsewhere

Location of Parents	Closeness to Either or Both Parents	Number of Respondents	Important Reasons for Keeping in Touch, in Per Cent				
			Enjoyment Only	Enjoy. and Obli.	Obligation Only	Neither Very Important	Total Pct.
Greensboro	Close to Both	(74)	46	50	3	1	100
	Close to One	(47)	30	40	19	11	100
	Close to Neither	(34)	12	24	38	27	101
Elsewhere	Close to Both	(145)	48	44	6	2	100
	Close to One	(93)	42	34	14	10	100
	Close to Neither	(51)	24	47	18	12	101

one parent, and neither parent, respectively. If the parents are close by, the same relationship appears, but much less distinctly. More than seven out of ten of the affectionally and residentially distant from their parents state that enjoyment is nevertheless an important factor in their continued contact. The hidden significance of this finding, as indicated above, is that the remote, because of their control over the initiation of contact, can keep interaction sufficiently infrequent that they are able to express enjoyment of the interaction they do have, even though they feel close to neither parent. The wife of a shipping clerk put it this way: "When I do see her I enjoy her more because I just don't see so much of her now."

There is a slight increase in the overt expression of general and/or specific obligation to parents when the respondent is affectionally close to one or neither parent. More important among the proximate, however, is the 27 per cent who assert that there is no important reason why they keep in touch with their parents. This confirms the conclusion drawn earlier that it is impossible for the proximate to avoid frequent contact with parents, even when they are affectionally distant or desire less interaction.

Verbal expression of underlying motives is always suspect to some degree, as Blumer asserts, but it is the opinion of the author that the investigation of subjective factors in relations with parents has yielded significant insights. The respondents have shown little hesitation in expressing a low feeling of closeness or obligation as a major reason for keeping in contact. More important, answers regarding such diverse subjective dimensions as affectional closeness, value consensus, interaction desires, and obligation or enjoyment form a consistent pattern, augmenting our understanding of the meaning of the contact patterns previously determined.

Section Four: Relations with Widows, Widowers, and Divorced Parents

To date, the effects of the absence of one parent upon the relations of an adult offspring with the remaining parent have received little attention. The widow, when studied, has been discussed almost exclusively in terms of her own economic and social circumstances, not in terms of the effect of her widowhood upon the adult child.[77] To initiate this brief discussion of the young adult as he relates to the widow, widower, or divorced parent, let us present two guiding observations: the first is that in modern urban-industrial society, obligation, when it is the prime attribute of a personal relationship, has a constraining effect upon the relation; second is the more central role of the female in kin relations.

Residential distance from a widow or from a pair of living parents is virtually identical in our Greensboro sample, there being no more than three percentage points difference in any distance category. However, the widower father is much *less* likely to live in Greensboro (22 per cent as compared to 35 per cent who have both parents alive and living together) and the divorced parent with whom the young adult maintains his most regular contact is much *more* likely to live in Greensboro (70 per cent of these parents reside locally). Thirty-two of the thirty-nine divorcees with whom the young adults have a closer relationship are their mothers; not a single young male in our sample reports keeping in close touch with a divorcee-father.

The distance of the parent or parents has an obvious effect upon the patterning of the various types of contact, as we stated above and as we note again in Table III-11, according to the sex of the young adult and his parent or parents. The widower father generally lives at the greatest distance, with the result that patterning is infrequent. At the other extreme, the divorced mother tends to live quite close by and there is a wide range of patterned contacts. The mother-daughter bond is demonstrated in Table III-11, where seven of the asterisks and only one of the minuses involve a daughter and her mother. Asterisks and minuses are evenly divided in cross-sex relationships, i.e., between a son and his mother or a daughter and father, while the relation of a son to a widower father is strictly one of non-involvement.

While many inferences could be drawn from the foregoing Table, the following comments will focus upon relations with a widowed mother as these compare with relations to a pair of living parents, thereby utilizing the greater portion of the available data.[78] When we observe rows one and three, and two and four, in Table

TABLE III-11

The patterned engagement of young adults and their parents in the contact types during the past two years, according to sex and to the marital status of the parents

Sex of Young Adult and of Parent(s), and Parents' Marital Status	Number of Respondents	Occurrence Several Times Yearly or More, in Per Cent						
		Home Visits	Activities	Organizations	Rituals	Communication	Aid Rec'd	Aid Given
Males: Parents Living Together	(187)	81	33	26	53	84	53	43
Females: Parents Living Together	(257)	78	44	28	51	91*	63	38
Males: Widowed Mother	(75)	77	19—	25	39—	83	39	60
Females: Widowed Mother	(109)	83	54*	38*	56	90*	59	60
Males: Divorced Mother	(11)	91	45	36	64	82	64	55
Females: Divorced Mother	(21)	95*	52*	10—	76*	76	67	67*
Females: Divorced Father	(7)	86	29	—	57	43	71	57
Males: Widower Father	(26)	69—	27	19	35—	69	8—	31—
Females: Widower Father	(31)	77	13—	16	35—	74	42	45

* Indicates a percentage which is important for its magnitude; — indicates a percentage which stands out due to its comparative smallness.

III-11 several important differences are apparent. Among the males, contact with the widowed mother is frequently restricted to helping her or to keeping in touch, either by dropping in or by the means of communication. The patterned receipt of help, the sharing of social activity, and ritual interaction are considerably less widespread between the male and a widowed mother than with a pair of living parents. The young married female, on the other hand, actually manifests *greater* likelihood of patterned social activity and organizational attendance with her mother, as well as in the giving of help to her, when her father is not alive. Of course, a portion of the explanation for such sex differences is that some of the adult male's social activity with parents is actually with the father to the exclusion of the mother.

Another important sex difference is in the receipt of help from the parents or mother. The males are less likely to receive help from a widowed mother, especially various services such as babysitting. There is in fact a modal change among the males from the *receipt* of aid predominating when both parents are alive, to the *giving* of aid predominating *vis-à-vis* a widowed mother. The female, while she is more likely to give patterned aid to a widowed mother than to a pair of parents, is almost as likely to receive services from her mother regardless of whether her father is living or deceased. In other words, males and females are almost equally likely to give a pattern of aid to a widow, but daughters are much more apt to be receiving services in return. Townsend found in his London study of the aged that daughters are the chief source of aid to their mothers. This, however, is not substantiated in Greensboro, even among the working-class respondents.[79]

The relationship of an adult son and his widowed mother, as it appears in contact patterns, seems characterized by an important obligatory element, both general and specific. Not common interests and activities, but obligation is central. The married daughter and her mother, by contrast, share various activities as well as a *reciprocal* helping pattern. Peter Marris, in one of the few detailed investigations of the widow, comments that an obligatory relationship becomes irksome to the widow, for she cannot reciprocate.[80] The irksomeness of a one-way relationship in which obligation is primary may hold for the adult son as well. If the effect of obligation is to strain relations with the widow, this should be apparent both in expressions of reasons for keeping in touch, and more importantly, in perception of affectional changes over the years as obligation has increased. In Table III-12 expressions of enjoyment and obligation, and of affection for the mother, are presented.

The first outstanding result is that more males do see obligation

TABLE III-12

Expression of enjoyment of and obligation to parents, or to a widowed mother, as important reasons for keeping in touch, and change in feelings of closeness to a widow or to the mother when the father is living, according to the sex of the young adult

Sex of the Young Adults	Which Parent(s) Living	Number of Respondents	Important Reasons for Keeping in Touch, in Per Cent		Change in Closeness Since Marriage, in Per Cent		
			Obligation	Enjoyment	Less Close	About the Same	Closer
Males	Both	(187)	51	76	27	36	37
	Widow	(75)	68	57	41	32	27
Females	Both	(257)	44	83	11	30	59
	Widow	(109)	50	72	28	25	47

as paramount in their relations with a widowed mother, while the daughters are more likely to see enjoyment as very important. Nevertheless, a comparison of the responses of those with both parents alive and those with only a widowed mother shows that both males and females are more likely to state that obligation is important in their relations with a widow than with a pair of parents. In daughter-widow relations, while enjoyment is paramount, it is not as decisively so as when both parents are living.

The attempt to ascertain perception of changes in feelings is also facilitated by the comparison. The results are strikingly similar to those on obligation and enjoyment. That is, both sexes are less likely to say that they are closer, and more likely to say they are less close, than formerly to a widowed mother than to a pair of living parents. In comparing the males and females, however, daughters still express as modal response that they are closer to their mother than before they married. The adult sons, on the other hand, again manifest a modal "flip-over." The largest percentage of males with both parents living indicate a greater closeness than formerly, but over 40 per cent of those with a widowed mother feel that they are less close to their mothers now than earlier.

Marris found in his London study that, from the widow's viewpoint, family contacts become no closer after the death of the husband. Though his finding was based upon simple interaction frequency, it is borne out in the present study, from the viewpoint of the adult offspring, with respect to attitudes. The male sees his relation to his mother as primarily obligatory, or obligatory and enjoyable, and tends to feel himself less close to her than he once was. The female is likely to find enjoyment and increased affection characterizing her involvement with her mother, and this is due to the wider range of activities shared by these female kin.

Young Adult-Parent Relations: Summary and Conclusions

Contact between young adult Greensboroites and their parents is a pervasive phenomenon. When the parents live in the same city, weekly interaction is the rule; when there is residential separation of offspring and parents, telephone calls, letters, or visits are exchanged monthly or more. The evidence is overwhelming that separation does not signify the isolation of these kin of orientation from each other.

Relations with parents involve primarily keeping in touch, with a secondary emphasis upon patterned mutual aid based upon need. Parents are not ordinarily social companions for the young adult; by this we mean that patterned engagement in social activities and in the same organization or association is infrequent. Instances of parents and their married children sharing the same occupation and work location are negligible.

Affection for parents is generally strong, being based upon an admixture of value consensus and positive concern for the parents.[81] The young adults usually initiate contact with their parents when they are separated residentially. Therefore, the remote are able to keep interaction to some degree in line with their desires and with their feelings about their parents, though this is truer for males than for females. Yet in general *contact frequency is but little associated with overt affection.* The link between feelings and contact is a strong sense of obligation to keep in constant touch with one's parents. Among the proximate, the major results of a weak affectional tie are a less frequent initiation of interaction by the young adult and a tendency to desire less frequent contact.

Is the strong general and specific obligation to parents considered oppressive or worthwhile by these young adults? Barrington Moore has commented that it is barbaric to have to give affection and attention "to a particular set of persons on account of the accident of birth."[82] Raymond Firth, on the other hand, contends that while such obligation may be irksome to some individuals, selective obligatory ties to kin may be one method the family uses to adapt to the urban, industrial environment.[83] More than once during the interviews our respondents asserted that kin are important to them because "my parents and sister are the only ones I can really count on," or some variation of this. It is obligatory concern which in fact makes it possible to "count on" one's parents. Obligation, when coupled with the other elements which comprise relations with parents, is not dysfunctional for subjective closeness. When, however, obligation and help become the primary elements, as in the case of males and a widowed mother, the tendency is toward a somewhat greater affectional distance.

The mother-daughter bond is strong in adulthood and is characterized by what we have termed "role convergence." The daughter marries, and as a housewife and mother she finds that she understands her own mother better and has much in common with her. In explaining why they feel as they do about their mother or parents now, 40 per cent of the young married females indicate either that they understand and appreciate them more, or have more similarity in values and interests now. A frequent comment is: "Now I know what she (my mother) went through in raising me, since I have children of my own." The young adult male, on the other hand, frequently asserts that his lesser closeness at present is because "my ideas on how to live are different from theirs," or "my family and work take up all my time." A uniformly high expression by females of value consensus with their mothers is illustrative of the role convergence between these kin of orientation. Lee Rainwater and associates note that blue-collar husbands and wives tend to go their separate ways, with a greater division of labor and interest than in the middle class.[84] One area of life in which this division of interest is apparent is in kin relations, the blue-collar husbands seemingly willing, but not always able, to leave these to his wife.

Occupational mobility and subsequent relationships with parents have received much attention in the foregoing investigation. Downward mobility is found detrimental to relations with parents in terms of affectional distance from the mother, despite frequent interaction, on the part of the male, whereas for the female the effect is for there to be less frequent interaction than residential distance would seem to allow. The accomplishment of upward mobility has been variously reported in the literature to be with the help and encouragement of both parents, the parents having adopted middle-class values and a middle-class style of life, or it may be the result of the influence of one parent or the other. Or mobility might be due to the young person, with the aid of school and peer group, lifting himself from a blue-collar milieu. This latter viewpoint, which might be labelled the "boot-strap" hypothesis, is widespread in the folklore of our society, but is probably least prevalent empirically. Its roots are in the same general conceptualization which produced the notion of the isolated urban family.[85] The Greensboro evidence points to the strong influence of the mother upon the upward mobility, through marriage, of a daughter, and the influence of either or both parents upon the upwardly mobile son. No interactional or attitudinal manifestations of greater ambivalence or shallower ties between upwardly mobile young adults and their parents than between stable middle-class adults and their parents have been detected. Of course, when compared with stable working-class adults there is somewhat less frequent interaction, since occupational demands often result in greater residential separation of the mobile. However, the upwardly mobile, like the stable middle class, make up for less interaction by the means of communication.

It is not, in the final analysis, isolation from parents which is either desired or accomplished by young adults in our society; it is independence and maturity. Our conclusion is very close to that of Cumming and Schneider: relations with parents are characterized by age or generational dissimilarity, help, and mutual concern—though not usually by dissimilarity of values. This is the typical, not the ideal or closest, relation with parents. The ideal relationship seems best exemplified in the relations of middle-class daughters and their mothers. This is an involvement based upon diffuseness of activity, or a wide range of patterned contacts, with enjoyment and affection central, and a secondary obligatory component manifested in extremely frequent contact and a willingness to help when needed.

Chapter IV

ADULT SIBLINGS:
INTEREST AND COMPARISON

Two kin relationships arise in the family of orientation, those between children and parents and between siblings. In many pre-industrial societies the sibling relationship has had a key role in social organization. For example, the joint family system of India is
predicated upon the sharing of economic position and of common
residence by male siblings and their wives and children. Where
they are a crucial element of the society's functioning, the relations
between siblings are carefully delineated by the norms. However, in
turning to siblings in urban, industrial society we face a somewhat
paradoxical situation. On the one hand, the sibling relationship has
recently been claimed by a few authors, among them Garigue,
Cumming and Schneider, and Farber, to be the most significant kin
tie among some groups in urban society and at certain stages of the
life cycle.[1] On the other hand, Donald Irish points out that sibling
interaction has generally been neglected in family research in favor
of that between parents and children. The preoccupation of researchers has been with parental responsibilities in socialization,
under the influence of Freudian thought, and with specific family
problems, resulting in the treatment of sibling relations as
incidental.[2] Of even greater importance to the present study is the
fact that, except for findings scattered through various kinship
studies, the analysis of siblings which has been done has involved
young children still in the parental home. Siblings who have
reached adulthood and left home are virtually ignored. Only with
the research of Garigue, Young and Willmott, Cumming and

93

Schneider and Farber, have students of urban society begun to demonstrate an awareness that sibling contacts are an area of social organization deserving of analysis.

Relations between siblings in the parental home are usually characterized as involving rivalry, or companionship, or both. These same relationship attributes may be found in the few sources dealing with adult sibling contacts. Garigue, for example, stresses that among the French Canadians the most important kin tie as a focus of activity is that between siblings. Sibling contact, assert Cumming and Schneider, is based upon resemblance and choice in adulthood.[3] In contrast, William H. Form and James A. Geschwender note, in their application of reference group theory to the study of job satisfaction, that the more satisfied have a higher occupational level than their brother, while the least satisfied are lower than their brother in occupational status. These manual workers are using their brother as a comparison or reference point to aid them in determining the meaning of their occupational position.[4] Throughout the ensuing discussion we shall be mindful of these two aspects of the sibling relationship—friendship or companionship and comparison or competition.

The 799 young Greensboro adults enumerated and located a total of 2236 siblings, 1173 brothers and 1140 sisters still living, and an additional 77 siblings whose whereabouts were unknown or who were deceased. The mean number of siblings per family of orientation, including the respondent, is 3.9, with a range from one to fourteen. Of course, the mean family size is larger than the national average due to the fact that aged families having no children were unrepresented in the sample. There are 165 young adults with only a brother or brothers, and 152 with only a sister or sisters. One hundred and two of the respondents are only children or else have no living sibling, leaving us with a total of 697 who have one or more brothers and/or sisters. These latter will be the focal point of Chapter IV.

It was decided that in each interview we should focus upon relationships with one specific sibling, referring to other brothers and sisters briefly or in passing. The determination of which sibling to discuss in detail had to be achieved without controlling sex, occupational stratum, residential distance, or the various attitudinal characteristics which are key factors in the investigation. It was also deemed important to explore relations with the sibling whom the respondent was likely to know as well or better than any other. In his study of coalitions in the triad, Theodore Caplow reports that "sibling coalitions appear to be based on similarity of sex, age, and interest rather than on the balance of strength in the triad."[5] Age is the only one of these three factors which is relatively tangential to our analysis, and therefore the respondents were asked to discuss—regardless of sex and occupational or other characteristics —the sibling who is closest to them in age, henceforth referred to as the "age-near sibling."

The following description will give some idea of the age-near siblings' characteristics. One hundred and seventy of the sibling combinations, i.e., respondent and age-near, are brothers, 203 are sisters, and 324 are cross-sex siblings, or a male and a female. These cross-sex siblings may be a brother discussing his sister, or a female reporting her relationship with her brother. As we might expect, 76 per cent of the age-near siblings are within four years of age of the respondent. The comparative age distribution includes 93 respondents whose sibling is five or more years older, 271 young adults whose sibling is four or less years older, ten sets of twins, 251 young adults whose sibling is four or less years younger, and 72 whose sibling is five or more years younger. Occupationally, 294 of the sibling pairs are white-collar or middle-class, 170 and blue-collar, 191 are occupationally disparate, i.e., one is white-collar and the other blue-collar, and in forty-two pairs either the respondent or his sibling, or both, have not yet established their occupational position.

Section One: Frequency of Contact with the Age-Near Sibling

If siblings are to be companions or the focus of activity in adulthood, they must live in reasonably close proximity to each other. Some 60 per cent of our respondents live within 100 miles of their parent or parents, and we now find that 29 per cent have their age-near sibling living in Greensboro, and another 23 per cent live 100 or less miles apart. That residential distance has not been biased by our choice of the age-near sibling is apparent in comparing the location of this sibling with the total number of living siblings located by the young adult. Twenty-eight per cent of all siblings live in Greensboro as compared with 29 per cent of the age-near, within 100 miles the comparisons are 24 and 23 per cent, beyond 100 miles in North Carolina, South Carolina, or Virginia are 21 per cent of all siblings and 20 per cent of the age-near, and elsewhere are located 26 and 28 per cent, respectively. Siblings, furthermore, are only slightly more proximate residentially than are kin as a whole (see Chapter II).

Once again, frequency of interaction is clearly limited by the distance separating the two siblings. When the sibling lives in Greensboro, slightly over half interact weekly or more, with all but 11 per cent seeing each other at least once a month. When the siblings live 100 or less miles apart, almost half interact monthly to weekly, and another large group interact several times a year. The majority of those whose age-near sibling lives from 100 to 250 miles away (56 per cent) see him or her several times yearly, while over three-fifths of those whose sibling is more than 250 miles away are in face-to-face contact with him yearly or less. It is noteworthy that the modal category of interaction frequency follows an orderly decline with each increase in residential distance.

Sex, Occupational Strata, and Frequency of Interaction with the Age-Near Sibling

The general tendency, noted in Chapter I, for females to be more instrumentally involved in urban kinship than males, should be manifested in sibling relations as follows: sister-sister contact should be most frequent, cross-sex sibling contact next, and brother-brother contact least frequent.[6] If this holds for Greensboro, as it did in Reiss' middle-class Boston sample, it is in spite of a slight tendency for brothers to live closer together than either sisters or cross-sex siblings. Thirty-six per cent of the age-near brothers both live in Greensboro, as compared with 29 per cent of the cross-sex siblings and 25 per cent of the sisters. Males are also found to live somewhat closer to their parents, and these two findings are in all likelihood attributable to the male's predominant role in occupational, and therefore geographical, choice.

Investigation of Reiss' assertion begins by noting that sisters, despite slightly greater separation, are nevertheless more likely to interact weekly or more. However, they are least likely to interact from monthly to weekly, the result being that the percentages of the three sex categories seeing each other monthly or more are almost identical (45, 44, and 42 per cent for brothers, sisters, and cross-sex siblings, respectively). In other words, when distance is ignored, interaction frequency between siblings varies only slightly between the three categories, with sisters a little more likely to interact as often as weekly.

In turning to occupational position, Stuckert reports that one reason for the isolation of the occupationally mobile from their kin is that they are also residentially mobile, and therefore not as integrated into either their kin network or their present community as are the occupationally stable.[7] This argument, however, overlooks the residential mobility or stability of the individual's kin, which is a function of *their* occupational orientation, not that of the respondent. Therefore, it is not surprising that the occupationally disparate, incorporating characteristics of both strata, are intermediate (53 per cent) between two white-collar (43 per cent) and two blue-collar (64 per cent) siblings with respect to living within 100 miles of each other.

Occupational mobility has a detrimental effect upon interaction with parents only among the downwardly mobile females, the other sex and stratum-mobility categories generally utilizing the opportunity afforded by their degree of proximity. However, Bott comments in her London study that the more distant a kin relationship is, the more objective differences receive consideration, and determine interaction.[8] When siblings are differentially mobile, so that one is white-collar and the other blue-collar, LeMasters finds much strain in the family or kin of orientation.[9] The mitigating influences of strong obligation to, and reception of achievement values from, parents are not likely to be operative to the same degree in sibling relations.

An additional factor which may influence sibling interaction is referred to by Willmott and Young. Contacts between fathers and sons are reduced by the son's mobility, but the other three relationships, i.e., between sons and their mothers or daughters and both parents, are not affected by mobility. More pointedly, the authors comment that women continue to have the same occupations: being a mother. Thus, they are little affected by occupational differentials between their husbands and fathers.[10] No evidence of father-son alienation due to mobility was found in Chapter III, but these findings may at least act as guiding hypotheses in the investigation of sibling interaction as well. It may well be that brothers who have been differentially mobile tend to go their separate ways socially, while the wives of occupationally disparate males are able to maintain a close relationship because of the lesser salience of occupation and the greater salience of their common adult roles. Table IV-1 presents both the interaction frequency between the various sex-stratum categories and the utilization of opportunity according to proximity.

Important distinctions by sex or occupational strata are difficult to discern in Table IV-1. The occupationally disparate brothers manifest no more tendency to infrequent interaction than do some other categories. Blue-collar brothers and blue-collar sisters make the least use of availability, though they are characterized by the greatest proximity. The only two categories in which 50 per cent or more see each other at least monthly are occupationally disparate sisters and blue-collar cross-sex siblings. The significance of these results is not immediately apparent, and it may require investigation of contact patterns and attitudes to understand the factors at work in simple frequency of interaction according to the sex and strata of siblings.

Communication and Total Contact Between Siblings

Residential separation, while it hinders interaction, does not prevent individuals from keeping in touch if they so desire. The mails and telephone, which are utilized so uniformly by young adults and their parents, are similarly available for sibling contact. Sussman and Burchinal speak of the "constant communication

TABLE IV-1

Frequency of interaction with the age-near sibling, and utilization of availability, according to sex and occupational strata

Sex and Occupational Strata of Siblings	Number of Respondents	Frequency of Interaction, in Per Cent					Sibling Within 100 Miles of Greensboro	Per cent Seeing Sibling Monthly+
		Weekly or More	Monthly-Weekly	Several Times Yearly	Yearly or Less	Total Pct.		
White-collar male with white-collar brother	(72)	17	26	35	22	100	43	43
Male with brother of opposite stratum*	(44)	14	32	23	32	101	57	46
Blue-collar male with blue-collar brother	(41)	24	22	29	24	99	76	46
White-collar respondent with white-collar cross-sex sibling	(132)	10	22	44	24	100	42	32
Respondent with cross-sex sibling of opposite stratum*	(91)	14	29	29	29	101	48	43
Blue-collar respondent with blue-collar cross-sex sibling	(83)	22	30	22	27	101	55	52
White-collar female with white-collar sister	(90)	14	20	48	18	100	46	34
Female with sister of opposite stratum*	(56)	27	27	23	23	100	57	54
Blue-collar female with blue-collar sister	(46)	26	22	26	26	100	67	48

* These are discussed in the text as "occupationally disparate" siblings.

among kin members" made possible by the telephone, and Young and Willmott note that siblings living at a distance still communicate with each other.[11] However, while over 50 per cent of the young Greensboro adults communicate with parents living outside Greensboro by telephone, by letter, or both at least monthly, only 21 per cent of the residentially separated siblings utilize the mails and 13 per cent the telephone as often as monthly.

Almost 95 per cent of the young adults are in some form of contact with their parents monthly or more. If the son does not frequently write his parents, his wife may. It is less likely that the wife will shoulder the burden of communicating frequently with her husband's siblings; nor is communication with siblings likely to be as frequent generally as with parents. Thus, in Greensboro contact with one's age-near sibling is drastically reduced for the majority by a residential separation which exceeds two to three hours driving time. Some form of contact at least once a month occurs between 93 per cent of those siblings who both live in Greensboro, but this per cent is reduced to 65, and then 38 and 39 when the sibling lives within 100 miles, elsewhere in the three-state area, and beyond that, respectively (see Table IV-2). Litwak commented that residential distance need not disrupt kinship relations, but it does in fact tend to lessen the contact between siblings substantially.[12]

We have investigated interaction frequency by sex and occupa-

TABLE IV-2

Frequency of the most frequent form of contact—whether face-to-face, telephone, or letter—between age-near siblings, by residential distance

Location of Sibling	Number of Respondents	Frequency of Most Frequent Contact, in Pct.				
		Weekly or More	Monthly-Weekly	Several Times Yearly	Yearly or Less	Total Pct.
Greensboro	(205)	64	29	4	2	99
—100 Miles	(158)	12	53	30	5	100
Beyond 100 Mi. in NC, SC, or Va.	(141)	1	37	49	13	100
Elsewhere	(193)	4	35	40	21	100

tional strata, and have uncovered few differences. Perhaps of greater importance is the question of who actually keeps in the most constant touch with his or her sibling. What, again, about contact between the occupationally disparate? The results of Table IV-3 are most instructive. Sisters and blue-collar siblings are in most frequent contact with each other, but for different reasons. The sisters do more corresponding by letter when they are separated, thereby compensating to some extent for infrequent interaction. The blue-collar siblings, on the other hand, tend to be more proximate, and their greater frequency of contact is thus due largely to more frequent face-to-face contact, as we observed in Table IV-1. The only surprising result of Table IV-3 is that the differentially mobile sisters, rather than being in less frequent contact than the stable, are considerably more likely to be in frequent contact. Approximately 20 per cent more of the occupationally disparate sisters are in touch monthly or more (columns one and two) than is true of the sisters who are similar in occupational status. At this stage of our inquiry it is impossible to do more than speculate as to the reason for the frequent contact between sisters whose husbands are in different occupational strata. A portion of the explanation is of course their similarity of interests due to their adult roles, but this does not differentiate them from the other categories of sisters. Litwak's concept of status gain and status deference is hypothetically applicable to this situation.[13] The occupationally stable may actually be rivals for the same family goals, such as approval of parents and the deference or help of kin. Or the relationship between these sisters may truly be reciprocal, in the sense in which Alvin Gouldner has employed the term. That is, the rights of one are accepted as duties by the other.[14] Mutual aid, either in terms of services or such intangibles as advice and emotional support, may link the occupationally disparate sisters in an even closer relationship than that between the occupationally similar. The investigation of contact patterns in the following section may elucidate these presumptions. A minimal conclusion is that, whether due to obligation or to enjoyment, interaction and contact frequency provide us with no evidence of the dissociative effects of differential mobility upon sibling relations.

TABLE IV-3

Frequency of the most frequent form of contact—whether face-to-face, telephone, or letter—between age-near siblings, according to sex and occupational strata

Sex and Occupational Strata	Number of Respondents	Frequency of Most Frequent Contact, in Pct.				
		Weekly or More	Monthly-Weekly	Several Times Yearly	Yearly or Less	Total Pct.
White-collar male with white-collar brother	(72)	18	33	43	6	100
Male with brother of opposite stratum*	(44)	18	41	23	18	100
Blue-collar male with blue-collar brother	(41)	32	32	20	17	101
White-collar respondent with white-collar cross-sex sibling	(132)	11	42	41	5	99
Respondent with cross-sex sibling of opposite stratum*	(91)	19	37	31	13	100
Blue-collar respondent with blue-collar cross-sex sibling	(83)	26	33	23	18	101
White-collar female with white-collar sister	(90)	20	43	33	3	99
Female with sister of opposite stratum*	(56)	41	43	11	5	100
Blue-collar female with blue-collar sister	(46)	35	28	22	15	100

* These three categories are those discussed in the text as occupationally disparate siblings, i.e., one white-collar and one blue-collar.

To summarize regarding frequency of sibling interaction, the major determinant—as between young adults and their parents—is the distance which separates them. Blue-collar siblings tend to live closer to each other and therefore to see each other more often. However, when residentially separated, it is only sisters who are likely to overcome the distance with extremely frequent utilization of the means of communication. For brothers and cross-sex siblings, a substantial separation comes close to producing isolation.

Occupationally disparate siblings, even brothers, do not manifest a lesser frequency of interaction or contact than two white- or blue-collar siblings. In fact, in many ways the cross-sex and occupationally disparate are merely intermediate categories, deriving their characteristics from the male and female, or from the white-collar and blue-collar, elements of which they consist. The prime exception is the occupationally disparate sisters whose frequency of total contact far exceeds that of any other category, though an explanation of this fact has not yet been confirmed.

Section Two: Types of Contact Between Age-Near Siblings

According to Garigue's study of French Canadians in Montreal, the most important kin tie as a focus of activity is that between siblings. The possibility of choice and personal preference, which is basic to sibling relations, results in more frequent and more meaningful contact with kin of the same generation than with those of the ascending generation.[15] While visiting, communication, and mutual aid are prime characteristics of young adult-parent contact, Garigue's findings, if they can be generalized suggest that recreation and other types of activities may feature or be significant attributes of sibling relations in an urban setting.

Despite Garigue's reference to sibling interaction, we are actually faced in this section with an instance of almost purely exploratory research. Dorothy Blitsten has commented in a recent book that husbands and wives may feel a sense of specific obligation, or "a limited responsibility toward their parents in case of need, but generally this sense of obligation does not extend to other relatives outside the nuclear unit."[16] The extent to which this obligation to help is manifested in sibling as well as parental relations has been investigated by Sussman in Cleveland, Ohio. He finds substantially less mutual aid between siblings than between young adults and their parents. Nevertheless, aid between siblings is still found to be quite widespread. Over 50 per cent of Sussman's sample of eighty Cleveland families had either given to or received from a sibling some form of aid within the month preceding the interview.[17] We are not likely to find quite so large a distribution in our Greensboro study, since attention is focussed upon a particular sibling relationship rather than siblings in general.

A third brief discussion of kinds of sibling contact is found in Young and Willmott's London study. Proximate siblings visit with considerable frequency, often at the home of their mother, and when separated they continue to communicate.[18] The frequency of this communication or visiting is not indicated, but there have at least been hints in these three sources concerning social activities, mutual aid, visiting, and communication between siblings.

The types of contact are once again employed to determine those aspects of daily life in which the age-near sibling may or may not play a significant role. These contact types include home visiting, social activities, organizational involvement, ritual or ceremonial get-togethers, communication by letter or telephone, working together at the same occupation and location, the giving of tangible aid or services to the sibling, and the receiving of such aid. Explanation of the activities incorporated in these contact types is found in the methodological section of Chapter I, and will not be repeated here. The greatest frequency of occurrence of any sub-activity, e.g., telephoning (under communication) or attending movies (under social activities), is considered to be the frequency with which that contact type is represented in sibling contact during the preceding two-year period. Table IV-4 shows the engagement of age-near siblings in the various contact types.

Communication and home visiting dominate the contact between siblings, both in terms of frequency and distribution in the sample. Between 60 and 70 per cent of the sample visit or communicate with the sibling, or do both, several times or more a year. No other

TABLE IV-4

Frequency of occurrence of the contact types in relations between age-near siblings during the past two years (N = 697)

Contact Types	Frequency of Occurrence, in Per Cent				
	Monthly or More	Several Times Yearly	Once or Twice a Year	Never	Total Pct.
Home Visits	26	35	24	16	101
Social Activities	8	19	22	52	101
Voluntary Organizations	7	5	9	78	99
Working Together	2	—	1	97	100
Ritual Occasions	5	21	36	39	101
Communication	41	26	15	18	100
Aid Received from Sibling	3	5	3	89	100
Aid Given to Sibling	4	5	2	88	99

type of contact, not even ritual occasions, is represented that often by more than 27 per cent of the age-near siblings. The sibling is no more, and in fact appears to be less, frequently used as a social companion than are the parents. However, in comparison to the exchange of mutual aid, social and organizational activity do appear relatively widespread. Although less aid was expected than that found by Sussman, the limited distribution of aid which is found in Table IV-4 was unanticipated. Only one out of six respondents reports *any* exchange of aid with the sibling within the past two years. We may summarize the results of this Table by stating that not one of the eight contact types either occurs as frequently or is distributed as widely between age-near siblings as between these young adults and their parents. The greatest divergences are in mutual aid, in frequent ritual reunions, and in less likelihood of monthly communication between siblings. The overall pattern is simply one of keeping in touch, and even this is not uniformly frequent. There are a minority who share social, organizational, and ritual interaction with moderate frequency, but the exchange of aid is to a great extent idiosyncratic. From the sharing of clothes or baby-sitting by adult sisters living close to each other to the loaning of $2,000 to a brother to invest in his business, it is the particular situation which elicits the help of a sibling. To speak of "patterns" of mutual aid between age-near siblings would be presumptuous. This, however, like most other aspects of contact, is governed largely by residential distance and by a lesser sense of specific obligation than in relations with parents.

When both the siblings live in Greensboro almost 50 per cent engage in patterned social activity and slightly over 50 per cent share a pattern of ritual interaction. However, even among the proximate, aid is patterned, i.e., several times a year or more, in either direction for only one in four sibling pairs, and what there is ordinarily consists of the exchange of baby-sitting or child care by sisters. The remote are characterized almost uniformly by simply keeping in touch in some manner.

Blue-collar cross-sex siblings are one of two sex-strata categories more than 50 per cent of whom interact monthly or more. These siblings, however, may be seen in Table IV-5 to be unlikely when residentially separated to have a pattern of frequent communication. Their interaction is primarily of the "drop-in" variety, i.e., seeing each other frequently for conversation but little else. The other category which is less likely to communicate when separated or to be social companions when proximate is the occupationally disparate males, this being our first sign that their relationship might be strained at all because of their occupational positions. Almost without exception, the occupationally disparate brothers who are involved in the same voluntary organization are attenders of the church but no other organization together. This is similarly true of the occupationally disparate sisters. These sisters, however, show other signs of a truly close relationship. They are not only in frequent interaction, they are the most likely of any category to share patterned social activities and ritual occasions, and are among the most frequent in manifesting patterned communication. Mutual aid, in other words, does *not* explain the relationship between occupationally disparate sisters, as we had postulated.

There is a working-class *mos* which obligates one to give shelter to or care for his relatives, according to Hollingshead.[19] It is apparent both in relations with parents and between siblings that blue-collar females are the major bearers of this obligatory responsibility. Twelve per cent more of the blue-collar sisters have a pattern

TABLE IV-5

Patterned engagement of age-near siblings in the contact types during the past two years, according to the sex and occupational strata of the siblings

Sex and Occupational Strata of Siblings	Number of Respondents	Occurrence Several Times Yearly or More, in Per Cent						
		Home Visits	Activities	Organizations	Rituals	Communication	Aid Received	Aid Given
White-collar male with white-collar brother	(72)	64	32*	7–	22	76	8	14
Male with brother of opposite stratum**	(44)	59	18–	23*	23	55	7	11
Blue-collar male with blue-collar brother	(41)	66	29*	2–	24	61	5	5
White-collar respondent with white-collar cross-sex sibling	(132)	56	19–	12	21	74	4	5
Respondent with cross-sex sibling of opposite stratum**	(91)	58	15–	12	24	58	6	8
Blue-collar respondent with blue-collar cross-sex sibling	(83)	61	16–	7–	24	46–	6	10
White-collar female with white-collar sister	(90)	61	37*	13	23	89*	13	12
Female with sister of opposite stratum**	(56)	55	45*	21*	39*	86*	13	5
Blue-collar female with blue-collar sister	(46)	74*	33*	15	30	59	22*	17*

* Indicates a percentage which is important for its magnitude; – indicates a percentage which stands out due to its comparative smallness.

** These are discussed in the text as the "occupationally disparate" siblings.

of giving or receiving aid, or both, than any other sex-strata category. We might summarize the relations between sisters thus: white-collar sisters are not likely to live close to each other, but they communicate frequently, and when together they go shopping or share other activities. Occupationally disparate sisters are frequent communicators as well as social companions, and blue-collar sisters visit each other, go shopping together, and/or help each other with their families or in other ways.

Summing the patterns in the eight contact types and dividing by the number of respondents, we once again are able to note, in a gross fashion, the patterned involvements of age-near siblings. Sisters have a mean number of contact patterns of 2.5-2.6, with no differences by strata. The white-collar males have a mean of 2.3, and the other five sex-strata groupings range from 2.0 down to 1.7, with the lowest mean being between blue-collar cross-sex siblings. Frequent interaction but a narrow range of contact types: this is the characteristic relationship between blue-collar cross-sex siblings. This finding is consistent with the division of labor and interests by sex in the working class noted by Rainwater *et al* and others.[20] Having little in common, they limit their contact to showing concern by dropping in, but patterned activity of any other sort is infrequent. Sisters, while having the widest range of contact patterns of any sex combination of siblings, do not demonstrate even as broad a scope of contact patterns as do blue-collar males and their parents, who are the least likely intergenerational kin of orientation to engage in several patterns.

In summary, the relationship between age-near siblings is predicated upon a basic family interest, upon the desire to know how and what one's brother or sister is doing. The role of social companion is seldom played by age-near siblings in the Greensboro sample, even when they live close enough to be good friends. Nor are these siblings a recurrent source of mutual aid. We arrive at the same general conclusion reached in the discussion of contact with parents: adult relations between siblings are to a great extent a continuation—mitigated by changing interests and distance considerations—of a relationship which has been developing during childhood and youth. It is a matter of interest, less often of companionship or help. Quite possibly the frequency of contact, as well as the sharing of various activities, is governed by affection and values, and by the lesser feeling of kin obligation found in sibling relations. Thus, the subjective factors in sibling involvement become the focus of Section Three.

Section Three: Subjective Aspects of Sibling Relations

Subjective Factors and Sibling Interaction

Close affectional ties to one's age-near sibling and perceived similarity of values are less often expressed than they are to parents. Newcomb and Svehla reported that siblings are less likely to share the same attitudes than are parents and children, and this is borne out in the present study.[21] Forty-five per cent of the young adults feel that they and their sibling have a high degree of value consensus, as compared to 54 per cent who expressed such a consensus with their parents. Forty-eight per cent indicate that they are affectionally close to this sibling, and the overall association between consensus and closeness is fairly high, 68 per cent of the respondents being high in both or low in both.

There is assumed by Cumming and Schneider, Garigue, and others, to be a greater degree of choice or personal preference contributing to sibling interaction than is found in relations with parents.[22] The young adult respondents indicate a modicum of association between affection and interaction with parents when moderately separated residentially, but no relation whatsoever under conditions of proximity or great distance. When affectional closeness and interaction frequency with the age-near sibling are related according to residential distance, there is a significant dissimilarity from parental relations. The range in which choice operates, although still somewhat limited, includes all residential categories (see Table IV-6). The same uniformly frequent interaction between proximate siblings is simply not demanded as it was in relations with one's parents.

The obligation to keep in touch with parents became even more apparent in the previous Chapter (see Table III-7) when we examined all forms of contact—communication as well as face-to-face.

TABLE IV-6

Expression of closeness to and frequency of interaction with the age-near
sibling, according to the sibling's residential location

Location of Sibling	Closeness to Sibling	Number of Respondents	Frequency of Interaction, in Per Cent				
			Weekly or More	Monthly-Weekly	Several Times Yearly	Yearly or Less	Total Pct.
Greensboro	Close	(102)	63	29	7	1	100
	Not Close	(103)	46	40	7	7	100
—100 Miles	Close	(89)	10	45	42	3	100
	Not Close	(69)	6	44	38	12	100
Beyond 100 Miles in NC, SC, Va.	Close	(58)	—	28	62	10	100
	Not Close	(83)	—	14	52	34	100
Elsewhere	Close	(87)	—	4	44	52	100
	Not Close	(106)	—	1	30	69	100

Daughters in particular feel constrained to communicate regularly
with parents regardless of how they feel affectionally toward them;
sons a little less so. In Table IV-7 an obvious difference in sibling
relations is that sisters are as likely as brothers to follow the dictates of their feelings in contact frequency. The cross-sex siblings
are noteworthy in that there is less variation in contact according to
expressions of closeness than there is between sisters or between
brothers, this being most evident in the right-hand column of the
Table. Perhaps cross-sex sibling contact is so much based upon kin
concern rather than common interests in any event that an expressed emotional attachment provides little basis for a wider range
of shared activities.

This interpretation, and other crucial differences in contact patterns which are dependent upon affectional closeness, may be better observed if we investigate patterning in the various contact
types according to the sex and affectional closeness of the siblings.

TABLE IV-7

Expression of affectional closeness to the age-near sibling and frequency of the most frequent form of contact—face-to-face, telephone, or letter—according to the sex of the siblings

Sex of Siblings and Affectional Closeness		Number of Respondents	Frequency of Contact, in Per Cent						Total Per Cent in Contact Monthly or More
			Weekly or More	Several Times Monthly	Monthly	Several Times Yearly	Yearly or Less	Total Pct.	
Brothers	Close	(66)	20	32	23	24	2	101	74
	Not Close	(104)	20	8	18	35	19	100	46
Cross-Sex	Close	(148)	22	14	27	30	7	100	64
	Not Close	(176)	17	12	22	34	15	100	51
Sisters	Close	(122)	37	21	23	19	1	101	80
	Not Close	(81)	22	11	21	30	16	100	54

Here (in Table IV-8) we note that the differences in patterned contact of various sorts between cross-sex siblings are not great according to closeness. Even when emotional attachment is strong, as inferred above, these siblings are not prone to engage in social activities, mutual aid, or frequent home visiting. However, expressions of affectional closeness or distance appear to make a substantial difference in visiting, communication, mutual aid, and activities between brothers or between sisters.

Intensive involvement with another person may result in perceiving the extent to which yours and their values diverge, as well as the extent of their similarity. Thus, it is not surprising that emotional attachment is more closely related to sibling interaction and contact than is value consensus. Without presenting a Table, we note that both in terms of the most frequent form of contact and the contact patterns, differences based on value consensus are in the same direction, but not as distinct, as when affectional closeness is employed.

Greater freedom of choice in sibling contact than in contact with parents is clearly manifested at two points. First, proximate siblings are free to interact somewhat less frequently and within a narrower range of contact types if they do not feel close to each other. Second, remote siblings, even sisters, who are not close in affection communicate much less often than do those characterized by a strong emotional bond. Presumably, this greater choice in sibling contact bespeaks a lesser or weaker feeling of general obligation than was found in relations with parents, and it is this aspect of sibling relations—the obligatory—which now demands our attention.

According to the verbal testimony of the young adult Greensboroites regarding their motives for keeping in touch with their age-near sibling, strong feelings of obligation are markedly less widespread than they are toward parents. Less than one-third see either general or specific obligation as fundamental to their relations with this sibling. Enjoyment is more likely to be stressed as very important to such sibling contact as they have, 70 per cent claiming this, but there are 21 per cent who feel that there is no really important reason or motive for keeping in touch with their age-near brother or sister.

TABLE IV-8

**Expression of closeness to the age-near sibling and patterned engagement
in the contact types, according to the sex of the siblings**

Sex of Siblings and Affectional Closeness		Number of Respondents	Occurrence Several Times Yearly or More, in Pct.						
			Home Visits	Activities	Organizations	Rituals	Communication	Aid Rec'd	Aid Given
Brothers	Close	(66)	77	44	12	29	83	15	17
	Not Close	(104)	55	21	11	19	54	3	8
Cross-Sex	Close	(148)	62	21	15	29	70	7	9
	Not Close	(176)	54	14	8	18	53	3	5
Sisters	Close	(122)	76	47	20	38	89	20	14
	Not Close	(81)	43	30	12	21	67	5	7

Insight into the expressed motivation for sibling contact may be increased by examining, as we did in Chapter III concerning parents, the relation of affectional closeness to enjoyment and obligation, according to the proximity or non-proximity of the sibling. The results once again accentuate the greater choice possible in sibling relations. Table IV-9 discloses lesser differences in enjoyment, among those with their sibling living in Greensboro, associated with degree of closeness than was true in the case of parents. The actual variation in interaction frequency between these siblings (Table IV-6), although not great, makes it possible for the siblings who are not affectionally close to nevertheless express an enjoyment of the contact which does occur. Furthermore, the expression of obligation is ordinarily low, rather than high, as it is between young adults and proximate parents.

As for siblings who live apart from each other, the interrelations between motives, closeness, and interaction are even more distinct. There is a pronounced positive relation between closeness and enjoyment, and a fairly strong negative relation between closeness and obligation. Notably the largest single category of affectionally distant, regardless of residential location, state that neither enjoyment nor obligation is an important reason for keeping in touch with the sibling. The affectionally and residentially distant, it will be recalled, interact less frequently and communicate less often than those who feel close. It is the 34 per cent, i.e., those who are neither proximate nor affectionally close and who see no important reason for keeping in touch, who are in face-to-face contact with their age-near sibling least often. Only 48 per cent of these 87 young adults see this sibling more than once a year.

In summary, on the one hand enjoyment of the sibling is quite similar to that expressed toward parents. Obligation, on the other hand, is usually not felt to be as great, and specific obligation, or obligation to help, is virtually non-existent. The freedom of the young adult to interact and communicate or not with the sibling, as he so desires, is much greater than in parental relations. This freedom, however, is not absolute. General obligation to keep in touch, while not dominant, is still an important aspect of sibling relations.

TABLE IV-9

Expression of closeness to the age-near sibling in relation to enjoyment of and obligation to the sibling, as important reasons for keeping in touch, according to whether the sibling lives in Greensboro or elsewhere

Location of Sibling	Closeness to Sibling	Number of Respondents	Important Reasons for Keeping in Touch, in Per Cent				
			Enjoyment Only	Enjoyment and Obligation	Obligation Only	Neither Very Important	Total Pct.
Greensboro	Close	(102)	54	33	4	9	100
	Not Close	(103)	31	27	10	32	100
Elsewhere	Close	(234)	65	24	4	7	100
	Not Close	(258)	31	20	15	34	100

The Sibling as a Reference Point

Sibling companionship and sibling rivalry are two themes with which we began the discussion of relations between age-near siblings. The companionship aspect, as manifested in contact patterns, is limited at best, but we have yet to investigate the possible continuation of sibling rivalry and/or identification into adulthood.

A few of the sex-strata findings in the present chapter include a close relationship between sisters, seen in a certain amount of aid and activity, as well as overall contact, a cross-sex relationship based upon interest rather than common activities, and a relation between occupationally disparate brothers founded primarily upon traditional ties such as those to the same church. The exploration of interaction and contact types has resulted in no clear-cut evidence of estrangement between any two sibling combinations according to sex or occupational strata. Such differences, if there are any, may be more readily observable in the subjective sphere since much sibling contact is influenced by distance and by the same, though less predominant, obligational tie which link children and parents.

Several indications are found in the kinship literature of the association between sibling affection and categories of sex and strata. LeMasters finds in a college sample that differentially mobile siblings are ambivalent toward each other during their college years, but Willmott and Young contend that in settled adulthood the common roles of female kin make occupational differences between their husbands essentially irrelevant to their relationship. Sisters express the closest affectional tie of any sibling combination, John Gulick and Charles E. Bowerman add.[23]

In the previous chapter we dwelt at length upon middle-class success values as a key factor in the relations of young adults and their parents, especially as regards affectional ties. Because kin are permanent, says Elizabeth Bott, they are used as bases for comparison and contrast with oneself.[24] Form and Geschwender illustrate this latter point in discovering that manual workers are more satisfied occupationally when they perceive their occupational position to be better than that of their brother, while the least satisfied are those whose occupational level is lower than their brother's.[25] Siblings are in fact the comparative reference group *par excellence,* being among one's effective kin from birth or soon thereafter, and being social givens, unlike friends. We are now prepared to suggest that middle-class success values, and personal comparisons and identifications in terms of them, are central to the relations between siblings in our urban, industrial society. To be more explicit, a young adult is more likely to feel close to, and possibly identify with, his sibling if the *sibling* is middle class than if he is working class. The middle-class sibling embodies, in adulthood, the societal definition of success, while the working-class does not. Our assumption, then, is that even though such differences were not apparent objectively or interactionally, that the success values will influence the subjective relations between siblings. While there is very likely an overall tendency for sisters to be closer than cross-sex siblings, and cross-sex closer than brothers, the sex and stratum categories should manifest the following pattern: white-collar respondents talking about a white-collar sibling and blue-collar respondents talking about a white-collar sibling should be closer affectionally and higher in identification than white-collar or blue-collar respondents talking about a blue-collar sibling. The extent to which these postulates hold within the Greensboro sample may be observed in Table IV-10.

The pattern of identification or non-identification and affection or non-affection is consistent with our presuppositions, except in the case of occupationally disparate brothers. These brothers are equally unlikely to identify with, or feel close to, each other. In this case it appears that occupation is too salient as a measure of personal success or failure to allow the working-class male to be subjectively close to his middle-class brother. To do otherwise would be to admit within the family his own occupational shortcoming. Similarity in other activities and interests does not occur often enough to overcome divergence in status as a determinant of subjective relations.

Affectional relations, and in some cases identification, between occupationally disparate sisters and cross-sex siblings may be interpreted as a one-way or non-reciprocated response to a family success. The blue-collar wife, while not seeking to purposely deprecate

TABLE IV-10

Expression of affectional closeness to and identification with or idealization of the age-near sibling, according to the sex and occupational strata of the siblings[26]

Sex and Occupational Strata of Siblings	Number of Respondents	Affectionally Close to Sibling	High in Idealization of Sibling
White-collar male with white-collar brother	(72)	47	22
White-collar male with blue-collar brother	(21)	24	14
Blue-collar male with white-collar brother	(23)	26	9
Blue-collar male with blue-collar brother	(41)	37	17
White-collar respondent with white-collar cross-sex sibling	(132)	54	30
White-collar respondent with blue-collar cross-sex sibling	(57)	30	21
Blue-collar respondent with white-collar cross-sex sibling	(34)	53	41
Blue-collar respondent with blue-collar cross-sex sibling	(83)	40	25
White-collar female with white-collar sister	(90)	72	30
White-collar female with blue-collar sister	(25)	36	16
Blue-collar female with white-collar sister	(31)	61	48
Blue-collar female with blue-collar sister	(46)	50	20

her own husband, is proud of the achievement of her brother or sister who is middle-class, and demonstrates her pride by subjective closeness to the higher status sibling. The same is true of the young blue-collar male whose brother-in-law has a higher status. Although in the interviews these males often expressed ambivalence or even jealousy of the brother-in-law, they were able to identify themselves indirectly with family success by means of a close relationship with the sister. No such identification or affectional tie appears in any of the white-collar categories discussing a blue-collar sibling. In fact, a certain disdain is often expressed for the brother or sister who did not achieve in middle-class terms. As expected, the mutually middle-class siblings tend to be subjectively closer than the mutually blue-collar siblings, although the greater closeness of sisters results in there being almost no difference between white-collar brothers and blue-collar sisters.

To what extent have the present feelings of these young adults toward their siblings been moulded by events, including occupational histories, since they left home? Many of the contact patterns, we have found, are a continuation of traditional or familial involvements into adulthood, altered in frequency by distance considerations. But what of attitudes; has there been a perceptible change in feelings toward the age-near sibling since marriage, since the commencement of settled adulthood? The respondents were asked, in retrospect, how they perceived their feelings to have changed toward this sibling since marriage. The result are contained in Table IV-11.

Three important aspects of this Table require comment. First, more than 50 per cent of the sisters feel that they are closer now than when they were growing up. This is especially true of the occupationally disparate sisters, which conforms with our argument that LeMasters' finding of sibling ambivalence during college cannot simply be generalized into adult kin relations. These sisters have often been quite far apart in ideas, interests, and affection during the adolescent years. However, with marriage and the coming of children they have drawn closer together.

A second important, but hardly unexpected, finding is the increasing adult disaffection of occupationally disparate brothers. Unlike sisters, these young adult brothers are characterized by occupational role divergence which simply continues the difference in ideas and feelings which in all likelihood began while they were still in the parental home. Only the blue-collar cross-sex siblings even approximate the disparate brothers in decreased closeness. The demarcation of male-female roles and interests in the working class, about which we shall have more to say in Chapter V, accounts for the lesser closeness and contact pattern dominated by brief conversation visits between the blue-collar cross-sex siblings.

TABLE IV-11

Expressed changes in closeness to the age-near sibling since
marriage, according to sex and occupational strata

Sex and Occupational Strata of Siblings	Number of Respondents	Changes in Closeness, in Per Cent			
		Closer to Sibling	About the Same	Less Close to Sibling	Total Pct.
White-collar male with white-collar brother	(72)	36	26	38	100
Male with brother of opposite stratum**	(44)	18	23	59*	100
Blue-collar male with blue-collar brother	(41)	22	46*	32	100
White-collar respondent with white-collar cross-sex sibling	(132)	34	35	31	100
Respondent with cross-sex sibling of opposite stratum	(91)	31	33	36	100
Blue-collar respondent with blue-collar cross-sex sibling	(83)	22	29	49*	100
White-collar female with white-collar sister	(90)	49	21	30	100
Female with sister of opposite stratum	(56)	61*	16	23	100
Blue-collar female with blue-collar sister	(46)	48	17	35	100

* Indicates a percentage which is important for its magnitude.
** These are discussed in the text as "occupationally disparate" siblings.

Robins and Tomanec, Farber, Bott, and others have referred to
the central role which women play in urban kin networks. It is,
therefore, little wonder that sisters are least likely to state that there
has been no change, positive or negative, in their feelings about
their age-near sister over the years. The very personal investment
of the young adult female in kinship relations mitigates against her
relation with her sister remaining unchanged, or dormant.

What reasons do these young adults give for their current feelings about this sibling? In the answers to this question we have a further key to understanding the changes in closeness expressed above. The complex and often idiosyncratic answers which are possible to an open-ended question have assumed a general pattern as follows: The occupationally disparate brothers are the most likely of any category to assert that they have little in common, or little basis for a close relationship. Another large group of them indicate that infrequent contact makes them less close than formerly. Of course, infrequent contact is an effect of earlier causes, especially a dissimilarity of values and interests since their youth. Over half of the disparate brothers either state little in common or infrequent contact as the reason for their present affectional distance. Also of interest are the eight young adult males who in Table IV-11 declare that they are closer to their occupationally disparate brother than formerly. Five of them feel that their competition has decreased, thereby increasing their enjoyment of each other's company, and the other three find that they have more in common now. It is these few who engage in social activities together, having developed a new basis for relationship which ignores their status differences. These eight, however, are the exceptions that "prove the rule"; the other thirty-six differentially mobile brother have been unable to establish more than an incidental relationship based upon traditional ties, drop-in or casual visits, and affectional distance.

It has been hypothesized that an important reason for the increasing feeling of closeness between sisters in young adulthood is the convergence or similarity of their adult roles. Almost 20 per cent of the females discussing their sister explain their present closeness as a function of having more in common now, often specified as marriage and children. In fact, 54 per cent of the young adults who gave this as the prime reason for their present affection are young adult females speaking of a sister. The other key rationale used by sisters to explain current closeness is enjoying each other more now. This was expressed variously as maturity decreasing competition, relationships have been renewed, and as enjoyment of activity increasing. It is the latter two which are expressed by 22 per cent of the sisters.

The white-collar siblings, regardless of sex, are decidedly more likely than the other two stratum combinations to say that they have always been close to their age-near sibling. Sixty per cent of the young adults who give this as the reason for their feelings are middle-class adults referring to a middle-class sibling. This reflects the claims of LeMasters and Hollingshead that the middle-class nuclear family is generally a "happy, well-knit group."[27]

Attempts at retrospect on the part of the respondents have resulted in a strengthening of the conclusions reached on the basis of expressions of identification with and affection for the age-near sibling. We close Section Three with a summary of the findings and conclusions concerning the subjective aspects of sibling relations.

Summary of Subjective Aspects of Relations with the Age-Near Sibling

Relations between age-near siblings tend to be less close subjectively in young adulthood than relations with parents. Sisters express the closest relationship, and the majority of young married females feel that they have grown closer to their sister in adulthood than they were while growing up. Cross-sex siblings and brothers are less likely to perceive themselves as close now or as having become closer since reaching adulthood. The divergent interests and adult roles of cross-sex siblings, and the concern of the males with their occupations and families of procreation (wife and children), are little inducement to an increased emotional investment in sibling relations.

Two major differences between sibling and parental relations are evident in the association of affectional closeness and contact, both differences accentuating the greater freedom of choice and preference operative in sibling relations. First, among proximate siblings affectional closeness and interaction frequency are associated; i.e., the affectionally distant, regardless of sex, interact less frequently on the average than do the affectionally close. This suggests that at close range frequent interaction with the age-near sibling can be avoided, whereas with propinquitous parents it was found to be virtually unavoidable. Secondly, the residentially separated siblings, including sisters, are not constrained to communicate as frequently if they do not feel close to their sibling. Such manifestations of choice are relative to the lack of choice vis-à-vis parents, but are not great in absolute terms. Cross-sex siblings are less divergent both in interaction frequency and in patterned engagement in a wide range of contact types according to subjective closeness, which exemplifies the fact that their interests and activities, regardless of emotional attachment, tend to be basically divergent.

Enjoyment as a motive for keeping in touch with the age-near sibling is similar to that expressed toward parents, but the general obligation to keep in touch, while present, is a less dominant feature of sibling relations. Garigue notes that there is a distinction between the obligation to interact with close relatives and that felt toward secondary relatives, which can often be satisfied by a yearly visit.[28] With parents the normative expectation seems to be monthly contact of some sort between the residentially separated and interaction weekly or more between the proximate. Siblings are apparently an intermediate category between parents and secondary kin with respect to the obligation to maintain contact. Periodic contact during the year will suffice for the remote and monthly contact for the proximate, with more frequent contact at the discretion of the siblings involved.

Opinion has been considerably divided concerning the effects of occupational mobility or differential occupational position upon kin relations. One reason for the divergent viewpoints has been the attempt to generalize regarding kin, instead of investigating individually the various degrees of kinship. The result has been that one or a few basic features tend to be stressed and others omitted. Those such as Litwak who focus upon the functionality of kin relations in urban society assert that they provide primary relations to the city dweller, including status gain or deference among the differentially mobile.[29] This statement, however, ignores the comparative or competitive aspects of kin, particularly sibling, relations and is therefore incomplete, emphasizing the positive elements to the exclusion of the strain which is likewise inherent in family relationships. Those authors such as Schneider and Homans or Stuckert who claim that mobility disrupts kin or results in shallow kin ties overlook the role of one or both parents in aspirations and the subsequent upward mobility of their child or children. They similarly overlook identification with successful kin as well as the lesser salience of the husband's occupation in adult female relationships.

To understand the effects of occupational disparity upon adult relations between siblings we must distinguish categories of kin, as Bott suggests, must understand the socialization process including its adult phase, and must be aware of the role which kin play as a comparative reference group for the modern urban individual. Occupational disparity between brothers generally signifies disaffection on the part of both the higher and lower status brother. Status differences between sisters and cross-sex siblings tend to result in greater subjective closeness of the lower status to the higher status sibling than *vice versa*. In fact, except for the occupationally disparate brothers, it appears that the status of the *sibling* and the sex of both are key determinants in subjective relations. That is, subjective relations tend to be closer if the sibling is white-collar than if he or she is blue-collar, and tend to be closest between sisters and least close between brothers.

Occupational status effects on sibling relations have been investigated without reference to the occupational position of the parents. We have ignored the issue of the influence of particular forms of mobility upon sibling relations, obscuring, for example, the distinction between two white-collar siblings whose parents are blue-collar and two white-collar siblings whose family background is also white-collar. Thus, consideration of the parents' occupational position in terms of sibling relations brings this section to a close.

Parents' or Sibling's Occupational Position: A Justification

The justification for discussing the occupational disparity or similarity of siblings apart from the parents' occupational position has not been made clear. Is there not a substantial difference between the relations of two white-collar siblings when their parents are of the same general status as the offspring and when there has been upward mobility on the part of the two siblings?

Interactionally, differences are negligible. Neither in frequency of contact nor in contact patterns between siblings is there any obvious divergence which might be attributable to the parents' posi-

TABLE IV-12

Expression of closeness to the age-near sibling by upwardly mobile and stable white-collar males and females (N = 397)[30]

Sex of White-collar Respondent	Respondent's Mobility or Stability	Status of Sibling	Affectionally Close to Brother		Affectionally Close to Sister	
			Number	Pct.	Number	Pct.
Males	Upward	White collar	(24)	54	(22)	59
		Blue collar	(18)	22	(18)	28
	Stable	White collar	(48)	44	(35)	60
		Blue collar	(3)*	33	(3)*	0
Females	Upward	White collar	(29)	48	(30)	63
		Blue collar	(21)	38	(22)	36
	Stable	White collar	(46)	50	(60)	77
		Blue collar	(15)	27	(3)*	33

* Percentages should not be figured on N's as small as these; it was done in order to demonstrate the overall pattern of percentage differences.

tion. This, however, is to be expected since the occupational histories of two upwardly mobile young adults do not differ greatly from the histories of two stable middle-class young adults, and the occupational histories affect residential distances which in turn affect contact frequency and types. Perhaps in the sensitive area of affectional response differences will be found which are dependent upon the upward or downward movement, or occupational stability, of one or both siblings in relation to their parents.

In Table IV-12 the stable white-collar and upwardly mobile young adults are compared in affectional closeness to their age-near sibling. Differences are much more dependent upon the siblings' present occupational positions than upon their family background. That is, when rows one and two are compared, as are three and four, and so on, it is apparent that the percentage differences range from ten to thirty-two, excluding those three compari-

sons involving small N's. These differences depend on the status of
the sibling. However, when rows one and three are compared, or
two and four, and so on, the percentage variations range from one
to fourteen. These comparisons are of course based upon the status
of the parents. Although not presented in Table IV-12, the same
general pattern results when the stable blue-collar and downward
mobile are compared. One exception, which is quite tentative due
to the small numbers, is that mutually downward mobile siblings
seem to be brought closer by their common experience, while at the
same time being affectionally distant from their parents. These siblings are simply much closer subjectively than are two stable
blue-collar siblings. Nevertheless, for the most part the present occupational position of one's sibling can be seen to be the key to
subjective relations rather than family background. The middle-
class success values of the society, as embodied or not embodied in
an adult sibling, are more directly associated with current relations
than is the occupational position of their parents or one's personal
pattern of mobility or stability *vis-à-vis* the parents. We have been
justified in virtually omitting consideration of parents' occupational
status from the investigation of sibling relations, and have thus discovered the closeness of mutually upward mobile siblings as compared to the situation in which one sibling is mobile and the other
is not.[31]

The evidence has not pointed to sibling resemblance and friendship, resulting in one's age-near sibling being the focus of his leisure activity, as the characteristic pattern. Instead, continuing interest and comparison appear to dominate sibling relations. However
siblings and parents comprise a sub-network, consisting of the kin
of orientation, within the kin network. Two questions regarding
this network demand some attention. First, it would be premature
to refer to sibling relations *in toto* on the basis of the preceding
analysis; we must admit the possibility that the young adult may
feel closer to, and spend more time with, a sibling other than the
one closest to him in age. Second, contact between siblings does
not occur *in vacuo*. Very often the parents are included, and, according to some authors, are likely to be the focal point of sibling

interaction. Thus, in the next section the "favorite" sibling and the possibility of "combination opportunities" will be investigated.

Section Four: The Favorite Sibling and Combination Opportunities

"Now tell me just a word or two about your other brothers and sisters. Do you have a brother or sister to whom you feel closer than you do to the one we have been talking about?"[32] With this question the respondents were given an opportunity to express preference for one sibling over the others. Some indicated that they are closer to another sibling, others responded that they are less close to the others, and a large number stated that they feel about the same toward all their siblings. The actual sample distribution is as follows: 22 per cent, or 153 individuals, have another sibling who is their favorite, 20 per cent (139 young adults) consider their age-near sibling as the one they are closest to, 32 per cent (226 respondents) have no special "favorite" sibling, and 26 per cent, 179 individuals, have only one sibling, i.e., they are from a two-child family of orientation.

The choice of a favorite sibling suggests possible differences both in subjective and objective relations. That favoritism is associated in absolute terms with feelings toward the age-near sibling may be observed in the left-hand portion of Table IV-13. When the age-near sibling is also the favorite a large majority indicate affectional closeness to him or her. Furthermore, inability to choose between one's siblings frequently signifies a moderately close relationship to all of them. Finally, the choice of another sibling as favorite often denotes an affectionally distant relation to the age-near sibling. These results, while predictable, once again demonstrate the coherence and value of the subjective data. More important, we are alerted to the possibility that the young adult who feels closer to another sibling may also interact more frequently and meaningfully with the favorite. Before considering favoritism and interaction, it should be stated that the sex of the young adult is not independently associated with expressions of favoritism, and occupational

TABLE IV-13

Expression of closeness to the age-near sibling, per cent in contact with this sibling monthly or more, and patterns of contact, according to the choice of a favorite sibling

Choice of a Favorite Among Siblings	Number of Respondents	Closeness to Age-Near Sibling, in Per Cent				Pct. in Contact Monthly or More	Occurrence Several Times Yearly or More, in Per Cent			
		Close	Fairly Close	Not Close	Total Pct.		Activities	Organizations	Aid Given	Aid Rec'd
Age-Near is Favorite	(139)	72	23	5	100	73	36	19	14	17
Only One Sibling	(179)	47	36	17	100	64	30	14	11	8
No Favorite	(226)	42	46	12	100	63	25	11	6	5
Another is Favorite	(153)	37	33	30	100	42	17	9	10	5

stratum is associated only in that the great majority of those with but one sibling are middle class. This, however, is a function of comparative family size by stratum and implies nothing regarding sibling preference.

Contact with the age-near sibling, it will be seen in the right-hand portion of Table IV-13, is most frequent when he or she is preferred over his brothers and sisters. It is, on the other hand, substantially less frequent with the age-near sibling when another is favorite. Also, patterned social activity, involvement in the same organization, and exchange of aid are all more widespread when the sibling being discussed is the favorite. Nevertheless, the overall picture of sibling contact patterns is altered but slightly by isolating the more intense sibling relations from the less intense. Interaction frequency and contact patterns with the 153 other siblings who are favorites resemble those with the age-near sibling when he or she is favorite. That is, even by looking at the favorite sibling as well as the age-near, siblings are still infrequently employed as social companions, although it now appears that some sibling may play such a role in the life of the young Greensboro adult about as often as do a parent or parents. Also, mutual aid between siblings is more widespread than just with the age-near sibling, but is still patterned only between about one-fifth of these young adults and any sibling. The characterization of sibling relations with which we closed Section Three persists even when the notion of favorite sibling is added to the discussion of the age-near.

A second issue which derives from the nature of parent and sibling relations as a sub-network is what we have called the "combination opportunity." Lee Robins and Miroda Tomanec, in their analysis of kin interaction, state as one reason for variations in kin interaction with relatives that the absolute time which any person has to spend in kin interaction is limited. Therefore, if he has many siblings, or children of his own, he has less time left over to spend with others of his kin.[33] This explanation, however, assumes that kin contacts are mutually exclusive. The cumulative effect of the residential proximity of many relatives is overlooked, and the fallacy of such an either-or conception of interaction is illustrated in Young and Willmott's study of Bethanal Green. The mother, they note, is a major link between siblings, their interaction often taking place at the "Mum's" home.[34] Thus, the parental home is not merely the locus of parent-child interaction, but is often a rendezvous for siblings and other kin. Young and Willmott's findings pertain to parents and siblings the majority of whom live in the same London borough, but the cumulative effects of proximity and the key role of parents in interaction between other kin may appear even when residential distance is greater.

Assuming with Young and Willmott that the parents are the focal point for much interaction between their adult children, inter-

TABLE IV-14

Frequency of interaction between age-near siblings, according to the relative location of sibling and parents, controlling for the residential location of the age-near sibling

Location of Sibling	Relative Location of Age-Near Sibling and Parents	Number of Respondents	Per Cent Who See Age-Near Sibling at Least Monthly
Greensboro	With or Within 50 Miles of Parents	(176)	91
	Over 50 Miles Apart	(17)	82
	Both Parents Deceased	(12)	75
−100 Miles	With or Within 50 Miles of Parents	(106)	64
	Over 50 Miles Apart	(41)	32
	Both Parents Deceased	(11)	27
			Per Cent Who See Age-Near Sibling Several Times Yearly or More
Beyond 100 Miles in NC, SC, or Va.	With or Within 50 Miles of Parents	(65)	82
	Over 50 Miles Apart	(65)	72
	Both Parents Deceased	(11)	64
Elsewhere	With or Within 50 Miles of Parents	(60)	47
	Over 50 Miles Apart	(118)	36
	Both Parents Deceased	(13)	39

action with the age-near sibling should be most frequent when he or she lives with, or within a few miles of, the parent or parents, so that both may be seen on a single visit. A lower frequency of inter-action with the sibling should occur when the children and parents are all separated by more than a few miles. Finally, interaction with the age-near sibling should be least frequent when both parents are deceased. In Table IV-14 we have arbitrarily employed a distance of fifty miles as a measure of close proximity to parents; the actual assumption is that any increase in residential separation between the three parties decreases interaction between the siblings. Thus, in Table IV-14 is presented frequency of interaction between age-near siblings according to the relative locations of the two siblings and of the age-near sibling and the parents. Within each residential distance category, the importance of proximity to parents for sibling interaction is evident.

Omission of such network analysis from considerations of the interaction of specific relatives appears to be a glaring weakness of much work in this area. Even as the "Mum's" home is a rendez-vous for children living in the same London borough, giving them the opportunity to combine sibling and parent contact, so is it a meeting place for siblings who are residentially separated from each other, but one of whom lives close to their parents. Combination opportunities are unquestionably a factor influencing frequency of interaction between siblings, and very likely between more distant relatives as well.

The Kin of Orientation and Other Systems: A Postcript

The family of orientation is related functionally, by means of socialization and consumership for example, to many of the other systems and institutions of modern, urban-industrial society. When they become the kin of orientation, i.e., when the children leave home, what happens to these links with the larger society? Up to now in our study the interrelations between kin and other societal systems have been referred to only in passing. However, the data do lend themselves to a brief analysis of such questions.

Perhaps the most interesting and best documented aspect of kinship in urban society is its relationship to the economic sphere. Individualistic economic motivations are apparent in the small numbers of young adults who follow in their fathers' occupations or who receive help in getting started occupationally from an uncle, older brother, or other relative. Less than 6 per cent of the present sample have received such help. Furthermore, the reactions of those who do work with kin in the same business or location is instructive. A school photographer who works with his brother and a cousin has this to say about the importance of relatives: "They are very important from a business standpoint. Socially, aside from business, they are unimportant." A young engineer who works in an engineering firm with his father and a brother makes the following comments on his lack of contact patterns with them: "We do very little except in a business way. We see enough of each other there. . . . I don't want to be really close to them because of business; business really keeps us apart." The ability to work with kin in the economic sphere seems to be predicated to a great extent in such cases on the ability of the parties involved to separate their economic from their social life.

Another aspect of economics which may impinge upon kin relations is the exchanging of tangible aid. A certain amount of this is acceptable to the young adult offspring. However, the respondents manifest some resentment when they receive what they perceive to be too much help, and, as noted above, when the necessity of their helping becomes the central activity it may have a weakening effect on the relationship.

Kin involvement in voluntary associations in the city appears to be restricted to those cases—in our sample about 10 per cent—where the kin of orientation attend the same religious organization. Other associations, such as clubs and unions, are represented by only a scattering of kin.

The general picture is not entirely one of either-or with respect to kinship and other institutions in urban-industrial society, but it is one in which the more active and apparently satisfactory relations between the kin of orientation are predicated upon a minimum of direct involvement—as kin—in other societal systems.[35] Interest or concern, continued contact, ritual occasions to renew ties, comparison, enjoyment, and help when needed—these are the factors which best characterize involvements among the kin of orientation.

Chapter V

THE BEST-KNOWN COUSIN AND SECONDARY KIN

"I don't see any use in keeping up with people you really don't care about or have time for, just because they are relatives." "No, relatives aren't the least bit important to me outside of my parents. We have never had a close-knit family." Young Greensboro adults report a median of about twenty-eight kin, with only five of them being kin of orientation. Yet the comparatively large numbers of recognizable secondary kin, i.e., aunts, uncles, cousins, grandparents, and so on, while clearly predominating over the kin of orientation, may not be indicative of their importance or unimportance in the life of the urban individual.

The kin group, contends Helen Codere, is localized in the immediate family. Kin responsibility, adds Blitsten, does not extend to other relatives outside the nuclear unit.[1] Even those studies which stress the functionality of kin in urban-industrial society, such as Sussman and Burchinal's and Eugene Litwak's, either refer specifically to the kin of orientation, as does the former, or refer to kin in general, as does the latter.[2] None of the urban samples, not even the kin-oriented French Canadians, manifest an elaborate involvement with secondary kin. Some have asserted that kin ties in the southern United States are both more intensive and more extensive than is generally true of Western societies. However, the guiding assumption with which we begin the discussion of secondary kin is that they are relatively unimportant in the lives and consciousness of young adult Greensboroites.

Several authors, notably Parsons and Robins and Tomanec, distinguish between relationships with various secondary kin. Based upon frequency of interaction, Robins and Tomanec find that grandparents are closer to Ego than are aunts and uncles, who are, in turn, closer than cousins. Both their sample and the orientation of the earlier discussion by Parsons, to which they are indebted, are predominantly middle-class, and one issue confronting us is the extent to which the occupational strata diverge in according relative importance to various categories of secondary kin. That there may be a difference is indicated by Garigue's sample of the working class, who tend to prefer and to engage in more frequent interaction with kin of the same rather than the ascending generation.[3]

Almost 10 per cent of the present sample know *no* secondary kin well enough to inform the interviewer about either subjective or objective relations with them. This means that among these seventy-five respondents little or no contact with secondary kin occurs, and subjectively there are feelings neither of affection for nor obligation to any such persons. Without dividing our sample by sex or occupational strata, the tendency is for aunts and uncles to be slightly more important interactionally than either grandparents or cousins. Those who spend more time with aunts and uncles than with cousins or grandparents total 223, or 28 per cent of the total sample. There is evidence that when the young adult has grandparents living they may be the focal point of substantial kin interaction. However, the majority of respondents have none of their four grandparents still alive. Only eighty, or 10 per cent, state that they interact more with a grandparent or grandparents than they do with other secondary relatives. Another eighty-seven young adults are with aunts, uncles, and grandparents more than they are with any cousins. Thus, nearly 50 per cent report spending more time with what Parsons calls the "first outer circle of relatives," i.e., those who are of *Ego*'s parents' family of orientation, than with cousins or more distant kin.[4] A fairly large minority are with the various categories of secondary kin equally frequently or infrequently, or spend more time with cousins, while almost ten per cent, as reported above, spend virtually no time with any secondary kin.

In order to focus the analysis of relations with these kin, the young adults were asked to think and talk about the cousin whom they feel that they *know* best.[5] It was felt that reference to the "best-known cousin" would provide insight into the effects of occupational status and mobility upon lateral, or same-generation, kin relations, while also indirectly furnishing information concerning relations with aunts and uncles, through whom one is related to his cousin. Once again, the attempt was made not to control either subjective or objective variables and, if anything, to maximize knowledge of and interaction with kin; hence the discussion of the best-known, rather than necessarily the best-liked, cousin.

Section One: Who Is the Best-Known Cousin?

How does one get to know his cousin in urban, industrial society —or does he? In a society with some form of extended or joint family, with siblings and their wives and children living under the same roof, getting to know one's cousin well is a concomitant of household arrangements. But the chances for intimacy between cousins in the United States are obviously slim unless relations between their parents are close, or some common interest or activity draws the cousins together, or they live in close proximity to each other. That is, the conditions must be just right for a cousin to become an important "other" in the individual's world. The identification of the best-known cousin and specification of the factors underlying this selection comprise the task of the present section.

Who Is He Genealogically?

The key role of the mother's brother and of other aunts and uncles in the life of the growing person in various societies influences significantly the relations between cousins. Anthropological literature abounds with references to relations between parallel cousins, i.e., children of sisters or brothers, and between cross cousins, i.e., children of cross-sex siblings. Variations range from avoidance to preferred marriage within a particular cousin relationship.

In Western urban society, the norm is kin bilaterality, with little functionality reported in relations between aunts and uncles and their nephews and nieces. Under unusual circumstances, such as the death of parents, an aunt and uncle may become parents or socializers of a nephew or niece. However, ordinarily preference and choice are assumed to operate in secondary kin relations in very much the same fashion as they do in the relations between old friends. Nevertheless, the "given" aspect of kinship is likewise operative, determining which kin are apt to have the opportunity for contact. Schneider and Homans postulate one distinction between secondary kin in this society, noting that first-name-alone designations are more often "applied to aunts and uncles on the mother's side than on the father's. . . ." Does this, they wonder, represent a tendency in this society for a person's close and warm ties to be with his mother's kin?[6] This, then, is one presupposition with which we may approach the genealogical relationship between "best-known" cousins.

The relations between cousins are influenced both by their own sex and the sex of their parents. While it is theoretically possible that, due to bilaterality and preference or choice, cousin involvement may be scattered randomly among the genealogical combinations, there is little reason to expect that this is so. Both sex differences and stratum differences may appear, with the result that a particular relationship, such as that between daughters of sisters, may be overrepresented among the best-known cousins. Because much of the relationship between cousins is dependent upon earlier contact between their parents, it is not surprising that the occupational stratum of the parents is more important than the present position of the young adult in determining the best-known cousin. Both among males and females, the upwardly mobile and stable blue-collar are quite similar, as are the downwardly mobile and stable white-collar, in their genealogical relations with their best-known cousin. Therefore, in Table V-1 categories are combined into a fourfold division based upon the sex of the young adult and the occupational stratum of his parents. Within these categories there are eight possible ways in which *Ego* may be related to a first cousin; i.e., the cousin may be the father's sister's son or daughter, the father's brother's son or daughter, the mother's sister's son or daughter, or the mother's brother's son or daughter.

In Chapter IV the strong bond between sisters became apparent,

TABLE V-1

The manner in which young Greensboro adults are related to the best-known cousin, according to their sex and their parents' occupational stratum

Sex of the Young Adult and the Parents' Occupational Stratum	Number of Respondents	Genealogical Relationship with the Best-Known Cousin, in Per Cent*									
		MSiSo	MSiD	MBSo	MBD	FSiSo	FSiD	FBSo	FBD	Other	Total Pct.
Males with white-collar parents	(115)	17	12	20	6	15	6	14	5	5	100
Males with blue-collar parents	(145)	12	9	16	5	19	6	26	3	4	100
Females with white-collar parents	(182)	11	27	6	13	7	11	8	11	5	99
Females with blue-collar parents	(212)	14	37	4	12	4	16	4	7	2	100

Sex of the Young Adult and the Parents' Occupational Stratum	Number of Respondents	Same-Sex or Cross-Sex Cousin (omitting "Other")		Related Through Mother or Father (omitting "Other")	
		Same-Sex	Cross-Sex	Through Mother	Through Father
Males with white-collar parents	(109)	69	31	58	42
Males with blue-collar parents	(139)	76	24	44	56
Females with white-collar parents	(172)	67	33	60	40
Females with blue-collar parents	(207)	73	27	69	31

* Omitted from this Table are 145 young adults who were unable to designate a particular cousin to discuss as best-known, or who failed to delineate their own or their parents' occupational position. The category abbreviations include: M for mother, F for father, Si for sister, B for brother, So for son, and D for daughter.

and this is emphasized again by the results of Table V-1. Almost one-third of all the cousins selected by young married females as the one they know best are their mother's sister's daughter, and over 45 per cent are either sons or daughters of the mother's sister. The preferential or choice aspect is seen in the predominance of same-sex cousins; this tendency is greatest among the males from a blue-collar family, and is much greater when the parents are blue-collar than when they are white-collar. Here is strong evidence of the division of activities and involvement by sex in blue-collar families. Male kin go their way and female kin theirs, being separated not only in marital and parental roles but in leisure and kin contacts much more completely in predominantly blue-collar kin networks than in white-collar. This is manifest in the fact that young adult males with blue-collar parents are more often related to their cousin through their father's siblings, while females from this stratum are overwhelmingly related through their mother. By comparison, both males and females with white-collar parents are a little more likely to have as best-known cousin an offspring of their mother's sibling, which is consistent with the greater involvement of middle-class females in kin relations, as well as Schneider and Homans' inference.

Basic findings emerging from the consideration of genealogy may be summarized as stemming from three factors: first is the open and unformalized operation of secondary kinship in urban, industrial society; second is the central role of females in kin involvement; and third is the greater separation of the sexes in the working class. The openness of secondary kinship is seen both in the broad distribution of best-known cousins in the various relationship categories and in the strong tendency to know best a cousin of one's own sex. Together, the distribution and same-sex tendency indicate that there is no formal avoidance or preference, but that within the context of a family's residential and cultural history a certain amount of choice based upon similarity is granted. Least likely to be known well are cross-sex cross or parallel cousins, e.g., the young male respondent selecting his mother's brother's daughter or father's sister's daughter. The shallow tie between cross-sex siblings, discussed in the previous chapter, provides a basis for understanding this result. The sharing of activity beyond simple visiting is seldom patterned between cross-sex siblings, and as they grow older their offspring, especially if they are also of different sexes, find little in common and spend too little time together to develop an intense relationship. Young married males of white-collar parents, although likely to know a same-sex cousin best, are particularly characterized by genealogical randomness, or true bilaterality, being almost equally likely to name a cousin related to them through their mother or father, and through a consanguineal aunt or uncle. Such randomness is probably more an indication of non-involvement on their part than anything else.

The central role of the female in kinship is apparent both in the prevalence of the daughters of sisters as best-known cousins, and in the fact that the most frequent occurrence of cross-sex cousin choice in Table V-1 is through the mother's sister.

Separation of working-class kin activity by sex is underscored by the findings regarding relation to the cousin being through one's mother or father. Despite the more focal role of females in kinship, young married males with working-class parents are more apt to trace the relationship to their best-known cousin through their father. Relationship through the mother strongly predominates among the females from a blue-collar family, while a similar but less pronounced relationship holds for young white-collar-background adults.

Was He a Childhood Companion?

One reason why a particular cousin is known better than other cousins may be because at a crucial stage of life close contact was afforded by residential proximity. Defining closeness of relationship by interaction frequency, Robins and Tomanec assert that "relatives who have lived in the same town with *Ego* (are) closer than those who have only lived away. . . ."[7] It is possible that frequent contact, especially in childhood, is characteristic of cousins who know each other best in adulthood.

Among young Greensboro adults, 85 per cent assert that they know at least one cousin well enough to talk about him or her. Of these 682 respondents who identify a "best-known cousin," 59 per cent lived in the same community with this cousin at least while they were growing up and many during adulthood as well. Included among best-known cousins, however, are all degrees of intimacy, from those who are known extremely well to those who are hardly known at all. Thus, it is instructive to note the association between residential histories of the cousins and current degree of intimate knowledge.[8] Almost seven out of ten of the 261 respondents who know this cousin quite or extremely well now were characterized by residential proximity in childhood, frequently continuing into adulthood. At the other extreme, about six out of ten who do not know their best-known cousin too well at present never lived close to this cousin at all or for more than a few years. Although not ascertained, it seems a logical assumption that those 100-plus respondents who were unable to discuss any cousin would be primarily distinguished by a lack of long-term proximity to cousins.

Childhood proximity does not overwhelmingly characterize relations between the cousins discussed by our respondents, but it is an aspect of the history of those best-known cousins who really know each other well at the present time. Not only interactionally but in terms of degree of intimate knowledge, Robins and Tomanec are correct in claiming that secondary kin are likely to have a closer relationship if they have been childhood companions, or at least have lived close to each other during their formative years.

Is He a Sibling-Surrogate?

In a perceptive discussion of sibling solidarity in American society, Cumming and Schneider comment that there is a tendency to add as intimates other kin as substitutes for a missing relationship. If an adult has no children, he is close to his nephews and nieces; if he has no siblings, he may be close to his cousins.[9] Their sample is fifteen persons between the ages of fifty and eighty which makes it problematic whether cousin substitution for a missing or non-existent sibling will be evident in a larger and more youthful sample such as ours.

Enlarging upon Cumming and Schneider's postulate, substitution might occur either when the individual has no siblings, as the authors affirm, or when the individual has no same-sex siblings. The

TABLE V-2

Knowledge of, affectional closeness to, and frequency to the most frequent form of contact—face-to-face, telephone, or letter—with the best-known cousin, according to whether the young adult has any siblings and any same-sex siblings

Sex of the Respondent and Sibling Relationship	Number of Respondents	Per Cent Who Know Cousin Fairly Well or Better	Contact with Cousin Several Times Yearly or More	Affectional Closeness, in Pct.	
				Close	Fairly or Close
Males with no siblings	(39)	74	54	18	54
Males with no brothers	(61)	74	51	10	57
Males with one or more brothers	(232)	67	44	9	41
Females with no siblings	(63)	83	68	21	68
Females with no sisters	(82)	78	68	23	63
Females with one or more sisters	(322)	70	54	19	53

latter would be consistent with the already-revealed tendency to identify a same-sex cousin as the one who is known best.

Precisely what might substitution signify? It could mean at least three things: (1) an intimate knowledge of the cousin, bordering on the sort of intimacy which exists between siblings; (2) an affectionally close feeling toward the cousin; (3) a frequency of contact with the cousin similar to that between siblings. In Table V-2 these possible interpretations are investigated among those young adults who have no siblings and those who have no same-sex siblings, comparing them with the large numbers who do have one or more same-sex siblings.

Differences between those with no siblings and those with cross-sex but no same-sex siblings are negligible. However, there is less likelihood of intimate knowledge of, reasonably frequent contact with, and fairly close affectional relations with the best-known cousin when the young adult has same-sex siblings than when he or she has none. Does this signify that the cousin is actually playing the role of a sibling-surrogate or substitute? The evidence leads to a negative conclusion. In this urban sample only a few of those with or without a same-sex sibling claim a close affectional relationship to their cousin. Thus, cousin closeness compares unfavorably even with the affectional relations between occupationally disparate brothers, who, it will be recalled, had the least intense relationship of any sibling combination. The point is this: to conclude that the best-known cousin frequently acts as a sibling-surrogate would be an incorrect or overstated interpretation of these data. Rather it would be more accurate to state that cousins are generally of but moderate consequence in the life of the young urban adult, being of even less importance when the individual has one or more same-sex siblings.

The identification of the best-known cousin, in summary, includes the fact that the cousin is ordinarily of the same sex as the respondent. The relationship is more often through the mother's kin, the exception to this being males from blue-collar families. Cousins who are known well have in most cases lived in the same community during childhood or longer. Finally, there is a tendency to somewhat greater cousin involvement when the young adult has no same-sex siblings. Even so, cousin involvement seems moderate at best, and it is to this involvement as exemplified in interaction which we now turn our attention.

Section Two: Contact Between Best-Known Cousins

Interaction with cousins is avoided by the 200 Vassar girls studied by Helen Codere. These girls, she reports,

> acknowledge the charms of a kin-group in which there is much sociability and hospitality, especially with their own age-mates, but they state again and again that they would not visit distant cousins or drop in on them to spend the night during an automobile trip, for instance, and some of them are painfully frank in stating that the reason is the potential dangers and bothers of reciprocity.[10]

TABLE V-3

Frequency of interaction with the best-known cousin, and frequency of the most frequent form of contact—face-to-face, telephone, or letter—according to the residential location of the cousin

Location of Cousin	Number of Respondents	Frequency of Interaction, in Per Cent				
		Weekly or More	Monthly-Weekly	Several Times Yearly	Yearly or Less	Totel Pct.
Greensboro	(140)	17	41	29	12	99
—100 Miles	(188)	4	23	45	27	99
Beyond 100 Miles in NC, SC, or Va.	(159)	1	4	44	51	100
Elsewhere	(195)	—	2	15	83	100
		Frequency of Most Frequent Contact, in Per Cent				
Greensboro	(140)	20	40	28	12	100
—100 Miles	(188)	4	26	46	24	100
Beyond 100 Miles in NC, SC, or Va.	(159)	2	8	45	45	100
Elsewhere	(195)	1	6	32	62	101

Garigue does not find this sort of avoidance of contact, but he does comment that very often yearly contact satisfies obligation to secondary kin.[11] Infrequent interaction is therefore the theme of the scattered literature on urban secondary kinship.

The best-known cousins frequently lived in the same community with our young adult respondents as they were growing up, but at present they are distributed widely. Twenty-one per cent are in Greensboro, another 28 per cent are within 100 miles, 23 per cent are beyond 100 miles in North Carolina, South Carolina, or Virginia, and the other 29 per cent are elsewhere. All but forty of these final 195 cousins are either in the Southern or Eastern United States.

Interaction with the cousin, as observed in Table V-3, is modally about monthly under conditions of close proximity, but there are large numbers of the proximate who interact less often than that. When the cousin lives outside Greensboro but within 100 miles, face-to-face contact is ordinarily several times during the year. Interaction with a cousin living beyond 100 miles is modally once a year or less, with the frequency decreasing with each increase in distance. For example, 35 per cent of those whose cousin lives more than 250 or so miles away have not seen him or her at all in the past two years. As a whole, the modal frequency category is yearly or less, although there are a large minority who see this cousin more often, some 150 of them monthly or more. Thus, there is a general agreement with Garigue's statement regarding yearly interaction sufficing, but the exceptions who are in more frequent interaction are numerous.

There is a resemblance between the best-known cousin and the age-near sibling in proximity to the young Greensboro adult, but both of these kin categories tend to live at a greater distance than the parents. When the parents are residentially distant from Greensboro, monthly contact is customarily maintained by means of the telephone and/or the mails. Such communication between remote siblings is less frequent, but nevertheless occurs in most cases several times or more during the year. Do cousins utilize the means of communication to sustain frequent contact when regular interaction is impossible? Our data indicate that the answer is no. Obligation to keep in touch with one's cousin seldom demands more than yearly communication between the remote. While numerous cousins do telephone and write each other from time to time, in most instances interaction and communication are similar in frequency, rather that the latter being employed—as in parent and sibling relations—as a substitute for the former (see the lower portion of Table V-3). Only a few of the remote use the means of communication to raise frequency of contact from yearly or less up to several times a year. It should also be recalled that we are discussing the best-known cousin, which, presumably, should come very close to maximizing objective or contact relations.

Type of Contact with the Best-Known Cousin

A death occurs in the kin group, and cousins converse briefly at the home of the deceased and sit together at the funeral. The young adult goes home to visit his parents, and during the visit his aunt

TABLE V-4

Frequency of occurrence of the contact types between young Greensboro adults and their best-known cousin during the past two years (N = 682)

Contact Types	Frequency of Occurrence, in Per Cent				
	Monthly or More	Several Times Yearly	Once or Twice a Year	Never	Total Pct.
Home Visits (including emergencies)	10	32	30	28	100
Social Activities	3	8	12	77	100
Voluntary Organizations	2	3	5	91	101
Working Together	2	—	—	98	100
Ritual Occasions	2	7	25	66	100
Communication	12	19	22	47	100
Mutual Aid (either way)	1	—	1	97	99

and uncle and their children drop in. Are these the prevalent types of contact between best-known cousins or are there others which predominate? Home visits, including emergencies, social activities, engagement in the same organization, ritual occasions, working together, communication by telephone and letter, and mutual aid: these are the types of contact which have been isolated for investigation in this study. Cousin contact is frequently, we find, a result of the combination opportunity, of incidental interaction appended to a visit with the kin of orientation (see Table V-4). The drop-in or conversation visit is the most widespread form of contact between best-known cousins, and even this is infrequent. Communication is the second most widespread contact type, but only slightly over 50 per cent of these young adult (less than 50 per cent of the total sample) have utilized the mails or the telephone to keep in touch with this cousin *at all* in the past two years. Family reunions or holidays have brought about one-third of these cousins together at least once in the two-year period, and slightly less than one in four have shared some form of social activity at least once. The other contact types—organizations, mutual aid, and working together—are almost non-existent between the respondent and his best-known cousin.

Engagement in the various contact types in a patterned or recurrent manner, i.e., several times a year or more, may best be summarized by stating that there are a small number who do many things together, and a large number who do almost nothing. All those who work together, help each other, or attend the same organization regularly also communicate and/or visit regularly as well. There are twenty-five individuals who share four or more contact patterns with their cousin, and another fifty-seven who share three. Hunting buddies, shopping partners, sharers of activity both at home and in the community: all but six of these eighty-two pairs of cousins spent their childhood in close proximity and developed through the years a companionship based upon common interests which exceeds the superficial obligation for secondary kin contact. These respondents refer to their cousin as "not just a relative, but a good friend." One or two contact patterns exist between 308 young Greensboro adults and their cousin, these patterns being comprised almost entirely of communication between the remote and visiting and sometimes telephoning between the proximate. Finally, there are 292, some 45 per cent, who have no specific type of contact more than once a year. Add to this the 117 who were unable to identify a cousin to discuss, and we find that less than 50 per cent of the total sample maintain patterned contact of any specific type with any cousin at all. It may be tentatively concluded that for all but a small minority, relations with the cousin who is known best could be characterized as circumstantial or *incidental,* involving the investment of little time and interest.

Sex, Occupational Stratum, and Cousin or Secondary Kin Contact

The association between the sex and occupational stratum of the young adult and contact with his best-known cousin or other secondary kin is predicated in the literature upon three postulates: females are more involved in kin affairs, the middle-classes are more mobile residentially, and the occupationally mobile tend to be isolated from, or maintain shallow ties with, their secondary kin. The first two assumptions have been amply documented thus far in the present study. Concerning the third point, Bott remarks that the more distant the relatives, the more objective differences in status receive consideration, and determine interaction.[12] Schneider and Homans add that shallowness characterizes the relations between the upwardly mobile and their kindred, while the downwardly mobile may be neglected by their kin.[13] The loss of contact between upwardly mobile French Canadians and their lateral kin, e.g., cousins, is noted by Garigue.[14]

Corresponding with the findings of previous chapters, it is those from a working-class background who tend to live somewhat closer to their best-known cousin, and it is the young adult females who interact with this cousin with somewhat greater frequency (see Table V-5). However, within the present sample the investigation of simple interaction frequency according to sex and stratum, and of the utilization of proximity for interaction, offer but meagre evidence of a uniquely shallow tie between the occupationally mobile and the best-known cousin. There is a perceptible, but slight, tendency for the stable white-collar respondents to utilize proximity to a greater extent and to be better able to identify a cousin for discussion than is true of the upwardly mobile. Yet it would be difficult on the basis of these results to build a case for the alienation of the occupationally mobile from their secondary kin. Furthermore, there are several difficulties which prevent our obtaining a clear picture of secondary kin relations from the above Table.

The first problem is apparent when we recall that status similarity or disparity between siblings is noticeably more important to their relationship than is their individual mobility or stability. A mistaken assumption inherent in Table V-5 and in many mobility investigations is that personal mobility means leaving a *strictly* blue-collar kin network, while personal occupational stability means that the individual and his kin are of the same stratum. In actuality, almost any kin network will cover a wide range of occupational statuses, though there is likely to be clustering at a particular level. In our sample, 85 per cent of the stable middle-class respondents and 70 per cent of the stable working-class who identify a cousin are discussing one of their own stratum. The upwardly mobile as well tend to claim as best-known cousin an individual of their current stratum, i.e., white collar, rather than of their parents'. Sixty-one per cent of the upwardly mobile males, and 51 per

TABLE V-5

Frequency of interaction with the best-known cousin, and a comparison of proximity and interaction frequency, according to the sex and occupational stratum and mobility of the young adult respondents

Sex	Occupational Stratum and Mobility	Number of Respon- dents	Frequency of Interaction, in Pct.					Comparison	
			Monthly or More	Several Times Yearly	Yearly-, or No Cousin	Total Pct.		Cousin –100 Miles	More Than Yearly
Males	Upward White Collar	(93)	20	23	57	100		43	43
	Stable White Collar	(111)	13	26	61	100		28	39
	Stable Blue Collar	(86)	26	20	55	101		49	45
	Downward Blue Collar	(26)	31	8	61	100		27	39
Female	Upward White Collar	(115)	12	30	57	99		35	43
	Stable White Collar	(160)	13	39	49	101		33	51
	Stable Blue Collar	(139)	22	32	46	100		58	54
	Downward Blue Collar	(38)	16	24	60	100		45	40

cent of the females, refer to a middle-class cousin. The downwardly mobile are equally likely to state that they know best a middle-class or a working-class cousin. Thus, the mobility or stability of the respondent is an inadequate index of the comparative occupational positions of any two specific secondary kin. The difficulty with statements concerning the effects of individual occupational and family position upon adult kin relations once again becomes evident. Within the kin network one is not alone in either his occupational or, as mentioned in the chapter on parents, his residential movement. The individual is apparently able to find one or several secondary kin, frequently from his own current occupational level, with whom a moderately viable relationship can be perpetuated.

Having ascertained the occupational position of the best-known cousin we face a second problem which is fundamental to Table V-5. Within categories of occupational mobility or stability and status, the investigation of interaction frequency according to the cousin's status still fails to produce broad variations attributable to differences in occupational status. Thus, for example, the upwardly mobile males are similar in their frequency of interaction with a white-collar or blue-collar cousin, and the same is true of the other mobility-stability categories as well. This does not, however, take into consideration the types of contact which occur, and it is to the various contact patterns that we now turn for insight into the operation of this lateral kin relationship. As we might expect from Table V-4, recurrent social activities and organizational attendance, most often the same church, are so infrequently and randomly patterned according to sex and stratum as to be virtually idiosyncratic in terms of these variables. The eighty-two respondents who were reported above to have patterned contact with their best-known cousin in three or more types are distributed randomly throughout the sex and stratum categories. Occupational mobility or stability simply does not explain those cases where cousins share a wide range of activity instead of the usual incidental and infrequent contact. Furthermore, the mean number of contact patterns, while slightly less for males and their cousins, manifests insignificant variation by individual occupational position. Stable white-collar males share a mean of .8 contact patterns with their best-known cousin, and the other categories of males .9; the upwardly mobile females have a mean of one contact pattern, with the stable white-collar and the blue-collar females having 1.1 and 1.2 patterns, respectively.

Although individual occupational history exhibits a negligible association with contact patterns, there is found in Table V-6 a fundamental tendency to keep in more frequent touch, by means of visits or communication, with one's cousin when he or she is of one's current occupational stratum. The white-collar females are much more likely to visit and communicate several times a year or more with a white-collar cousin than with a blue-collar, even when this blue-collar cousin is perceived as the one they know best. A similar same-stratum tendency is evident in the communication of stable white-collar males with their cousins and in home visiting between stable blue-collar males and their cousins. The general result is therefore consistent with Bott's inference that among distant kin objective differences in occupational position do inhibit patterned contact. In summary, the individual's family background and present position disclose little regarding patterns of contact with the best-known cousin, but the similarity or disparity of the occupational strata of the two cousins is related to regular visiting and/or communication.

There is yet a third factor—besides the strata of the two cousins and the contact types—which is obscured by Table V-5 and which may aid us in understanding cousin contact. This factor is comparative contact with other secondary kin. Robins and Tomanec, and Parsons earlier, have contended that contact is more frequent with aunts, uncles, and grandparents than with cousins. Their assertion pertains to the urban middle class, and diverges from Garigue's finding that among the French Canadians he studied, most of whom are working class, contact is more frequent within the same generation.[15] According to the Greensboro data, both viewpoints are correct. Sixty per cent of the stable middle class have one or more aunts, uncles, or grandparents with whom they interact more frequently than with any cousin. Conversely, 56 per cent of the stable working class spend more time with cousins than with other secondary kin. The upwardly and downwardly mobile manifest

TABLE V-6

Patterned contact with the best-known cousin, according to the cousin's occupational stratum and the sex and occupational mobility or stability of the respondent*

Sex and Occupational Stratum and Mobility	Cousin's Stratum	Number of Respondents	Occurrence Several Times Yearly or More, in Per Cent				
			Home Visits	Activities	Organizations	Rituals	Communication
Males							
Upward White Collar	White Collar	(43)	37	12	—	14	28
	Blue Collar	(27)	41	11	4	4	22
Stable White Collar	White Collar	(70)	30	10	3	3	30**
	Blue Collar	(12)	33	—	8	8	17
Stable Blue Collar	White Collar	(18)	39	6	11	11	11
	Blue Collar	(40)	60**	13	8	3	10
Females							
Upward White Collar	White Collar	(40)	48	5	3	15	50**
	Blue Collar	(38)	40	5	—	8	32
Stable White Collar	White Collar	(107)	48**	11	5	7	49**
	Blue Collar	(19)	32	11	5	11	16
Stable Blue Collar	White Collar	(28)	54	7	7	14	32
	Blue Collar	(68)	54	13	6	16	28

* This Table omits the few downwardly mobile.
** Indicates key percentage differences according to the cousin's stratum.

their transitional character in this regard, being equally likely to have more secondary kin interaction with cousins (lateral kin) or with aunts, uncles, and grandparents (ascending kin). The result is that by introducing comparative interaction frequencies with secondary kin the few differences in interaction frequency which appear in Table V-5 are virtually eliminated.

Earlier the frequency of contact between cousins was seen to be primarily a function of their interaction, the means of communication seldom being employed to increase contact (see Table V-3). However, in Table V-6 it becomes apparent that the female and her best-known cousin are more likely to communicate, i.e., telephone and write letters, regularly than are males. More specifically, forty-five of the young wives, approximately 10 per cent of the female sample, communicate several times a year or more when they are unable to see their cousin over once a year. On the other hand, just eleven males, less than 4 per cent of the total male sample, communicate with their cousin with greater frequency than they interact. The overall result is that 45 per cent of the young married males keep in some form of contact with their best-known cousin more than once a year, as compared with nearly 60 per cent of the females. Differences in total contact by stratum are virtually nonexistent, the range for the four categories of males being from 44 to 46 per cent, and for the females from 55 to 63 per cent. Consideration of communication with secondary kin reveals little more than another manifestation of the adult female's greater temporal involvement in kinship.

How may we summarize and conclude the investigation of sex, occupational stratum, and contact between secondary kin? First, blue-collar interaction with secondary kin is more frequent, which is due to greater proximity. Second, female contact, including communication, with secondary kin is more frequent—a function of their generally greater kin involvement. Thirdly, there is a discernible tendency toward more lateral kin contact within the blue-collar network, and more contact with ascending generations in the predominantly white-collar network. The effect of upward mobility upon secondary kin contact is to inhibit it slightly, since the majority of one's kin are likely to be of the other stratum. This lesser involvement is manifested among the upwardly mobile either in terms of less frequent contact with the best known cousin or in less likelihood of being in touch with other secondary kin more than with this cousin. However, as we saw in Chapter Two, this characteristic of the upwardly mobile concerns the intensity of secondary kinship, not its extensiveness, for these persons claim the largest numbers of recognizable kin. A second caution regarding the notion of attenuated ties among the mobile is that these respondents seem to be able to find kin of their own current stratum with whom to pursue the occasional contacts characteristic of secondary kinship among young adult Greensboroites. The term "occasional" implies a final factor complicating the discussion of mobility and these kin. Patterned contact of various sorts is randomly distributed among the sex and stratum-mobility categories. In fact, secondary kin contacts are so uniformly incidental or occasional in adulthood, occurring less for their own sake than as adjuncts to a parental visit or as aspects of a family ritual or emergency, that meaningful differences according to sex or status are kept to a minimum.

Section Three: Subjective Aspects of Cousin and Secondary Kin Relations

Cousins appear to invest little time and interest in the sharing of interaction, and it is expectable that this lack of involvement on the part of young urban adults will include such subjective factors as affectional closeness, value consensus, and identification as well. Only 126 young adult respondents indicate an affectional relationship to their cousin which is quite or extremely close, approximately 15 per cent of the total sample. Value consensus is more difficult to ascertain reliably in cousin relations, since its expression depends upon a fairly high level of personal knowledge. That is, you must know someone fairly well to be able to determine whether you and they hold the same values. In the case of parents and siblings, familiarity, upon which perception of value consensus or dissensus must be based, is seldom a problem. There are, however, ninety-two males and 117 females, over one-fourth of the sample, who either know no cousin or else feel that they are not acquainted well enough to assess the extent of their similarity in values and opinions. Another 50 per cent feel that they and their cousin have little in common, which leaves but 21 per cent of the males and 25 per cent of the females expressing a substantial value consensus with their cousin. Identification is only slightly more than half as likely as is value consensus in relations with the best-known cousin, i.e., about 11 per cent of the males and 14 per cent of the females idealizing or identifying with him or her.

Throughout this chapter it must be constantly borne in mind that cousin involvement has been purposely maximized by talking of the best-known cousin rather than cousins in general. The findings regarding affection and value consensus are consonant with the incidental nature of cousin interaction. While affection, value consensus, and identification are all low, almost half again as many respondents assert that value consensus is high than that either affection or identification is high, indicating the basically superficial emotional connection between cousins even when common interests and ideas are perceived as shared.

An examination of the motivations for cousin contact reinforces the delineation of the relationship which has been emerging throughout the discussion. Expression of a strong sense of obligation to keep in touch is found among but sixty-three of the young adults (8 per cent of the total sample), of whom forty are currently middle-class wives. Another 25 per cent feel that there is at least some obligation to keep in touch with their cousin, but the result is that nearly 70 per cent either have no cousin-acquaintance or else are unable to express any sense of obligation to them whatsoever. Enjoyment is given as an important reason for keeping in touch with the best-known cousin by almost 40 per cent of the sample. Although, 41 per cent of the respondents claim that either enjoyment or obligation, or both, are important reasons why they and their best-known cousin maintain contact with each other. The result is that over half perceive *no important reason* for cousin contact. Furthermore, when expression of enjoyment is compared with actual frequency of contact, it becomes apparent that what many are saying is that they "enjoy" having infrequent contact with their cousin. As in the case of siblings—only more visibly—cousin contact is geared to desires, so that such contact as there is may be considered enjoyable.

The relationship between desires and contact referred to in the previous sentence is discernible in Table V-7, where affectional closeness is seen to be highly associated with frequency of contact regardless of the young adult's sex. Almost half of those who feel

TABLE V-7

Frequency of the most frequent form of contact—face-to-face, telephone, or letter—with best-known cousin, according to the sex of the young adult and expression of affectional closeness to the cousin

Sex of Young Adult	Closeness to Cousin	Number of Respondents	Frequency of Contact, in Per Cent			
			Monthly or More	Several Times Yearly	Yearly or Less	Total Pct.
Males	Quite or Extremely	(34)	47	27	27	101
	Fairly Close	(117)	33	41	27	101
	Not Close	(125)	16	19	65	100
Females	Quite or Extremely	(92)	49	38	13	100
	Fairly Close	(175)	25	52	23	100
	Not Close	(139)	14	29	58	101

close to their cousin are in some form of contact monthly or more, while 60 per cent of those expressing little or no affection for this cousin are in contract yearly or less, many not at all. The very weakness of the obligatory link between cousins makes possible a close association between feelings toward him or her and frequency of contact.

Who are likely to be affectionally close to their best-known cousin? It is primarily those young adults who lived in the same community with this cousin during childhood or longer. Seventy per cent of those who are quite close or closer to their cousin have been characterized by such propinquity, and most of the others either spent summers together while growing up or lived in the same community for a few years. Nevertheless, 407 respondents and their cousins did live close to each other while they were being raised, but less than half of these are affectionally close at present. It might therefore be contended that childhood proximity is a quasi-necessary, but far short of a sufficient, condition for affectional closeness between cousins in adulthood.

A second condition for closeness to one's cousin in adulthood is value consensus, or similarity of ideas and interests. Nearly all of those who are affectionally close also express a high degree of value similarity with this cousin. Apparently, as kin concern and obligation are less, a kinship tie will either take on the characteristics of a friendship or will simply remain in the category of "nominal" kin—kin in name only. That is, a close lateral secondary kin tie is very likely to be based upon common interests and ideas and minimal obligation, the same attributes considered to be crucial to friendship relations. A close tie between kin of orientation, although it may include interests and ideas, also frequently involves concern and even obligation.[16]

Childhood proximity and common interests and values are two conditions which are more likely to produce close adult relations between cousins. A third factor in cousin closeness, it may be recalled, is that affection for the best-known cousin is somewhat more likely if the individual has no same-sex sibling. However, only one in five having no such sibling indicates that he feels affectionally close to his cousin.

The negative aspects of these data clearly outweigh the positive, the result being that no single condition, nor complex of conditions, appears to guarantee or be sufficient for cousin closeness in our urban society. It is not that Codere's cousin avoidance is the rule, but simply that affection is likely to be weak, and interaction kept in line with the individual's desires. Childhood proximity, while the best predictor of adult closeness, is far short of being a sufficient condition for it. Having the same values, being of the same stratum, and having no same-sex sibling all help in predicting adult closeness, but with percentage differences which are less than definitive.

Relations with aunts and uncles are likely to be closer than with cousins, especially among middle-class urbanites. When they are close, however, they tend to be based less upon a friendship pattern than upon family tradition, rituals, and a moderate sense of obligation. There are also indications that grandparents, when living, are a focal point of much ritual kin interaction.

Occupational stratum is referred to in the foregoing paragraph, and it should be stated that the occupationally similar are consistently closer in affection and value consensus, and are more likely to see enjoyment as an important reason for cousin contact, than are the occupationally disparate. Yet as a whole the upwardly mobile males are more likely to be close affectionally, similar in values, and high in enjoyment of their cousin, regardless of the cousin's occupational position, than are either the stable white-collar or stable blue-collar males toward their cousin (see Table V-8). The young stable white-collar females are somewhat more likely to be high in affection, consensus, idealization, and enjoyment, but the differences between the female categories are not definitive. Throughout the investigation of cousins and other secondary kin, unmistakable indications of shallower ties between the upwardly mobile and their secondary kin have simply not been forthcoming. Bott is basically correct in asserting that objective status differences are more determinative of actual relationships between secondary kin than between the kin of orientation, especially parents. However, she misses the fact that the individual is ordinarily able to find kin of his own stratum with whom to cultivate relations. In addition, interests and activities may make for a viable relationship in some cases where objective statuses differ.

Summary of Cousin and Secondary Kin Relations

Discussions of kinship relations in urban society have primarily, often exclusively, focussed upon the nuclear family. Isolated references to secondary kinship in several sources, particularly papers by Garigue, Codere, Parsons, and Robins and Tomanec, have furnished research leads, but the present investigation has been virtually exploratory in nature. Under such conditions summarization of results is essential if we are to avoid concluding with a complex and disjointed series of findings. Our summary will review the iden-

TABLE V-8

Affectional closeness, value consensus, idealization, and obligation and enjoyment as important reasons for keeping in touch with the best-known cousin, according to the sex and occupational stratum of the young adult

Sex	Occupational Stratum and Mobility	Number of Respondents	Pct. Affectionally Close	Pct. High in Value Consensus	Pct. High in Idealization	Pct. Obligation Impt.	Pct. Enjoyment Impt.
Males	Upward White Collar	(93)	10	25	13	4	38
	Stable White Collar	(111)	7	22	10	5	31
	Stable Blue Collar	(86)	6	19	9	7	27
	Downward Blue Collar	(26)	19	17	15	—	32
Females	Upward White Collar	(115)	18	27	10	15	48
	Stable White Collar	(160)	26	29	16	12	54
	Stable Blue Collar	(139)	17	17	14	3	48
	Downward Blue Collar	(38)	8	27	8	7	47

tification of the best-known cousin and its implications, fundamental characteristics of secondary kinship, and the association of occupational status and secondary kin relations.

Eighty-five per cent of young Greensboro adults know one or more cousins well enough to describe them at least in minimal fashion. The cousin known best is ordinarily of the same sex as the respondent, and is generally known better when the two individuals lived close to each other during childhood and when the respondent has no same-sex sibling. Contact between proximate siblings is fairly frequent, but is largely of an incidental nature, not involving mutual aid, or social activities, or patterned contacts other than brief visits and less frequently communication. When the young adult and his cousin are separated residentially, the mails and telephone are seldom used regularly for keeping in touch as they are with siblings and parents. Affectional closeness, value consensus, idealization, and feelings of obligation to keep in contact with the cousin all bespeak a generally insignificant subjective bond between these kin. Enjoyment is expressed as a motive for keeping in touch in terms of relatively infrequent contact, not so extremely as to illustrate Codere's "cousin avoidance," but demonstrating that cousin contact is usually kept within the bounds of personal desires.

Young adult females tend to be linked to their secondary kin in a more substantial way than are males. This is apparent but slightly according to simple interaction frequency, but the various forms of contact are employed more often by females, the result being that they are usually in more frequent over-all touch with these kin. Affectional closeness to and enjoyment of the cousin are both somewhat more widespread among the urban females. Nevertheless, patterned contact of the various types is seldom evident even among the female respondents.

The greater closeness of female relatives is also manifested in the analysis of cousin genealogy. The most frequently occurring genealogical link between cousins is that between sister's daughters, who comprise nearly one-third of the female cousin relationships identified. Furthermore, the most prevalent cross-sex cousin as best-known is related to the respondent through his mother's sister.

There is a much more random genealogical relation between males and their cousins than between females and theirs in choosing the best-known. Openness and non-formalized preference or avoidance are the rule, with choice being based primarily, of course, upon residential and genealogical availability, i.e., whether such a cousin exists or not, but after this upon similarity of sex, similarity of values, and other aspects of personal preference.

Two basic distinctions between secondary kin relations are dependent upon the primarily blue-collar or white-collar character of the network. First, from the investigation of genealogy we discover the greater separation of the sexes in the blue-collar network. When they are of white-collar parents, both males and females (about 60 per cent) tend to be related to their cousin through their mother's sibling. Even a larger percentage (70 per cent) of the blue-collar background females are thus related. However, the young adult males whose parents are blue-collar predominantly identify as their best-known cousin one to whom they are related through their father's sibling. This points up the greater separation of the sexes among working-class persons than among middle-class, which is true not only in kin relations but in friend and marital relationships as well. A second basic middle-class—working-class distinction in secondary kinship concerns the category with whom contact is most frequent. Within the sample as a whole, contact is somewhat more frequent with aunts and uncles than with either grandparents or cousin. This relationship is strong among the young adults from a white-collar background, but those whose parents are blue-collar indicate that they spend more time with their lateral kin. It seems likely that urban working-class kin networks come closer to reproducing rural or pre-industrial patterns than do urban middle-classes, both in terms of sex separation and lateral versus ascending kin.

The question of the effect of occupational mobility upon secondary kin relations has claimed considerable attention in the present Chapter. When the testimony concerning number and distribution of kin, contained in Chapter Two, is considered along with the foregoing analysis, there is no appreciable evidence to substantiate the claim that the upwardly mobile keep shallower ties with secondary kin than do stable white- and blue-collar individuals. Neither contact nor affection indicate in a clear-cut fashion that the mobile lose touch with or interest in these kin. The explanation for the inconsequential nature of mobility differences is two fold. First, the young adult is able to find kin of his current stratum with whom reasonably viable relations can be maintained even in a network which is principally of the other stratum. A fallacy in the literature stressing the dissociative effects of upward mobility is the covert assumption that all others in one's kin network are of his parents' occupational level. While it is true that occupational disparity between secondary kin does seem to preclude intense relations, this fact is relatively independent of the occupational mobility or stability of the individual. Secondly, and more important, the secondary kin relations of young adult Greensboroites are so uniformly shallow or incidental as to exhibit only small variations attributable to social or occupational status. That is, secondary kinship is basically superficial regardless of stratum, and such differences as exist tend to be between moderate involvement and negligible involvement. A small number of respondents do sustain a relationship characterized by emotional intensity and a wide range of activities with their best-known cousin or other secondary relative, but these are distributed almost randomly according to the sex-stratum categories. Such engagement in secondary kinship is primarily a result of the personal and family histories of the two kin, including the intensity of mutual concern between previous generations, the propinquity of the respondent and his kinsman through the years, and the development of common interests and/or concern resulting in a degree of friendship or kin concern which exceeds the demands of secondary kin obligation in urban society.

What is the response of young Greensboro adults to the shallowness of secondary kinship? A few are troubled by it. The wife of a bus terminal clerk complains: "It is distressing that distance is pulling families apart so. Seeing relatives was very important when I was young and I miss it now. It bothers me that my children don't know their cousins and play with them like I did." The vast majority, however, are quite satisfied to be free from what Moore calls the barbaric "obligation to give affection as a duty to a particular set of persons on account of the accident of birth."[17] Such an obligation, if it was ever strong toward secondary kin in our society, is clearly not so among young adult Greensboroites today.

Chapter VI

URBAN KIN RELATIONS: SUMMARY AND CONCLUSIONS

Economic structures and motivations dominate urban, industrial society, being basic to many of its central characteristics. The a-personal nature of many social contacts, the relative ease of residential movement, and the mass educational system, are all geared to serve the needs of the economy. At many points these same structures and values are seen to be consistent with the variety and style of kinship relations found in the city. The scatter of kin networks, the use of the means of communication for keeping in touch with close kin, and the weak and preferential or volitional nature of secondary kinship (i.e., "my secondary kin contacts are with whom and as frequent or infrequent as I want them"): all these characteristics and more "make sense" in the urban, industrial setting.

In this work we have set ourselves the task of characterizing the kin involvements of residents of one urban place. The attempt has been made to answer many of the open questions regarding urban kinship, including the kinds of and occasions for contact which occur, the subjective attributes of kin relations, differences in relations according to degree of kinship, the dimensions of the network, and the problem of occupational mobility effects upon kin relations. The summary which follows should make it possible to perceive the extent to which we have achieved at least provisional answers to any or all of these questions.

163

Parents, Siblings, and Secondary Kin

Relations between young adults and their kin are dominated by involvement with their parents. The parents are objects of extremely frequent contact among our Greensboro respondents. These intergenerational kin of orientation perform several functions on each other's behalf. Foremost is the provision of primary relations, including intimate communication and relationship for its own sake, in the midst of the segmental and often economically motivated social contacts of the urban setting. Contact patterns indicate that a mutual affection and obligation dominate the relation of parents and their adult offspring, the relationship focussing in a basic *concern* for each other's welfare. This concern finds a tangible and intangible outlet in the various forms of mutual aid, either financial or services, which are shared periodically as well as when a specific need is perceived, and also in the aforementioned frequent contact. The underlying obligation to keep in touch with parents is so pervasive, though not always overt, that the result is little association between one's expressed feelings toward his parents—be they close or distant—and frequency of contact with them. For even when affectional ties are weak, general obligation results in the maintenance of regular contact with parents by whatever means are available.

Adult sibling relations may be best characterized by the terms *interest* and *comparison*. The term "interest" signifies less of the positive, active element of concern than was apparent in relations with parents. Thus, the sharing of mutual aid is infrequent, being virtually idiosyncratic to a specific situation. Nevertheless, fairly frequent contact is maintained, demonstrating the interest which siblings ordinarily have in how the other is getting along. Sibling contact among a majority of our sample does not manifest the characteristics of social companionship; rather, it consists of home visiting, communication, and family ritual occasions. The primary subjective factor in sibling relations is a result of comparison and/or identification. The question "how am I doing?" can be quickly and readily answered by comparing oneself with his sibling or siblings. Such rivalry or comparison appears crucial, particularly in brother relations, even in adulthood. Due to a less intense feeling of obligation to keep in touch with siblings than with parents, contact tends to be somewhat more frequent if the young adult is affectionally close to his sibling than if he is not. *In toto,* the relations between young adult siblings seem constrained to some extent by divergent values and interests, but there is a concurrent tendency, especially among females, to reaffirm ties when both siblings are married and have children. Whether the later stages of the life cycle see an increased development of the friendship aspects of sibling relations, as Cumming and Schneider hypothesize, remains for other research to determine.[1]

When attention turns from parents and siblings, the kin of orientation, to cousins and other secondary relatives, one is hard-pressed to find great significance in such relationships among young adult Greensborites. A small minority, just slightly over 10 per cent of the respondents, state that both objectively and subjectively their relations with certain secondary kin are valued. However, on the whole the young adults consider these relationships—to aunts, uncles, cousins, and so on—to be functionally irrelevant. Thus, we may characterize secondary kin ties in Greensboro as for the most part circumstantial or *incidental.* Incidental relations are thus contrasted with intentional, in which perpetuation would be for the sake of the relationship itself, either as a result of common interests or of concern for the other's welfare. Kin obligation, at least insofar as it demands frequent or diverse types of contact, is seldom a part of the relationship of these young married persons and their secondary kin.

The contrasts between relations with parents, siblings, and secondary kin which we have just summarized are elucidated in Table VI-1. Here we observe that frequency of contact, feelings of affection, and a sense of obligation are congruent. Affection for one or both parents tends to be strong, feelings of obligation are present and often important, and contact is modally—in fact almost universally—monthly or more. Siblings are less likely to be objects of close affectional ties, only about one in three of the age-near siblings are the focal point of a strong overt sense of obligation, and contact frequency ranges from two or three up to a dozen times a year ordinarily. Cousins are seldom recipients of either strong af-

TABLE VI-1

Expression of affection, obligation, frequency of the most frequent form of
contact—face-to-face, telephone, or letter—and contact patterns with
parent or parents, age-near sibling, and best-known cousin

Kin Category	Number of Respondents	Pct. Affectionally Close	Pct. Obligation Impt.	Pct. Contact Monthly or More	Pct. Contact Sev. Times a Yr. or More	Mean No. of Contact Patterns
Parent(s)	(724)	75	50	94	98	3.8
Age-Near Sibling	(697)	48	32	61	90	2.1
Best-Known Cousin	(682)	18	10	27	63	1.0

fectional or obligational sentiments, and the frequency of contact is
modally once or twice a year. Of course, the respondents are in
some cases more involved with another sibling or other secondary
kin than with the age-near sibling or best-known cousin. However,
the increases in total involvement with these two categories, as
noted in Chapters IV and V, are relatively minor. For, in fact,
there is a great amount of overlap in secondary kin involvement, so
that the same respondents who are subjectively and objectively
close to their best-known cousin are likely to be concerned about
aunts or grandparents as well. Contact patterns, i.e., contacts of a
specific type at least several times a year, typically include home
visits, communication, mutual aid, and either rituals, organizations,
or recreational contact with parents. With the age-near siblings, contact patterns, as stated above, are usually restricted to home visits
and communication, with a minority engaging in social activities or
ritual interaction, or some other contact type. Some cousins visit
and/or communicate in a patterned fashion; many do neither.

One qualification and two extensions are pertinent to the foregoing general conclusions. A brief comment by Haller, and the inferences of other authors, have been noted to the effect that in the
large metropolis there are now being reborn—or may still be found
—the meaningful secondary kin networks of earlier rural-agricul-
tural days. The ghetto, the ethnic mutual aid kin association, and
other megalopolitan kin groups—these may be important, if not

emerging, phenomena. However, while the present author would grant the existence and importance of a few such networks in urban settings, he is not prepared to accept the generalizability to urban place of the functionally significant *wider* kin network, i.e., secondary kin as well as the kin of orientation, much beyond the 10 to 15 per cent of urbanites found in the Greensboro study. Of course, further evidence to the contrary would be both of interest and theoretically significant.[2]

Two extensions of the categorical conclusions presented above may help to explicate further the characteristics of urban kin networks, especially the interrelations between degrees of kinship. First, we recall from Chapter Two the important position which the aging apparently occupy in the kin network. Aging parents play a particularly central role both in perpetuating their nuclear families of procreation, i.e., in linking siblings together after they leave the parental home, and in maintaining their family of orientation, or ties with their own aging siblings and their children. They further serve to relate their families of procreation and orientation to each other, so that young adults at least keep posted on the activities of, if they don't keep in touch with, aunts, uncles, and cousins, as well as their siblings. After the death of the older generation there is likely to be loss of interest on the part of young adults in their secondary kin, i.e., their parents' family of orientation. They, in turn, are apt to begin to focus upon *their* nuclear families of orientation and procreation, and extensions of these in children, as they grow older. The effective kin network is thus continually expanding by birth and contracting by death and loss of contact on the part of the aging. One important hub of such kin involvement in urban society is the aged or grandparental generation, and the other is the females in the network.

A second extension of our findings by means of comparisons of categories of kin concerns one's orientation toward them. Everett Rogers and Hans Sebald, in a study of Iowa and Ohio farm families, demonstrate that familism, or strong family concern and involvement, while a useful concept, is basically ambiguous unless a distinction is drawn between the nuclear family and the "extended kinship group."[3] We would now propose that the results of this present study indicate that instead of a dichotomy between family and kin a trichotomy is necessary in order to comprehend the empirical family-kinship actualities. Many, if not a majority, of our respondents state that their parents, brothers, and sisters are important to them, while none or a small number of secondary kin are considered significant. Among the familistic should therefore be distinguished three types: (1) the *nuclear familistic,* whose dominant values and interests include concern for their spouse and children but little concern for other kin; (2) the *"kin of orientation" familistic,* who are actively engaged in perpetuating ties with parents and siblings, their kin of orientation, as well as with their families of procreation; and (3) the *wider kin oriented,* who are involved in a complex network of contact with and concern for kin of various degrees of relationship. These ideal types would, of course, contrast with non-familistically oriented individuals who either have no family ties or little family concern, e.g., the man who is "lost in his work." It seems quite possible, in view of the data on kin importance presented in Chapter II, that in our urban society the majority of married females could be characterized as kin of orientation familistic, while the males would be divided between kin of orientation and nuclear familistic. These latter husbands are likely to assert that "what matters to me is my work, my wife, and my children." As is true of many other findings of this study, the predominance of these orientations toward family and kin is open for further testing in various social settings, such as rural areas and other cities. Nevertheless the fourfold typology may be helpful in reconciling some of the divergent opinions found in the literature on kinship in urban society. What occurs is that some researchers have generalized a great amount of kin involvement from the observation of young adult-parent relations, and others, viewing the *total* network, have concluded that urban kin ties are weak. Each approach, we are implying, is apt to be only partially correct in its results.

Distance, Sex, Occupational Position and Kinship

Residential distance is stated by Reiss and others to be unquestionably the prime determinant of, or limiting condition upon, frequent interaction between kin. Our findings are relatively consistent with this conclusion, but qualifications must be added to the influence of distance upon kin affairs. Not only does distance limit interaction frequency, but it also determines the kinds of interaction and the occasions upon which face-to-face contact occurs. The greater the residential separation, the more likely is interaction to be restricted to vacation or holiday reunions. We have, in addition to noting the restrictive effects of distance upon interaction, discovered unmistakably that, as Litwak asserted, distance does not necessarily limit or determine total contact, due to the availability of the telephone and postal service. Nor does distance prevent the exchange of tangible aid, or emotional involvement or primary relations between kin, or the perception of kin as important to the individual. However, here again the degree of kin relationship is associated with distance effects: the closer the kin relationship, the less likely is increasing distance to affect adversely total contact frequency, exchange of aid, and emotional ties. Thus, it is primarily for parents, and secondarily for siblings, that the concept of the "isolated nuclear family" fails to hold among the residentially mobile.[4] Degree of relationship alters distance effects in another way also. Face-to-face contact with parents living within 100 miles of Greensboro but outside the city is more frequent than with secondary kin living in Greensboro, and the same comparison holds for other distance categories. Our conclusion is that if kin desire to maintain contact and keep concern active, as is true of the majority of young adults and their parents, distance is but a qualifier, not a deterrent.

Kin affairs according to the sex of the young urban adult may be summarized rather briefly. The strength of the mother-daughter bond, so central to Young and Willmott's studies in England, is likewise observable in Greensboro, North Carolina. However, differences between males and females in relations with parents are discernible primarily in the subjective sphere; contact frequencies are quite similar. The close mother-daughter bond may be extended further to indicate that females play a more dominant role in the kin network than do males. Young wives tend to express a closer affectional relation to all degrees of kin, are in slightly more frequent contact with siblings and secondary kin, and are more likely to feel that kin are an important part of their lives. Females and the aging, we have said, are the foci of urban kin affairs.

A variable which has been of much concern in the present study is occupational status and mobility. One reason for this is the divergence of viewpoints in the literature regarding the effects of social mobility upon kin relations. As is true of other studies, the blue-collar kin networks are characterized by less residential dispersion, the result being that more frequent blue-collar interaction with various kin occurs. When there is residential separation it is the middle-classes who make the most use of the means of communication to sustain kin contact. We recall that Parsons' paper, which referred to the middle-classes, asserted that the chances of residential separation from kin are great, and intimated that separation really means isolation.[5] This should be altered to read that the chances of middle-class separation from kin are moderately great, but that this eventuality does not result in isolation from kin of orientation. On the other hand, working-class migration and separation from kin, though less frequent, is apt to result in virtual isolation from all kin except parents when it does occur.

There is a basic working-class division by sex in secondary kin affairs which does not appear in the middle classes. Blue-collar male kin are ordinarily more involved with each other, and females with each other. Even in the case of parents such sex divisions occur among the working classes. This is apparent in correspondence between young married adults and their parents. Regardless of occupational stratum the female tends to serve as family correspondent; the result is that the middle-class wife writes both sets of parents, while the working-class wife concentrates upon her own. The close female relations in blue-collar kin networks are also apparent in the great amount of mutual aid shared between mothers and daughters, and even in some cases between blue-collar sisters.

The divergent opinions on occupational mobility and kinship relations are exemplified in articles by Schneider and Homans and by Litwak. The former authors comment, in their discussion of kin terminology, that "upward mobile persons keep only shallow ties with members of their kindred, if they keep them at all; downward mobile persons may be neglected by their kindred." Litwak, on the other hand, states that in his sample even a movement from manual to business or professional, or vice versa, does not distinguish with regard to frequency of interaction.[6] The first result of our study concerns interaction. Frequency of interaction is intimately associated with residential distance, which is, in turn, related to one's occupational position. The occupationally mobile person is an individual of one stratum whose kin network is likely to be characterized by the majority being of the other stratum. Therefore, the mobile tend to form a middle category between white-collar offspring of white-collar parents and blue-collar offspring of blue-collar parents with respect to both distance from and frequency of interaction with various kin. Whether the occupationally mobile are perceived as having strong or weak kin ties is thus likely to be a function of the group with whom they are compared. Comparing the upwardly mobile with the stable blue collar in interaction frequency with kin, our conclusion would resemble that of Schneider and Homans, i.e., the mobile have weaker or shallower kin ties. But if the comparison is made between the upward mobile and the occupationally stable members of their new stratum, it can only be concluded that the interactional ties of the mobile to their kin are as strong, if not stronger, than those of the stable middle class.

This finding provides an introduction to the dominant theme which pervades the investigation of occupational mobility and kinship: individual movement or non-movement in the economic-occupational system is not the key factor in determining kin relations in adulthood. Rather, the middle-class success values of the society, and the *current* occupational positions and concomitant value systems of the parties involved, appear more determinative of present relationships. Upward mobility is not a "boot-strap" phenomenon; it requires social support from parents and often from other kin, particularly for the male. Thus, the influence of both parents upon the upwardly mobile male and of the mother upon the upwardly mobile female result in close adult relations with parents, rather than the rejection which is inherent in Schneider and Homans' comment. Sibling relations are likewise affected by differential achievement, so that occupational or status disparity between brothers usually means an affectional distance and non-identification, and between cross-sex siblings and sisters often means a non-reciprocated identification of the lower-status sibling with the "family success." In contrast, mutually upward or downward mobile siblings are drawn together, not apart. Similarity of life circumstances, whether successful or deprived, and mutual support result in strengthened bonds, especially between the downward mobile who have, in effect, been failed by their parents.

Looked at as a network, the foregoing parent and sibling relations illustrate the importance of middle-class success values and present status in relations between the kin of orientation. Parsons asserts, concerning our occupational and kinship systems, that the open, isolated, nuclear or conjugal family system seems most functional for our mobile occupational system and urban living.[7] The results of the Greensboro investigation imply that the economic values of urban, industrial society do influence considerably the integration of the family of orientation when the children reach adulthood. Cleavages and solidarities occur which are most readily accountable in terms of such societal values. This may be demonstrated by Figure 1. Mutually downward mobile siblings (Diagram 1) are affectionally close while manifesting affectional distance from their parents, particularly their mothers. When only one of the children is downwardly mobile (Diagram 2) he or she is affectionally distant from parents and the sibling. Although the numbers are too small to be definitive, these young adults appear most likely to have attenuated kin networks, including a shallow relation with their kin of orientation.

The stable blue-collar adult whose sibling is upwardly mobile tends to identify with his sibling's achievement, but may blame his parents for the fact that he was not also mobile (Diagram 3). However, occupational salience and open competition prevent even such one-way identification and affection between occupationally disparate brothers (Diagram 3a).

The upwardly mobile devise different solutions to the problem of integration with the kin of orientation. Mutually upward mobile siblings are relatively close to each other in their mutual achievement, and in addition respond positively to their parents' efforts on

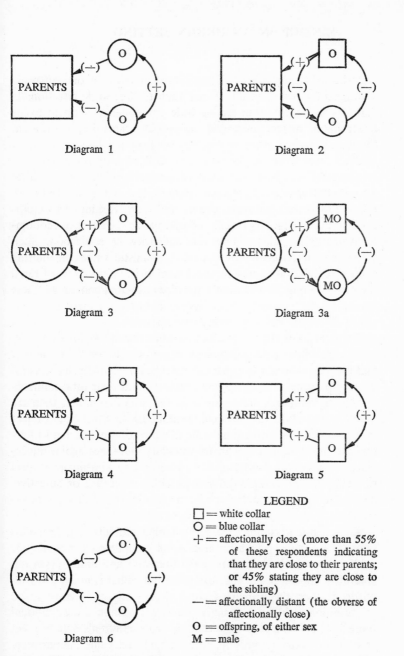

Diagram 1

Diagram 2

Diagram 3

Diagram 3a

Diagram 4

Diagram 5

Diagram 6

LEGEND

☐ = white collar
O = blue collar
+ = affectionally close (more than 55% of these respondents indicating that they are close to their parents; or 45% stating they are close to the sibling)
— = affectionally distant (the obverse of affectionally close)
O = offspring, of either sex
M = male

FIGURE VI-1. Affectional relations with the kin of orientation, according to comparative occupational positions.[8]

their behalf (Diagram 4). The upward mobility of one offspring (Diagram 3) results in this young adult tending to be affectionally close to his parents, but feeling little emotional attachment to his lower status, or less successful, sibling. Diagrams 5 and 6 present the typical mutual affectional closeness of stable white-collar kin of orientation and distance of stable blue-collar kin of orientation.

There are variations according to the sex of the individual, either young adult or parent, especially in the role convergence and close relation of working-class daughters and their working-class mothers. Yet these diagrams reveal and summarize the effect of economic-occupational values upon kin solidarity in adulthood. Such values characteristically override kin familistic values in altering subjective relations between the kin of orientation. Nevertheless, the general obligation to, and often circumstantial contact of, these immediate kin causes the quantity of contact to be maintained despite variation in both its quality and types.

Secondary kin affairs are likewise not affected negatively by the upward mobility of the individual. The upward mobile are able to find kin with whom to perpetuate a modicum of involvement—frequently persons of their current stratum—and their total numbers of kin acquaintances are no smaller, and are often larger, than are the networks of the occupationally stable. Either through kin rejection or feelings of inadequacy, the downwardly mobile tend to relinquish ties with many of their secondary kin. Once again, the incidental or circumstantial nature of secondary kinship in general results in few observable differences, either subjective or objective, which might be accounted for by occupational stability or movement.

An attempt to summarize occupational mobility and kin relations confronts us with a multiplicity of complicating factors. The guiding hypothesis drawn from the literature and based upon degree of relationship and the sex of the individual is much too simplistic. Rather, the primary factors include migratory history and the resulting residential distances, society's economic-occupational success values, the role of parents in their children's achievement or non-achievement, present occupational and value similarity or divergence between siblings, and the basically incidental nature of secondary kinship.

Future Research and Functional Centrality: A Postscript

The primary purposes of the present study have been two-fold. First and foremost, the endeavor has been made to piece together the scattered and often fragmentary materials on urban kinship into a generally unified picture, including both its subjective and objective attributes. A second purpose coincides with the exploratory nature of much of the analysis, especially of adult sibling and secondary kin relations. That is, besides the general characterization there are numerous hypotheses and areas of study which merit further, more detailed, investigation. The depth of our findings could be increased in several directions. (1) What are the values upon which perceived consensus or dissensus in the kin network is based? Political attitudes, optimism or pessimism, success orientation, religious outlook, reactions to minorities or children—these are some of the ideas that respondents may be thinking about when they say that they and a relative have the same opinions or different opinions on things that matter. On the basis of extemporaneous comments, it seems likely that the two crucial sets of values which are salient to kin relations are *economic* and *moral*. By economic we mean feelings that "he works hard," or "he is a good provider," or "she doesn't care if she goes down." Some of the ways in which such economic values impinge on the kin network have already become apparent. By moral values we mean feelings that "he is a good man," or "he drinks a lot," or "she is religious and tries to live the right kind of life for her children." Other attitudes, such as political among upper-middle-class males, are apt to be less universally salient to kin relations in urban-industrial society than these.

A second direction for increased depth would be to attempt a fuller investigation of downward mobility. (2) The either-or choice between husband and family of orientation is apt to be greater for the downwardly mobile female than for the male. The downwardly mobile male has made his own choice, due perhaps to school difficulties and involvement with lower status friends, while the female has simply chosen a husband. But downward mobility is far from a settled issue as regards its relation to kin affairs.

The extent of knowledge of urban kinship could be expanded in many directions. Further breakdown in status categories, marital relations and kinship, kin and other societal systems, and change —all these are of interest and importance. Do upper class persons still have the strong kin networks that are attributed to them in the literature? (3) I would hypothesize that the old upper classes would have such networks—non-localized—but that the "nouveau riche" and upper-middle-classes would come closest to epitomizing the "nuclear familistic" described above. Also, the lower-blue-collar are likely to have looser knit kin networks than the true urban working classes, i.e., the industrial or semi-skilled workers. In any case, further occupational and status breakdown is needed.

What is the relation of marital power relations to involvement with one or both kin networks? (4) It is quite possible that the agreement of both spouses that they should be close to both sets of kin, or neither, or one and not the other, is enough to keep peace within the couple and with kin and in-laws. However, a struggle for power may be manifested in those cases where a choice must be made regarding settling near one set of kin or the other. Much needs to be done on marital interaction and kin involvement.

It seems to this author that the two most fruitful aspects of urban kinship for future concern are change and interrelations with other systems. How does kinship affect and adapt to the urban-industrial environment? (5) One way to study this would be to follow longitudinally the characteristics of urban in-migrants, such as those from Eastern Kentucky into Southern Ohio, as they change over a period of years. It would be well to parallel this with an investigation of a minority group of urban migrants, to note whether minority status results in more emphasis being put on the maintenance of kin ties for the sake of mutual survival and a greater chance of societal success.

The question of interrelations and the societal role of kin requires somewhat more extended comment before leaving the subject of urban kinship. (6) Litwak and Sussman, as well as our study, have rather convincingly demonstrated that being part of an urban society signifies neither uniformly great distance from one's kin, nor does remoteness, when it does occur, necessarily signal isolation in terms of lack of contact. But isolation from kin is not the principle issue of either Parsons' or Wirth's discussions of urban kinship. These authors are saying that, in historical and societal perspective, our kinship system does not appear to be as functionally central, or as crucial an element, in the total society as it has been in many other times and places. Parsons, for example, makes this explicit when he states that at marriage the individual is drastically segregated, in comparison with other societies, from his parents and siblings.[9] Parsons' concern here is with kinship in the "contemporary United States" in a comparative way. His critics, on the other hand, have collected data which are significant in their own right, and have replied to Parsons in the following vein: "See, the kinship system does 'function' in urban settings. Relatives interact, keep in touch, celebrate happy occasions, and parents and their adult children even help each other from time to time." Parsons and his critics, in their conceptions of functionality, are in fact talking past each other. The major concern of Parsons and the Chicago school is with the relation of the part to the whole, of the kin network to the society. Sussman, Litwak, Greer, Axelrod, and the present study have largely dealt with the functioning of the part. We have generally agreed with these latter studies regarding the function of parents in providing primary relations and aid to their adult offspring, and have noted the comparative function performed by siblings. But to generalize from such findings to the functional role of kin in the total society would be presumptuous. Were we to infer societal functionality from our findings regarding nepotism, total aid exchanged between kin, mutual involvement in voluntary organizations, or the few instances of parents or other kin residing with a respondent, we would be inclined to agree with Parsons. Adult kin relations do appear, in comparison to other societies historically and to other institutional spheres in modern urban society, to be functionally peripheral to the ongoing of the total structure. But our study has not probed very far into the functional comparisons or interrelations between institutional spheres, nor have we sought to resolve cross-cultural or historical issues—these remain to be removed from the literature and investigated in the empirical arena.

Ours has been primarily a characterization of kin relations in one urban place, and that task is at an end. Relations with kin, we have found, should be generalized with reference to a specific kin category, not to the total network. Parents are objects of positive concern, which includes frequent contact, readiness to help, and strong feelings of affection and obligation. Siblings are objects of continuing interest and comparison in urban society. Finally, secondary kin are commonly objects of but little concern and incidental contact.

FOOTNOTES

Chapter I

1. Many of the best studies of urban kinship to date have been carried out by anthropologists: Raymond Firth, "Family and Kinship in Industrial Society," *The Development of Industrial Societies,* Paul Halmos, editor (The Sociological Review Monograph No. 8, Keele: University of Keele, 1964), pp. 65-87; Michael Young and Peter Willmott, *Family and Kinship in East London* (Baltimore, Md.: Penguin Books, 1964); Philip Garigue, "French Canadian Kinship and Urban Life," *American Anthropologist,* Vol. 58 (December, 1956), pp. 1090-1101. The centrality of kinship in Anthropology is noted by George and Louise Spindler, in Ernest L. Schusky, *Manual for Kinship Analysis* (New York: Holt, Rinehart, and Winston, Inc., 1965), p. vi.
2. By this we do not mean to imply that the Western kinship system did not also play an active role in urban, industrial development. On this, see Sidney Greenfield, "Industrialization and the Family in Sociological Theory," *American Journal of Sociology,* Vol. 67 (November, 1961), pp. 312-322; John W. Bennett and Leo A. Despres, "Kinship and Instrumental Activities," *American Anthropologist,* Vol. 62 (April, 1960), pp. 254-267.
3. There is a tendency, with some substantiation, for warmer ties to be with the female's kin; see David M. Schneider and George C. Homans, "Kinship Terminology and the American Kinship System," *American Anthropologist,* Vol. 57 (December, 1955), pp. 1194-1208.
4. Sources for the "classical urban theory" include: Louis Wirth, "Urbanism as a Way of Life," *American Journal of Sociology,* Vol. 44 (July, 1938, pp. 1-24; Talcott Parsons, "The Kinship System of the Contemporary United States," *American Anthropologist,* Vol. 45 (January-March, 1943), pp. 22-38; Ralph Linton, "The Natural History of the Family," *The Family: Its Function and Destiny,* Ruth Nanda Anshen, editor (New York: Harper and Brothers, Publ., 1949), pp. 18-38; Robert Redfield, "The Folk Society," *American Journal of Sociology,* Vol. 52 (November, 1947), pp. 293-308.
5. Wirth, "Urbanism as a Way . . . ," pp. 12, 21.
6. Parsons, "The Kinship System . . . ," p. 27.
7. Joel Smith, William H. Form, and Gregory P. Stone, "Local Intimacy in a Middle-Sized City," *American Journal of Sociology,* Vol. 60 (November, 1954), p. 283; see also Floyd Dotson, "Patterns of Voluntary Association Among Urban Working-Class Families," *American Sociological Review,* Vol. 16 (October, 1951), pp. 687-693; Morris Axelrod, "Urban Structure and Social Participation," *American Sociological Review,* Vol.

21 (February, 1956), pp. 13-18; Wendell Bell and Marion D. Boat, "Urban Neighborhoods and Informal Social Relations," *American Journal of Sociology,* Vol. 62 (January, 1957), pp. 391-398; Scott Greer and Ella Kube, "Urbanism and Social Structure: A Los Angeles Study," *Community Structure and Analysis,* Marvin B. Sussman, editor (New York: Thomas Y. Crowell Company, 1959), pp. 93-112; William H. Key, "Rural-Urban Differences and the Family," *The Sociological Quarterly,* Vol. 2 (January, 1961), pp. 49-56; Marvin Sussman, "The Isolated Nuclear Family: Fact or Fiction?," *Social Problems,* Vol. 6 (Spring, 1959), pp. 333-340; J. P. Sutcliffe and B. D. Crabbe, "Incidence and Degrees of Friendship in Urban and Rural Areas," *Social Forces,* Vol. 42 (October, 1963), pp. 60-67.

8 Albert J. Reiss, Jr., "Rural-Urban Status Differences in Interpersonal Contacts," *American Journal of Sociology,* Vol. 65 (September, 1959), pp. 182-195, compares rural and urban interpersonal contacts. On urban primariness, see Eugene Litwak, "Occupational Mobility and Extended Family Cohesion," *American Sociological Review,* Vol. 25 (February, 1960), p. 20; Bert N. Adams, "Interaction Theory and the Social Network," *Sociometry,* Vol. 30 (March, 1967,) pp. 64-78.

9. On mutual aid, see Harry Sharp and Morris Axelrod, "Mutual Aid Among Relatives in an Urban Population," *Principles of Sociology,* Ronald Freedman and associates, editors (New York: Henry Holt and Co., 1956), pp. 433-439; Gordon F. Streib, "Family Patterns in Retirement," *The Journal of Social Issues,* Vol. 14 (Spring, 1958), pp. 46-60; Marvin B. Sussman, "The Help Pattern in the Middle-Class Family," *American Sociological Review,* Vol. 18 (February, 1953), pp. 22-28; Sussman and Lee Burchinal, "Parental Aid to Married Children: Implications for Family Functioning," *Marriage and Family Living,* Vol. 24 (November, 1962), pp. 320-332; Sussman and Burchinal, "Kin Family Network: Unheralded Structure in Current Conceptualizations of Family Functioning," *Marriage and Family Living,* Vol. 24 (August, 1962), pp. 231-240. On migration and the stem family, see Leonard Blumberg and Robert R. Bell, "Urban Migration and Kinship Ties," *Social Problems,* Vol. 6 (Spring, 1959), pp. 328-333; James S. Brown, Harry Schwarzweller, and Joseph J. Mangalam, "Kentucky Mountain Migration and the Stem Family: An American Variation on a Theme by Le Play," *Rural Sociology,* Vol. 28 (March, 1963), pp. 48-69.

10. Studies noting degree of involvement with various kin include: Parsons, "The Kinship System . . . ," pp. 25-26; Garigue, "French Canadian Kinship . . .," pp. 1094, 1095; Young and Willmott, *Family and Kinship* . . ., pp. 78-84; Elizabeth Bott, *Family and Social Network* (London: Tavistock Publications, Ltd., 1957), pp. 129, 147; Paul J. Reiss, "The Extended Kinship System: Correlates of and Attitudes on Frequency of Interaction," *Marriage and Family Living,* Vol. 24 (November, 1962), p. 334; Lee N. Robins and Miroda Tomanec, "Closeness to Blood Relatives Outside the Immediate Family," *Marriage and Family Living,* Vol. 24 (November, 1962), pp. 342-343.

11. Peter Willmott and Michael Young, *Family and Class in a London Suburb* (London: Routledge and Kegan Paul, 1960), p. 78. Specifically

working class or middle class studies also underscore this difference: Reiss, "The Extended Kinship . . . ,' p. 333; Young and Willmott, *Family and Kinship* . . ., pp. 36, 88.

12. Reiss, "The Extended Kinship . . .," pp. 336, 334; Garigue, "French Canadian Kinship . . .," p. 1093; Willmott and Young, *Family and Class* . . ., p. 127.

13. General sources on kinds of interaction are few, and seldom supported by data. Such sources include: Bernard Farber, *Family: Organization and Interaction* (San Francisco: Chandler Publishing Company, 1964), pp. 196f; Donald Gilbert McKinley, *Social Class and Family Life* (New York: The Free Press of Glencoe, 1964), p. 23; Alvin L. Schorr, *Filial Responsibility in the Modern American Family* (Washington, D.C.: Social Security Administration, U. S. Department of Health, Education, and Welfare, 1960), p. 18; Sussman and Burchinal, "Kin Family Network . . .," pp. 235, 238-239.

14. Tamotsu Shibutani, "Reference Groups as Perspectives," *American Journal of Sociology*, Vol. 60 (May, 1955), p. 563.

15. References to identification and comparison with kin include: Eugene Litwak, "Geographic Mobility and Extended Family Cohesion," *American Sociological Review*, Vol. 25 (June, 1960), p. 388; Bott, *Family and Social* . . ., p. 155; William H. Form and James A. Geschwender, "Social Reference Basis of Job Satisfaction: The Case of Manual Workers," *American Sociological Review*, Vol. 27 (April, 1962), p. 232.

16. Leonard Berkowitz and Louise R. Daniels, "Affecting the Salience of the Social Responsibility Norm: Effects of Past Help on the Response to Dependency Relationships," *Journal of Abnormal and Social Psychology*, Vol. 68 (March, 1964), pp. 275-281.

17. The notion of reciprocity is discussed in Alvin W. Gouldner, "The Norm of Reciprocity: A Preliminary Statement," *American Sociological Review*, Vol. 25 (April, 1960), pp. 161-178.

18. Barrington Moore, Jr., *Political Power and Social Theory* (Cambridge, Mass.: Harvard University Press, 1958), p. 193.

19. Firth, "Family and Kinship . . .," p. 85.

20. Reiss, "The Extended Kinship . . ," p. 334; Bott, *Family and Social* . . ., p. 122.

21. See John Mogey, "Family and Community in Urban-Industrial Societies," *Handbook of Marriage and the Family*, Harold T. Christensen, editor (Chicago: Rand McNally and Company), pp. 501-529, for a discussion and excellent bibliography on kin and community.

22. Helen Codere, "A Genealogical Study of Kinship in the United States," *Psychiatry*, Vol. 18 (February, 1955), p. 68; Reiss, "The Extended Kinship . . .," p. 333; Robins and Tomanec, "Closeness to Blood . . .," p. 341; Garigue, "French Canadian Kinship . . .," p. 1091; Firth, "Family and Kinship . . .," p. 81.

23. A. O. Haller, "The Urban Family," *American Journal of Sociology*, Vol. 66 (May, 1961), p. 621; Parsons, "The Kinship System . . .," p. 27.

24. Mogey, "Family and Community . . .," p. 505, points out that the only persons with similar kindreds are siblings.

25. Schneider and Homans, "Kinship Terminology . . .," p. 1207; Robert P.

Stuckert, "Occupational Mobility and Family Relationships," *Social Forces,* Vol. 41 (March, 1963), pp. 301-307, generally agrees with Schneider and Homans.

26. Young and Willmott, *Family and Kinship . . .,* p. 184; Litwak, "Occupational Mobility . . .," pp. 9-21; Streib, "Family Patterns in . . .," p. 52.

27. Willmott and Young, *Family and Class . . .,* p. 167.

28. Bott, *Family and Social . . .,* p. 147.

29. William J. Goode, "Family and Mobility," *Class Status, and Power,* Reinhard Bendix and Seymour Martin Lipset, editors (New York: The Free Press of Glencoe, 1966 ed.), p. 600.

30. United States Department of Commerce, Bureau of the Census, *United States Census of Population: 1960,* North Carolina: General Social and Economic Characteristics PC(1)-35C (Washington: U. S. Government Printing Office, 1961), Table 33.

31. This is reported, among other places, in Paul C. Glick, *American Families* (New York: John Wiley and Sons, Inc., 1957), chapter 8.

32. For a detailed listing of these types of contact, see questions A50-A62, A71-B8, B27-B39, and C9-C21, in Appendix A.

33. The rationale for this procedure has been so carefully worked out and presented in two sources that we feel it unnecessary to explicate the omission of tests of significance. Instead we refer the reader to two discussions: Seymour Martin Lipset, Martin Trow, and James Coleman, *Union Democracy* (Garden City, N.Y.: Doubleday Anchor Books, 1962), pp. 480-485; and Gerhard Lenski, *The Religious Factor* (Garden City, N.Y.: Doubleday and Co., Inc., 1961), pp. 331-340.

Chapter II

1. This three-fold distinction between kin is presented in Raymond Firth and J. Djamour, "Kinship in South Borough," *Two Studies of Kinship in London,* Raymond Firth, editor (London: London School of Economics Monographs on Social Anthropology, No. 15, 1956), p. 45f.

2. Paul J. Reiss, "The Extended Kinship System: Correlates of and Attitudes on Frequency of Interaction," *Marriage and Family Living,* Vol. 24 (November, 1962), p. 333.

3. Philip Garigue, "French Canadian Kinship and Urban Life," *American Anthropologist,* Vol. 58 (December, 1956), p. 1091.

4. Raymond Firth, "Family and Kinship in Industrial Society," *The Development of Industrial Societies,* Paul Halmos, editor (The Sociological Review Monograph No. 8, Keele: University of Keele, 1964), p. 81. Other studies reporting numbers of kin include: Helen Codere, "A Genealogical Study of Kinship in the United States," *Psychiatry,* Vol. 18 (February 1955), p. 68; Lee Robins and Miroda Tomanec, "Closeness to Blood Relatives Outside the Immediate Family," *Marriage and Family Living,* Vol. 24 (November, 1962), p. 341.

5. For a recent summary of the literature on family size by socio-economic

status and religion, see Robert F. Winch, *The Modern Family* (New York: Holt, Rinehart, and Winston, 1963 edition), pp. 203-210, 212-216.

6. Michael Young and Peter Willmott, *Family and Kinship in East London,* (Baltimore, Md.: Penguin Books, 1964), p. 84.
7. David M. Schneider and George C. Homans, "Kinship Terminology and the American Kinship System," *American Anthropologist,* Vol. 57 (December, 1955), pp. 1194-1208; Garigue, "French Canadian Kinship . . .," p. 1097.
8. Eugene Litwak, "The Use of Extended Family Groups in the Achievement of Social Goals," *Social Problems,* Vol. 7 (Winter, 1959-1960), p. 184.
9. Reiss, "The Extended Kinship . . .," *loc. cit.*
10. Seymour Martin Lipset and Reinhard Bendix, *Social Mobility in Industrial Society* (Berkeley: University of California Press, 1964), p. 216.
11. See question C74, Appendix A, for the wording of this question.
12. Elizabeth Bott, *Family and Social Network* (London: Tavistock Publications, Ltd., 1957), p. 129.

Chapter III

1. The word "contact," in this and subsequent chapters, signifies both face-to-face interaction and non-face-to-face contact, such as communication by mail or telephone. Communication plus interaction equals contact.
2. Examples are Joel Smith, William H. Form, and Gregory P. Stone, "Local Intimacy in a Middle-Sized City," *American Journal of Sociology,* Vol. 60 (November, 1954), pp. 276-284, where frequency of interaction is used to indicate intimacy; and Lee Robins and Miroda Tomanec, "Closeness to Blood Relatives Outside the Immediate Family," *Marriage and Family Living,* Vol. 24 (November, 1962), pp. 340-346, in which the concept of "closeness" to various kin is determined by actual interaction, not by expression of affection.
3. Paul J. Reiss, "The Extended Kinship System: Correlates of and Attitudes on Frequency of Interaction," *Marriage and Family Living,* Vol. 24 (November, 1962), pp. 334, 337.
4. Elizabeth Bott, *Family and Social Network* (London: Tavistock Publications, Ltd., 1957), p. 128; the importance of location in friendship patterns is affirmed in Leon Festinger, Stanley Schachter, and Kurt W. Back, *Social Pressures in Informal Groups* (New York: Harper and Brothers, 1950), pp. 33-59; see also George Casper Homans, *Social Behavior: Its Elementary Forms* (New York: Harcourt, Brace, and World, Inc., 1961), Chapter 11.
5. The tendency for kin to follow other kin in migration is discussed in James S. Brown, Harry K. Schwarzweller, and Joseph J. Mangalam, "Kentucky Mountain Migration and the Stem Family: An American Variation on a Theme by Le Play," *Rural Sociology,* Vol. 28 (March,

1963), pp. 48-69; and Leonard Blumberg and Robert R. Bell, "Urban Migration and Kinship Ties," *Social Problems*, Vol. 6 (Spring, 1959), pp. 328-333.

6. For statements of the greater closeness of females to their parents, see, among others: Robert M. Gray and Ted C. Smith, "Effect of Employment on Sex Differences in Attitudes Toward the Parental Family," *Marriage and Family Living*, Vol. 22 (February, 1960), pp. 36-38; Dorrian Apple Sweetser, "Assymetry in Intergenerational Family Relationships," *Social Forces*, Vol. 41 (May, 1963), p. 347; Mirra Komarovsky, "Continuities in Family Research: A Case Study," *American Journal of Sociology*, Vol. 62 (July, 1956), p. 46.

7. Michael Young and Peter Willmott, *Family and Kinship in East London*, (Baltimore, Md.: Penguin Books, 1964), p. 61; Mirra Komarovsky, *Blue-Collar Marriage* (New York: Random House, 1964), p. 242; Peter Townsend, *The Family Life of Old People* (London: Routledge and Kegan Paul, 1957), p. 33.

8. William M. Smith, "Family Plans for Later Years," *Marriage and Family Living*, Vol. 16 (February, 1954), p. 40; Reiss, "The Extended Kinship . . .," p. 336.

9. These comparative percentages persist whether the husband or the wife is interviewed regarding parents and parents-in-law.

10. Komarovsky, *Blue-Collar Marriage*, p. 241.

11. Young and Willmott, *Family and Kinship* . . ., p. 36, italics mine.

12. Robins and Tomanec, "Closeness to Blood . . .," p. 342; Smith, "Family Plans . . .," *loc. cit.;* Reiss, "The Extended Kinship . . .," p. 334.

13. Young and Willmott, *Family and Kinship* . . ., pp. 45, 131.

14. Peter Willmott and Michael Young, *Family and Class in a London Suburb*, (London: Routledge and Kegan Paul, 1960), p. 78; Young and Willmott, *Family and Kinship* . . ., p. 36; Komarovsky, *Blue-Collar Marriage*, p. 241.

15. Talcott Parsons, "The Kinship System of the Contemporary United States," *American Anthropologist*, Vol. 45 (January-March, 1943), p. 27.

16. A. O. Haller, "The Urban Family," *American Journal of Sociology*, Vol. 66 (May, 1961), p. 621.

17. An interesting, albeit tangential, issue concerns the reasons for the prevalence—even as a "straw" man—of the idea of the isolated urban nuclear family. William Key indicates how he feels the position of Parsons and the Chicago school may have arisen: "It seems likely . . . that the hypothesis of the disintegration of the extended family developed early in the history of urban sociology when attention was focussed on recent immigrants to the city, and before these individuals had had an opportunity to establish families." Later the impersonality of the city increased, rather than decreased, kin interaction. William H. Key, "Rural-Urban Differences and the Family," *Sociological Quarterly*, Vol. 2 (January, 1961), p. 56. Another relatively obvious, although neglected, aspect of the explanation may lie in the somewhat biased perception of the academician. As Joel Gerstl documents, the kin experience of the professor or researcher is far from typical of his society, or even of

professionals. In fact, the academician tends to be near one end of the spectrum of kin involvement. Particularly is the productive scholar—whose work we read—likely to have forsaken such ties for his profession. See Joel Gerstl, "Leisure, Taste, and Occupational Milieu," *Social Problems*, Vol. 9 (Summer, 1961), pp. 61-62.

18. For example, see Robins and Tomanec, "Closeness to Blood . . .," p. 344; or Young and Willmott, *Family and Kinship . . .*, p. 184.

19. Carson McGuire, "Conforming, Mobile, and Divergent Families," *Marriage and Family Living*, Vol. 14 (May, 1952), p. 110; see also Ralph H. Turner, "Some Family Determinants of Ambition," *Sociology and Social Research*, Vol. 46 (July, 1962), p. 398.

20. McGuire, "Conforming, Mobile, . . .," *loc. cit.;* the role of the father in the arousal of aspirations in the son is reported in Joseph A. Kahl, "Educational and Occupational Aspirations of 'Common Man' Boys," *Harvard Educational Review*, Vol. 23 (Summer, 1953), pp. 186-203; the influence of the mother whose status outranks that of the father is stressed in Robert A. Ellis and W. Clayton Lane, "Structural Supports for Upward Mobility," *American Sociological Review*, Vol. 28 (October, 1963), pp. 743-756.

21. E. E. LeMasters, "Social Class Mobility and Family Integration," *Marriage and Family Living*, Vol. 16 (August, 1954), p. 229; on the generally disruptive effects of mobility, see Russell R. Dynes, Alfred C. Clarke, and Simon Dinitz, "Levels of Occupational Aspiration: Some Aspects of Family Experience as a Variable," *American Sociological Review*, Vol. 21 (April, 1956), p. 215.

22. Robert P. Stuckert, "Occupational Mobility and Family Relationships," *Social Forces*, Vol. 41 (March, 1963), pp. 304-306.

23. Eugene Litwak, "Occupational Mobility and Extended Family Cohesion," *American Sociological Review*, Vol. 25 (February, 1960), pp. 11, 16. See also Paul H. Glasser and Lois N. Glasser, "Role Reversal and Conflict Between Aged Parents and Their Children," *Marriage and Family Living*, Vol. 24 (February, 1962), p. 49; Young and Willmott, *Family and Kinship . . .*, p. 184.

24. Eugene Litwak, "Geographical Mobility and Extended Family Cohesion," *American Sociological Review*, Vol. 25 (June, 1960), p. 387; William J. Goode, *World Revolution and Family Patterns* (New York: The Free Press of Glencoe, 1963), p. 369; Alvin L. Schorr, *Filial Responsibility in the Modern American Family* (Washington, D.C.: Social Security Administration, United States Department of Health, Education, and Welfare, 1960), p. 15; Marvin B. Sussman and Lee Burchinal, "Kin Family Network: Unheralded Structure in Current Conceptualizations of Family Functioning," *Marriage and Family Living*, Vol. 24 (August, 1962), p. 239.

25. Litwak, "Geographical Mobility and . . .," p. 386.

26. Letter writing is by family, not by the individual respondent. In most families (59 per cent of the present sample) the wife carries the burden of personal letter writing. A bias is thus avoided if we consider how frequently either spouse writes, rather than the respondent only. Telephoning means talking together; it is not the number of times the young

adult has called his or her parents, but includes calls from as well as to the parents.

27. Alan D. Coult and Robert W. Habenstein, "The Study of Extended Kinship in Urban Society," *Sociological Quarterly*, Vol. 3 (April, 1962), p. 144.

28. Donald Gilbert McKinley, *Social Class and Family Life* (New York: The Free Press of Glencoe, 1964), p. 23.

29. Bernard Farber, *Family: Organization and Interaction* (San Francisco: Chandler Publishing Company, 1964), pp. 196f.

30. Reuben Hill, J. Joel Moss, and Claudine G. Wirths, *Eddyville's Families* (Chapel Hill, N.C.: Institute for Research in Social Science, University of North Carolina, 1953), pp. 168, 170.

31. Sussman and Burchinal, "Kin Family Network . . .," p. 235, Morris Axelrod, "Urban Structure and Social Participation," *American Sociological Review*, Vol. 21 (February, 1956), p. 17.

32. Ruth Albrecht, "The Parental Responsibilities of Grandparents," *Marriage and Family Living*, Vol. 16 (August, 1954), p. 203; Litwak, "Occupational Mobility and . . .," p. 20.

33. Goode, *World Revolution and . . .*, p. 76.

34. Schorr, *Filial Responsibility in . . .*, p. 18.

35. Young and Willmott, *Family and Kinship . . .*, p. 49; Townsend, *The Family Life . . .*, p. 116.

36. Marvin Sussman, "The Isolated Nuclear Family: Fact or Fiction," *Social Problems*, Vol. 6 (Spring, 1959), p. 337.

37. Marvin Sussman, "The Help Pattern in the Middle Class Family," *American Sociological Review*, Vol. 18 (February, 1953), pp. 25, 27.

38. Sussman, "The Isolated Nuclear . . .," pp. 335-337.

39. Harry Sharp and Morris Axelrod, "Mutual Aid Among Relatives in an Urban Population," *Principles of Sociology*, Ronald Freedman *et al.*, editors (New York: Henry Holt and Company, 1956), pp. 433-439. A weakness in both Sussman's and Sharp and Axelrod's studies is their use of the terms "frequent," "more," and "pattern." In Sussman's Cleveland study, he asked respondents if they had given or received a form of aid within the past month. On the basis of the replies, he then described the middle classes as giving "more" of this or that form of aid. He would have been correct if he had stated that a particular help was more widespread or more widely distributed among middle-class respondents, but he presented no information either on how often or how much aid was given. Sharp and Axelrod even more blatantly misuse the terms denoting frequency. Their question is recorded as follows: "In which of these ways have you *ever* given any help to relatives?" (Italics are mine.) The authors then proceed to discuss "patterns" and "frequencies" of mutual aid. Having given or received something once does not indicate a pattern, and nothing whatsoever can be ascertained concerning frequency from answers to the question "ever." Sharp and Axelrod may legitimately observe, along with Sussman, the distribution of the various forms of aid which prevails within their sample. To talk of frequencies would require specifying the period of time, as Sussman did, but also an enumeration of events.

40. See Gordon Streib, "Family Patterns in Retirement," *The Journal of So-

cial Issues, Vol. 14 (February, 1958), p. 56, for an excellent discussion of this point. Other sources on aid include: Albrecht, "The Parental Responsibilities . . .," p. 201; Sussman, "The Isolated Nuclear . . .," p. 336; Townsend, *The Family Life* . . ., p. 61. On advice and emotional support, see Sussman, *loc cit.,* and Streib, *loc. cit.* On nepotism, see Sussman, "The Help Pattern . . .," p. 25, and Sussman and Lee Burchinal, "Parental Aid to Married Children: Implications for Family Functioning," *Marriage and Family Living,* Vol. 24 (November, 1962), p. 331.

41. Sussman, "The Isolated Nuclear . . .," p. 337.
42. Ethel Shanas, *Family Relationships of Older People* (Chicago: Health Information Foundation, 1961), p. 7; Townsend, *The Family Life* . . ., p. 52.
43. Mirra Komarovsky, "Functional Analysis of Sex Roles," *American Sociological Review,* Vol. 15 (October, 1950), p. 513.
44. Urie Bronfenbrenner, "The Changing American Child—A Speculative Analysis," *The Journal of Social Issues,* Vol. 17 (February, 1961), p. 11.
45. See Sussman, "The Help Pattern . . .," pp. 24-25, where the author notes the necessity for parents to use discreet means of helping their married children financially. For a fuller treatment of this, see also Bert N. Adams, "Structural Factors Affecting Parental Aid to Married Children," *Journal of Marriage and the Family,* Vol. 26 (August, 1964), pp. 327-331.
46. Eugene Litwak, "The Use of Extended Family Groups in the Achievement of Social Goals: Some Policy Implications," *Social Problems,* Vol. 7 (Winter, 1959-1960), p. 184.
47. Hilde T. Himmelweit, "Socio-Economic Background and Personality," *International Social Science Bulletin,* Vol. 7 (January, 1955), pp. 29-34, reported in Turner, "Some Family Determinants . . .," p. 398.
48. This is also noted in Young and Willmott, *Family and Kinship* . . ., p. 190.
49. Litwak, "Occupational Mobility and . . .," p. 9.
50. George Casper Homans, *Social Behavior: Its Elementary Forms* (New York: Harcourt, Brace, and World, Inc., 1961), p. 187; see also, Theodore M. Newcomb, "The Prediction of Interpersonal Attraction," *The American Psychologist,* Vol. 11 (November, 1956), pp. 578-579.
51. Herbert Blumer, "Attitudes and the Social Act," *Social Problems,* Vol. 3 (October, 1955), pp. 60, 64.
52. Reinhard Bendix and Bennett Berger, "Images of Society and Problems of Concept Formation in Sociology," *Symposium on Sociological Theory,* Llewellyn Gross, editor (Evanston, Ill.: Row, Peterson, and Company, 1959), p. 100.
53. Bendix and Berger, "Images of Society . . .," p.111.
54. Homans, *Social Behavior* . . ., p. 215; Newcomb, "The Prediction of . . .," p. 577. For the interview questions used to discern affectional closeness to or value consensus with parents, see Chapter I or Appendix A, questions A39, A41, A43, and A45. Questions concerning closeness to parents and value consensus with them were separated in the interview in order to minimize the deliberate duplication of responses.
55. The closer subjective relations between mothers and daughters are noted

by Komarovsky, *Blue-Collar Marriage,* pp. 252, 366; Sweetser, "Asymmetry in Intergenerational . . .," p. 347; Young and Willmott, *Family and Kinship* . . ., pp. 194 *et passim.*

56. Theodore Newcomb and George Svehla, "Intra-family Relationships in Attitude," *Sociometry,* Vol. 1 (July-October, 1937), p. 200.
57. Komarovsky, *Blue-Collar Marriage, loc. cit.*
58. Melvin L. Kohn and Eleanor E. Carroll, "Social Class and the Allocation of Parental Responsibilities," *Sociometry,* Vol. 23 (December, 1960), pp. 391-392.
59. McKinley, *Social Class and* . . ., p. 116.
60. Kahl, "Educational and Occupational . . .," Ellis and Lane, "Structural Supports for . . .," pp. 744, 747.
61. Willmott and Young, *Family and Class* . . ., p. 167.
62. Willmott and Young, *Family and Class* . . ., p. 84.
63. Komarovsky, Blue-Collar Marriage, p. 253, refers to this fact.
64. Parsons, "The Kinship System . . .," p. 31.
65. Schorr, *Filial Responsibility in* . . ., p. 17; Robert M. Dinkel, "Parent-Child Conflict in Minnesota Families," *American Sociological Review,* Vol. 8 (August, 1943), p. 419.
66. Elaine Cumming and David M. Schneider, "Sibling Solidarity: A Property of American Kinship," *American Anthropologist,* Vol. 63 (June, 1961), p. 505; Philip Garigue, "French Canadian Kinship and Urban Life," *American Anthropologist,* Vol. 58 (December, 1956), p. 1090; August Hollingshead, "Class Differences in Family Stability," *The Annals,* Vol. 272 (November, 1950), p. 45; Reiss, "The Extended Kinship . . .," p. 336; Donal E. Muir and Eugene A. Weinstein, "The Social Debt: An Investigation of Lower-Class and Middle-Class Norms of Social Obligation," *American Sociological Review,* Vol. 27 (August, 1962), pp. 532-539.
67. Robins and Tomanec, "Closeness to Blood . . .," p. 345; Muir and Weinstein, "The Social Debt . . .," p. 535. The latter authors justify an all-female sample for the study of social debts with the assertion that "many (if not most) of the family's social obligations are probably contracted, repaid, and generally 'administered' by the wife."
68. Maria Rogers, "The Human Group: A Critical Review with Suggestions for Some Alternative Hypotheses," *Sociometry,* Vol. 14 (February, 1951), p. 27.
69. On initiation of interaction between adult offspring and their parents, see further E. Grant Youmans, *Aging Patterns in a Rural and an Urban Area of Kentucky* (Lexington, Ky.: University of Kentucky Agricultural Experiment Station, Bulletin 681, 1963), pp. 43-44.
70. Cumming and Schneider, "Sibling Solidarity: . . .," *loc. cit.;* Reiss, "The Extended Kinship . . .," p. 336; Robert M. Dinkel, "Attitudes of Children Toward Supporting Aged Parents," *American Sociological Review,* Vol. 9 (August, 1944), p. 379; Marvin R. Koller, "Studies of Three-Generation Housholds," *Marriage and Family Living,* Vol. 16 (August, 1954), p. 206; Sussman and Burchinal, "Parental Aid to . . .," p. 332.
71. Garigue, "French Canadian Kinship . . .," p. 1095.

72. For the order and wording of these questions in the interview, see Appendix A, questions A67-A70.
73. Hollingshead, "Class Differences in . . .," *loc. cit.*
74. Muir and Weinstein, "The Social Debt . . .," pp. 537-538.
75. On concern as a component of affectional closeness, or the primary relationship, see Bert N. Adams, "Interaction Theory and the Social Network," *Sociometry,* Vol. 30 (March, 1967), pp. 64-78.
76. Dinkel, "Parent-Child Conflict . . .," p. 419.
77. Peter Marris, *Widows and Their Families* (London: Routledge and Kegan Paul, 1958); Elaine Cumming and William E. Henry, *Growing Old: the Process of Disengagement* (New York: Basic Books, Inc., 1961).
78. For a more complete discussion of this subject, see Bert N. Adams, "The Middle-Class Adult and His Widowed or Still-Married Mother," forthcoming in *Social Problems.*
79. Townsend, *The Family Life . . .,* p. 52. In the Greensboro study, the percentages of blue-collar females giving any aid at all and aid monthly to a widowed mother are 68 and 32, respectively. Corresponding figures for blue-collar males are 70 and 30. We have ignored occupational status distinctions throughout this discussion since, aside from the greater prominence of patterned contact among the blue-collar kin, objective and subjective relations with widows are similar by sex across occupational lines.
80. Marris, *Widows and Their . . .,* p. 49.
81. Adams, "Interaction Theory and . . ."
82. Barrington Moore, Jr., *Political Power and Social Theory* (Cambridge, Mass.: Harvard University Press, 1958), p. 163.
83. Raymond Firth, "Family and Kinship in Industrial Society," *The Development of Industrial Societies,* Paul Halmos, editor (The Sociological Review Monograph No. 8, Keele: University of Keele, 1964), p. 85.
84. Lee Rainwater, Richard P. Coleman, and Gerald Handel, *Workingman's Wife* (New York: Oceana Publications, Inc., 1959), p. 76.
85. Litwak, "Occupational Mobility and . . .," p. 10, notes the assumptions of differing values and lack of kin interest which underlie the theory of the isolated urban family.

Chapter IV

1. Philip Garigue, "French Canadian Kinship and Urban Life," *American Anthropologist,* Vol. 58 (December, 1956), p. 1092; Elaine Cumming and David M. Schneider, "Sibling Solidarity: A Property of American Kinship," *American Anthropologist,* Vol. 63 (June, 1961), p. 499; Bernard Farber, *Kinship and Family Organization,* (New York: John Wiley and Sons, 1966), pp. 69-70, 255.
2. Donald P. Irish, "Sibling Interaction: A Neglected Aspect in Family Life Research," *Social Forces,* Vol. 42 (March, 1964), pp. 286-287.

3. Garigue, "French Canadian Kinship . . .," p. 1092; Cumming and Schneider, "Sibling Solidarity: . . .," p. 505.
4. William H. Form and James A. Geschwender, "Social Reference Basis of Job Satisfaction: The Case of Manual Workers," *American Sociological Review*, Vol. 27 (April, 1962), pp. 228-237.
5. Theodore Caplow, "Further Development of a Theory of Coalitions in the Triad," *American Journal of Sociology*, Vol. 64 (March, 1959), p. 493.
6. Paul J. Reiss, "The Extended Kinship System: Correlates of and Attitudes on Frequency of Interaction," *Marriage and Family Living*, Vol. 24 (November, 1962), p. 334.
7. Robert P. Stuckert, "Occupational Mobility and Family Relationships," *Social Forces*, Vol. 41 (March, 1963), p. 306.
8. Elizabeth Bott, *Family and Social Network* (London: Tavistock Publications, Ltd., 1957), p. 147.
9. E. E. LeMasters, "Social Class Mobility and Family Integration," *Marriage and Family Living*, Vol. 16 (August, 1954), p. 229.
10. Peter Willmott and Michael Young, *Family and Class in a London Suburb* (London: Routledge and Kegan Paul, 1960), pp. 167, 84.
11. Marvin B. Sussman and Lee Burchinal, "Kin Family Network: Unheralded Structure in Current Conceptualizations of Family Functioning," *Marriage and Family Living*, Vol. 24 (August, 1962), p. 239; Michael Young and Peter Willmott, *Family and Kinship in East London* (Baltimore, Md.: Penguin Books, 1964), p. 81.
12. Eugene Litwak, "Geographical Mobility and Extended Family Cohesion," *American Sociological Review*, Vol. 25 (June, 1960), p. 385.
13. Eugene Litwak, "The Use of Extended Family Groups in the Achievement of Social Goals," *Social Problems*, Vol. 7 (Winter, 1959-1960), pp. 177f.
14. Alvin W. Gouldner, "The Norm of Reciprocity: a Preliminary Statement," *American Sociological Review*, Vol. 25 (April, 1960), p. 172.
15. Garigue, "French Canadian Kinship . . .," pp. 1092, 1090.
16. Dorothy R. Blitsten, *The World of the Family* (New York: Random House, 1963), p. 34.
17. Marvin Sussman, "The Isolated Nuclear Family: Fact or Fiction," *Social Problems*, Vol. 6 (Spring, 1959), p. 336.
18. Young and Willmott, *Family and Kinship . . .*, pp. 78, 81.
19. August B. Hollingshead, "Class Differences in Family Stability," *The Annals*, Vol. 272 (November, 1950), p. 45.
20. Lee Rainwater, Richard P. Coleman, and Gerald Handel, *Workingman's Wife* (New York: Oceana Publications, Inc., 1959), p. 76.
21. Theodore Newcomb and George Svehla, "Intra-family Relationships in Attitude," *Sociometry*, Vol. 1 (July-October, 1937), p. 202.
22. Cumming and Schneider, "Sibling Solidarity . . .," p. 505; Garigue, "French Canadian Kinship . . .," p. 1090.
23. LeMasters, "Social Class Mobility . . .," p. 229; Willmott and Young, *Family and Class . . .*, p. 84; John Gulick and Charles E. Bowerman, *Adaptation of Newcomers in the Piedmont Industrial Crescent* (Chapel

Hill, N.C.: Institute for Research in Social Science, University of North Carolina, 1961), p. 50.
24. Bott, *Family and Social . . .*, p. 155.
25. Form and Geschwender, "Social Reference Basis . . .," p. 232.
26. This table is reprinted with permission from Bert N. Adams, "Occupational Position, Mobility, and the Kin of Orientation," *American Sociological Review*, Vol. 32 (June, 1967), p. 371.
27. Hollingshead, "Class Differences in . . .," p. 44; LeMasters, "Social Class Mobility . . .," p. 227.
28. Garigue, "French Canadian Kinship . . .," p. 1095.
29. Eugene Litwak, "Occupational Mobility and Extended Family Cohesion," *American Sociological Review*, Vol. 25 (February, 1960), p. 21.
30. This table is reprinted with permission from Adams, "Occupational Position, Mobility . . .," p. 373.
31. Carson McGuire, "Conforming, Mobile, and Divergent Families," *Marriage and Family Living*, Vol. 14 (May, 1952), p. 110, speaks of mobile families as those in which both parents are oriented toward upward mobility for their offspring. LeMasters, "Social Class Mobility . . .," p. 229, points out that the Type II family, which moves up together, is well integrated, whereas the family with differentially mobile siblings (type III) is characterized by ambivalence and strain. These findings, while not synonymous with ours, are parallel.
32. Question B50, Appendix A.
33. Lee Robins and Miroda Tomanec, "Closeness to Blood Relatives Outside the Immediate Family," *Marriage and Family Living*, Vol. 24 (November, 1962), p. 343.
34. Young and Willmott, *Family and Kinship . . .*, p. 78.
35. Litwak, "The Use of Extended . . .;" in this article the author discusses some of the ways in which the kin network aids the individual in adapting himself to or integrating himself into the larger society.

Chapter V

1. Helen Codere, "A Genealogical Study of Kinship in the United States," *Psychiatry*, Vol. 18 (February, 1955), p. 78; Dorothy R. Blitsten, *The World of the Family* (New York: Random House, 1963), p. 34.
2. Marvin Sussman, "The Isolated Nuclear Family: Fact or Fiction," *Social Problems*, Vol. 6 (Spring, 1959), pp. 333-340; Sussman and Lee Burchinal, "Kin Family Network: Unheralded Structure in Current Conceptualizations of Family Functioning," *Marriage and Family Living*, Vol. 24 (August, 1962), pp. 231-240; Eugene Litwak, especially "Geographic Mobility and Extended Family Cohesion," *American Sociological Review*, Vol. 25 (June, 1960), pp. 385-394.
3. Talcott Parsons, "The Kinship System of the Contemporary United States," *American Anthropologist*, Vol. 45 (January-March, 1943), pp. 22-38; Lee N. Robins and Miroda Tomanec, "Closeness to Blood Rela-

tives Outside the Immediate Family," *Marriage and Family Living,* Vol. 24 (November, 1962), p. 342; Philip Garigue, "French Canadian Kinship and Urban Life," *American Anthropologist,* Vol. 58 (December, 1956), p. 1090.

4. Parsons, "The Kinship System . . .," p. 25.
5. Question B70, Appendix A.
6. David M. Schneider and George C. Homans, "Kinship Terminology and the American Kinship System, *American Anthropologist,* Vol. 57 (December, 1955), p. 1199.
7. Robins and Tomanec, "Closeness to Blood . . .," p. 343.
8. See Question B71, Appendix A.
9. Elaine Cumming and David M. Schneider, "Sibling Solidarity: a Property of American Kinship," *American Anthropologist,* Vol. 63 (June, 1961), p. 504.
10. Codere, "A Genealogical Study . . .," p. 70.
11. Garigue, "French Canadian Kinship . . .," p. 1095.
12. Elizabeth Bott, *Family and Social Network,* (London: Tavistock Publications, Ltd., 1957), p. 147.
13. Schneider and Homans, "Kinship Terminology . . .," p. 1207.
14. Garigue, "French Canadian Kinship . . ., p. 1097.
15. Robins and Tomanec, "Closeness to Blood . . .," p. 342; Parsons, "The Kinship System . . .," p. 25; Garigue, "French Canadian Kinship . . .," p. 1090.
16. For a further discussion of the components of kinship and friendship relations, see Bert N. Adams, "Interaction Theory and the Social Network," *Sociometry,* Vol. 30 (March, 1967), pp. 64-78.
17. Barrington Moore, *Political Power and Social Theory* (Cambridge, Mass.: Harvard University Press, 1958), p. 163.

Chapter VI

1. Elaine Cummings and David M. Schneider, "Sibling Solidarity: a Property of American Kinship," *American Anthropologist,* Vol. 63 (June, 1961), p. 502 *et passim.*
2. Personal conferences with Jewish students from New York, Detroit, and other megalopolitan centers indicate that an exception to our generalization regarding the incidental nature of secondary kinship may very well be found in the Jewish kin networks of these urban complexes. One pattern seems to be for the successful individual to help nephews and sometimes nieces, and not just his own children, in their attempts to achieve in society. A book just off the press, Hope Jensen Leichter and William E. Mitchell, *Kinship and Casework,* New York: Russell Sage Foundation, 1967, should increase our understanding of kinship in such settings.
3. Everett M. Rogers and Hans Sebald, "A Distinction Between Familism, Family Integration, and Kinship Orientation," *Marriage and Family Living,* Vol. 24 (February, 1962), pp. 25-30.

4. This concept, i.e., the isolated nuclear family, can be looked upon, we have said, as a construct of the lag between migration and communication theories, the former simply pre-dating the latter. Distance does not imply isolation in urban-industrial society.
5. Talcott Parsons, "The Kinship System of the Contemporary United States," *American Anthropologist,* Vol. 45 (January-March, 1943), pp. 27, 35.
6. David M. Schneider and George C. Homans, "Kinship Terminology and the American Kinship System," *American Anthropologist,* Vol. 57 (December, 1955), p. 1207; Eugene Litwak, "Occupational Mobility and Extended Family Cohesion," *American Sociological Review,* Vol. 25 (February, 1960), p. 16.
7. Parsons, "The Kinship System . . .," p. 37.
8. This figure is reprinted with permission from Bert N. Adams, "Occupational Position, Mobility, and the Kin of Orientation," *American Sociological Review,* Vol. 32 (June, 1967), p. 375.
9. Parsons, "The Kinship System . . .," p. 30.

DATA COLLECTION INSTRUMENT: "A STUDY OF PEOPLE AND THEIR RELATIVES"

A4. Sex of Respondent
———— 1. Male
———— 2. Female

A5. How many years have you been married?
———— 1. Less than one year.   ———— 4. 6-9 years.
———— 2. One or two years.   ———— 5. 10-15 years.
———— 3. 3-5 years.   ———— 6. 16-20 years.

This is your first marriage, isn't it? If unmarried, or married 21 or more years, or if this is not their first marriage, *terminate* interview.

A6. Which of the following age groups are you in?
———— 1. Under 20.   ———— 4. 30-34.   ———— 7. 45-49.
———— 2. 20-24.   ———— 5. 35-39.   ———— 8. 50-59.
———— 3. 25-29.   ———— 6. 40-44.   ———— 9. 60 or over.

A7. How many children do you have?
———— 0. None.
———— (Simply write in number of children; if none, skip to q. A9).

A8. Are any of your children three years of age or younger?
———— (Write in the number: 0, 1, 2, etc.)

A9. Does anyone live with you besides your wife (husband) and children?
———— 0. No one.
———— 1. Your parent(s).
———— 2. Your spouse's parent(s).

_____ 3. Another relative of yours.
_____ 4. Another of your spouse's relatives.
_____ 5. One or more non-relatives.

A10. How far did you go in school?

_____ 1. 0-6 years.
_____ 2. 7-9 years.
_____ 3. Some high school, but did not gradu-ate.

_____ 4. High school graduate.
_____ 5. Some college, or voca-tional training.
_____ 6. College graduate.
_____ 7. Post-graduate study.

A11. What kind of work do you (does your husband, if talking to wife) do? (Describe in detail. If both husband and wife work, describe both of their occupations). ....
....

A12. How long have you lived in this community (city)?

_____ 1. All your life.
_____ 2. Ten or more years, but not all your life.

_____ 3. Between 3 and 9 years.
_____ 4. One or two years.
_____ 5. Less than one year.

A13. Where was the place located that you moved here from?

_____ 1. Within 50 miles.
_____ 2. 50-100 miles away.
_____ 3. Elsewhere in North Carolina.
_____ 4. South Carolina or +100 miles in Vir-ginia.

_____ 5. Another Southern state.
_____ 6. Northeastern U.S.
_____ 7. Midwestern U.S.
_____ 8. Far Western U.S.
_____ 9. Elsewhere (Specify: ... .).

A14. Did you live:

_____ 1. On a farm.
_____ 2. Outside of town, but not on a farm.
_____ 3. In a town of less than 5,000.
_____ 4. In a town of 5,000-25,000 people.
_____ 5. In a town of 25,000-100,000 people.
_____ 6. In a city of over 100,000 people.

A15. Altogether, how many different communities have you lived in since your marriage which were 50 or more miles from here and from each other? (Exclude present city of residence). _____ (Simply insert number)

A16. Have you ever lived in the same community with your parents since you have been married?

_____ 1. No.
_____ 2. Yes, but not during the past two years.

———— 3. Yes, up until very recently.
———— 4. Yes, the whole time.
———— 5. Yes, for the last year or so.
———— 6. Yes, off and on.
———— 7. Yes, for the past several years.

A17. How do you feel in general about moving?
———— 1. I would not want to move if I could possibly help it.
———— 2. Moving bothers me some, and I would rather not do it.
———— 3. I don't mind moving if there is a good reason.
———— 4. I think moving every so often from place to place is a valuable experience.

A18. How would you say you feel about being with people?
———— 1. Enjoy it very much.
———— 2. Enjoy it to some extent.
———— 3. Do not enjoy it too much.

* * *

A33. We have been talking about you and your spouse up to now. Let's talk some about the rest of your family. Do you believe you and your spouse agree on how frequently you should be in touch with any of *your* relatives?
———— 1. Yes, we agree completely.
———— 2. We agree for the most part.
———— 3. We disagree to some extent.
———— 4. We disagree completely.

A34. Are your parents still living?
———— 1. Yes, both are liv-   ———— 3. Mother only is living.
ing.   ———— 4. Neither parent is alive.
———— 2. Father only is liv-
ing.
(If neither is living, skip to q. *A38,* and then to *B11.* If only one is living, ask questions pertaining to that one).

A35. If both are living, are they living together?
———— 1. Yes.
———— 2. No. (If no, talk about the one with whom contact is most frequent)

A36. Where are they (he, she) living?
———— 1. In this city.   ———— 5. South Carolina or
———— 2. Within 50 miles.   +100 miles in Vir-
———— 3. 50-100 miles.   ginia.
———— 4. Elsewhere in No.   ———— 6. Another Southern state.
Carolina.   ———— 7. Northeastern U.S.

———— 8. Midwestern U.S.   ———— 0. Other (Specify: ....
———— 9. Far Western U.S.   ....).

A37. Do they (he, she) live:
———— 1. On a farm.
———— 2. Outside of town, but not on a farm.
———— 3. In a town of less than 5,000.
———— 4. In a town of 5,000-25,000 people.
———— 5. In a town of 25,000-100,000 people.
———— 6. In a city of 100,000 plus people.

A38. What kind of work does (did) your father do? (Ask even if not
living). ....
(If father dead, skip to q. *A43*).

A39. How close would you say you are in your feelings toward your
father?
———— 1. Not too close.   ———— 4. Quite close.
———— 2. Somewhat close.   ———— 5. Extremely close.
———— 3. Fairly close.

A40. How far did your father go in school?
———— 1. 0-6 years.   ———— 4. High school graduate.
———— 2. 7-9 years.   ———— 5. Some college, or voca-
———— 3. Some high school,   tional training.
        but did not gradu-   ———— 6. College graduate.
        ate.   ———— 7. Post-graduate study.

A41. Do you and your father agree in your ideas and opinions about the
things *you* consider really important in life?
———— 1. Yes, completely.   ———— 3. Yes, to some extent.
———— 2. Yes, to a great ex-   ———— 4. No, very little.
        tent.

A42. Would you like to be the kind of person your father is?
———— 1. Not at all.   ———— 4. In most ways.
———— 2. In just a few ways.   ———— 5. Yes, completely.
———— 3. In several ways.
(If mother is dead, skip to q. *A47*).

A43. How close would you say you feel to your mother?
———— 1. Not to close.   ———— 4. Quite close.
———— 2. Somewhat close.   ———— 5. Extremely close.
———— 3. Fairly close.

A44. How far did your mother go in school?
———— 1. 0-6 years.   ———— 5. Some college, or voca-
———— 2. 7-9 years.   tional training.
———— 3. Some high school.   ———— 6. College graduate.
———— 4. High school gradu-   ———— 7. Post-graduate study.
        ate.

A45. Do you and your mother agree in your ideas and opinions about the things *you* consider to be really important in life?

_____ 1. Yes, completely.   _____ 3. Yes, to some extent

_____ 2. Yes, to a great ex-   _____ 4. No, very little.
tent.

A46. Would you like to be the kind of person your mother is?

_____ 1. Not at all.   _____ 4. In most ways.

_____ 2. In just a few ways.   _____ 5. Yes, completely.

_____ 3. In several ways.

A47. In the past two years or so, about how often have you seen your parents (or the one we are talking about)?

_____ 1. Every day.   _____ 6. Several times a year.

_____ 2. More than once a   _____ 7. About once a year.
week.   _____ 8. Less than once a year.

_____ 3. Once a week.   _____ 9. Never.

_____ 4. More than monthly.

_____ 5. About once a
month.

A48. If you have not seen them (him, her) at all, how long has it been since you have seen them? (Insert no. of years). _____ (Skip to q. *A63*).

A49. Whose idea is it usually that you get together?

_____ 1. Your idea.

_____ 2. Your spouse's idea.

_____ 3. Your parents' idea.

_____ 4. Sometimes your idea, and sometimes your parents.

_____ 5. No one suggests it; we get together from habit or tradition.

A50-A62. In the past two years or so (or since moving here, if less than two years), how often have you and your parent(s) engaged in the following types of activities together? (1 = more than once a month, 2 = several times a year, 3 = once or twice, 4 = never).

_____ A50. Commercial recreation.

_____ A51. Home recreation, such as picnics, card playing, etc.

_____ A52. Outdoor recreation, such as fishing, hunting, or camping.

_____ A53. Brief drop-in visits for conversation.

_____ A54. Vacation visits.

_____ A55. Large family reunions (including aunts, uncles, cousins).

_____ A56. Emergencies of any sort (sickness, death, etc.).

_____ A57. Working together at the same location, or occupation.

_____ A58. Baby sitting.

_____ A59. Happy occasions, such as birthdays or Christmas.

_____ A60. Attending the same church or religious group.

_____ A61. Shopping together.

_____ A62. Other (Specify: ....).

A63. Do you wish you could see your parents more or less often than you do?
_____ 1. Much less often.
_____ 2. A little less often.
_____ 3. You see them just often enough.
_____ 4. A little more often.
_____ 5. Much more often.

A64. How often do you (your spouse) write letters to *your* parents.
_____ 1. Never.
_____ 2. Only on special occasions, such as birthdays or Christmas.
_____ 3. Several times a year.
_____ 4. About once a month.
_____ 5. Several times a month.
_____ 6. Once a week or more.

A65. Do you ever talk to your parents on the telephone?
_____ 1. No, never.
_____ 2. Yes, on special occasions, or in emergencies.
_____ 3. Several times a year.
_____ 4. About once a month.
_____ 5. Several times a month.
_____ 6. Once a week or more.
(If never, omit q. *A66*).

A66. Do you usually call them, or do they call you?
_____ 1. You almost always call them.
_____ 2. You call a little more often.
_____ 3. You and they call equally often.
_____ 4. They call a little more often.
_____ 5. They almost always call you.

A67-A70. Now I want us to look a little deeper into your relations with your parent(s), to see if we can get at *why* you keep in touch. There are several reasons people might give for keeping in touch with their parents. As I read each of the following reasons, tell me if it is very important, somewhat important, or unimportant, in your relation with your parents:

	Very Impt.	Some. Impt.	Unimpt.
A67. First, you feel you ought to, or have an obligation to keep in touch.	1. _____	2. _____	3. _____
A68. You need their help in some way.	1. _____	2. _____	3. _____
A69. They need your help in some way.	1. _____	2. _____	3. _____

A70. You simply enjoy keeping in
touch.   1. _____ 2. _____ 3. _____

A71-A78. In the past two years or so, how often have you received the following kinds of help from your parents? (Use 1, 2, 3, or 4).

_____ A71. Advice on a decision you had to make.

_____ A72. Help on special occasions, such as childbirth, sickness.

_____ A73. Help in caring for your children, such as baby sitting.

_____ A74. Financial assistance, such as money or a loan.

_____ A75. Gifts, other than the reciprocal occasions.

_____ A76. Hand work: such as garden produce, sewing, yard work.

_____ A77. Job placement.

_____ A78. Other (Specify: ....).

B5-B8. In the past two years or so, have you given your parents any specific help you can think of? If so, how often? (1, 2, 3, or 4).

_____ B5. Help in their home or yard.

_____ B6. Taking them to the doctor, or caring for them when sick.

_____ B7. Financial aid.

_____ B8. Non-reciprocal gifts, or other miscellaneous.

B9. Would you say you feel closer to your parents now than you did when growing up, or not as close?

_____ 1. Don't feel as close.

_____ 2. Feel closer to father, but not to mother.

_____ 3. Feel closer to mother, but not to father.

_____ 4. Feel closer to both parents.

_____ 5. Feel about the same.

B10. Why would you say you feel as you do about them now? ....
....

*   *   *

B11-B12. How many brothers and sisters do you have? (Insert number).

_____ B11. Brothers.

_____ B12. Sisters. (If no brothers or sisters, skip to q. B66).

B13. What is the first name of the brother or sister who is *closest* to you *in age?* 1. Brother _____. 2. Sister _____.

B14. Where does he (she) live?

_____ 1. In this city.

_____ 2. Within 50 miles.

_____ 3. 50-100 miles.

_____ 4. Elsewhere in No. Carolina.

_____ 5. South Carolina or +100 miles in Virginia.

_____ 6. Another Southern state.

_____ 7. Northeastern U.S.

_____ 8. Midwestern U.S.

_____ 9. Far Western U.S.

_____ 0. Other (Specify: ....).

B15. Is your brother (sister) older or younger than you?
———— 1. Five or more years older.
———— 2. Four or less years older.
———— 3. A twin.
———— 4. Four or less years younger.
———— 5. Five or more years younger.

B16. What is your brother's (sister's) marital status?
———— 1. Unmarried, living with parents.
———— 2. Unmarried, not living with parents, but within 50 miles.
———— 3. Unmarried, living more than 50 miles from parents.
———— 4. Married, living within 50 miles of parents.
———— 5. Married, living more than 50 miles from parents.
———— 6. Married, parents not living.
———— 7. Unmarried, parents not living.
(If unmarried, skip to q. *B19*)

B17. How would you say you feel about his wife (her husband)?
———— 1. Like her (him) a lot.
———— 2. Like her (him) some.
———— 3. Don't feel one way or the other about her (him).
———— 4. Dislike her (him) a little.
———— 5. Dislike her (him) a lot.

B18. Why would you say you feel as you do about her (him)? ....
....

B19. What kind of work does your brother (brother-in-law, unmarried sister) do? ....

B20. How close would you say you feel toward your brother (sister)?
———— 1. Not too close.   ———— 4. Quite close.
———— 2. Somewhat close.   ———— 5. Extremely close.
———— 3. Fairly close.

B21. How far did your brother (sister) go in school (or expect to go)?
———— 1. 0-6 years.   ———— 5. Some college or voca-
———— 2. 7-9 years.   tional training.
———— 3. Some high school.   ———— 6. College graduate.
———— 4. High school gradu-   ———— 7. Post-graduate study.
       ate.

B22. Do you and your brother (sister) agree in your ideas and opinions about the things which *you* consider important in life?
———— 1. Yes, completely.   ———— 3. Yes, to some extent.
———— 2. Yes, to a great ex-   ———— 4. No, very little.
       tent.

B23. Would you like to be the kind of person your brother (sister) is?
——— 1. Not at all.   ——— 4. In most ways.
——— 2. In just a few ways.   ——— 5. Yes, completely.
——— 3. In several ways.

B24. Within the past two years, how often have you seen your brother (sister)?
——— 1. Every day.   ——— 6. Several times yearly.
——— 2. More than once a   ——— 7. About once a year.
     week.   ——— 8. Less than once a year.
——— 3. Once a week.   ——— 9. Never.
——— 4. More than monthly.
——— 5. About once a
     month.

B25. If you have not seen him (her) at all, how long has it been since you have seen him (her)? (Insert no. of years). ...... (Skip to q. *B40*).

B26. Whose idea is it usually that you get together?
——— 1. Your idea.
——— 2. Your spouse's idea.
——— 3. Your sibling and/or his wife's (her husband's) idea.
——— 4. Sometimes your idea, and sometimes theirs.
——— 5. Someone else's idea, such as parents, or circumstantial.

B27-B39. In the past two years or so, how often have you and your brother (sister) engaged in the following types of activities together? (Use 1, 2, 3, or 4).
——— B27. Commercial rec-   ——— B34. Working at the same
     reation.   location or job.
——— B28. Home recreation.   ——— B35. Baby sitting.
——— B29. Outdoor recrea-   ——— B36. Happy occasions.
     tion.   ——— B37. Attending the same re-
——— B30. Brief conversa-   ligious group.
     tion visits.   ——— B38. Shopping together.
——— B31. Vacation visits.   ——— B39. Other (Specify: .....
——— B32. Large family re-   ....).
     unions.
——— B33. Emergencies of
     any sort.

B40. Do you wish you could see your sibling more or less often than you do?
——— 1. Much less often.   ——— 4. A little more often.
——— 2. A little less often.   ——— 5. Much more often.
——— 3. You see them just
     often enough.

B41-B42. In the past two years or so have you given any help to, or received help from your brother (sister)? For example, financial, advice, etc. (Note how often). ....

B43. How often do you (your spouse) write to your brother (sister)?
——— 1. Never.   ——— 4. About once a month.
——— 2. Only on special oc-   ——— 5. Several times a month.
          casions.   ——— 6. Once a week or more.
——— 3. Several   times   a
          year.

B44. Do you ever talk with your brother (sister) on the telephone?
——— 1. No, never.   ——— 4. About once a month.
——— 2. Yes, on special oc-   ——— 5. Several times a month.
          casions   or   emer-   ——— 6. Once a week or more.
          gencies.
——— 3. Several   times   a
          year.
(If never, omit q. *B45*).

B45. Do you usually call him (her), or does he (she) call you?
——— 1. You almost always call him (her).
——— 2. You call a little more often.
——— 3. You and he (she) call about equally often.
——— 4. He (she) calls a little more often.
——— 5. He (she) almost always calls you.

B46-B47. Once again, let's try to get at *why* you keep in touch with your brother (sister). How important would you say the following reasons for keeping in touch with your brother (sister) are to you?
B46. You feel you ought to, or   *Very Impt. Some Impt. Unimpt.*
have an obligation to keep
in touch.   1. ——— 2. ——— 3. ———
B47. You simply enjoy keeping
in touch.   1. ——— 2. ——— 3. ———

B48. Would you say that you feel closer to your brother (sister) now than you did when you were growing up, or not as close?
——— 1. Don't   feel   any-   ——— 3. About the same.
          where near as close. ——— 4. A little closer.
——— 2. Not quite as close.   ——— 5. Very much closer.

B49. Why do you think you feel as you do now about him (her)? .....
    ....
(If respondent has but one sibling, skip to q. *B66*).

*   *   *

B50. Now tell me a word or two about your other brothers and sisters. Do you have a brother or sister to whom you feel closer than you do to the one we have been talking about?

—— 1. Yes, a brother.
—— 2. Yes, a sister.
—— 3. No, I feel less close to the others.
—— 4. I feel about the same toward all my brothers and sisters.
(If *no* or *same*, skip to q. *B55*).

B51. Why do you feel as close to him (her) as you do? . . . .
. . . .

B52. Where does he (she) live?
—— 1. In this city.
—— 2. Within 50 miles.
—— 3. 50-100 miles.
—— 4. Elsewhere in No. Carolina.
—— 5. South Carolina or +100 miles in Virginia.
—— 6. Another Southern state.
—— 7. Northeastern U.S.
—— 8. Midwestern U.S.
—— 9. Far Western U.S.
—— 0. Other (Specify: . . . .).

B53. What is your relation to this brother (sister)? Is he (she) your:
—— 1. Oldest brother.
—— 2. Older brother.
—— 3. Younger brother.
—— 4. Youngest brother.
—— 5. Oldest sister.
—— 6. Older sister.
—— 7. Younger sister.
—— 8. Youngest sister.

B54. How often do you see him (her)?
—— 1. Every day.
—— 2. More than once a week.
—— 3. Once a week.
—— 4. Several times monthly.
—— 5. About once a month.
—— 6. Several times a year.
—— 7. About once a year.
—— 8. Less than once a year.
—— 9. Never.

B55. Where do you come in relation to your brothers and sisters? You are:
—— 1. Oldest child.
—— 2. Next to oldest child.
—— 3. A middle child.
—— 4. Next to youngest child.
—— 5. Youngest child.

B56-B65. We have talked about one or two of your brothers and sisters. Where do the others, not talked about, live? (Insert number).

_____ B56. In this city.

_____ B57. Within 50 miles.

_____ B58. 50-100 miles.

_____ B59. Elsewhere in No. Carolina.

_____ B60. South Carolina or +100 miles in Virginia.

_____ B61. Another Southern state.

_____ B62. Northeastern U.S.

_____ B63. Midwestern U.S.

_____ B64. Far Western U.S.

_____ B65. Other, including deceased (Specify: ....).

B67-B69. Let's talk a few minutes about some of your other relatives. Think about the grandparents, aunts, uncles, cousins, etc., that you have. Where do those whom you would recognize if you passed them on the street live? (Just own relatives and their affines, not spouse's relatives. Insert number).

_____ In this city.

_____ Within 50 miles.

_____ 50-100 miles.

_____ Elsewhere in No. Carolina.

_____ South Carolina in +100 miles in Virginia.

_____ Another Southern state.

_____ Northeastern U.S.

_____ Midwestern U.S.

_____ Far Western U.S.

_____ Other (Specify: ....).

B66. Let's see now, that totals up to .... Does that sound about right)?

B70. Now, think of the cousin whom you *know* the *best*. What is his or her first name, so we can talk about him (her)? ....
In what way is he (she) related to you?

_____ 1. Mother's sister's son.

_____ 2. Mother's brother's son.

_____ 3. Mother's sister's daughter.

_____ 4. Mother's brother's daughter.

_____ 5. Father's sister's son.

_____ 6. Father's brother's son.

_____ 7. Father's sister's daughter.

_____ 8. Father's brother's daughter.

_____ 9. Other cousin (Specify relation: ....).

B71. You have said that you know this cousin best. Just how well do you know him (her)?

_____ 1. Not well at all.

_____ 2. Not too well.

_____ 3. Fairly well.

_____ 4. Quite well.

_____ 5. Extremely well.

B72. Where does he (she) live?
———— 1. In this city.
———— 2. Within 50 miles.
———— 3. 50-100 miles.
———— 4. Elsewhere in No. Carolina.
———— 5. South Carolina or +100 miles in Virginia.
———— 6. Another Southern state.
———— 7. Northeastern U.S.
———— 8. Midwestern U.S.
———— 9. Far Western U.S.
———— 0. Other (Specify: ....
......................).

B73. Did you ever live in the same community with him (her)?
———— 1. No, never.
———— 2. No, but have lived within 50 miles.
———— 3. No, but spent summers together while growing up.
———— 4. Yes, for a few years.
———— 5. Yes, while you were growing up.
———— 6. Yes, most of your life.

B74. Is your cousin older or younger than you?
———— 1. 5+ years older than you.
———— 2. 4— years older.
———— 3. 4— years younger.
———— 4. 5+ years younger.

B75. What kind of work does your cousin (cousin's husband) do? .....
....

B76. How close would you say you feel toward your cousin?
———— 1. Not too close.
———— 2. Somewhat close.
———— 3. Fairly close.
———— 4. Quite close.
———— 5. Extremely close.

B77. How far did your cousin (or does your cousin expect to) go in school?
———— 1. 0-6 years.
———— 2. 7-9 years.
———— 3. Some high school.
———— 4. High school graduate.
———— 5. Some college or vocational training.
———— 6. College graduate.
———— 7. Post-graduate study.
———— 8. Don't really know.

B78. Do you and your cousin agree in your ideas and opinions about the things *you* consider important in life?
———— 1. Yes, completely.
———— 2. Yes, to a great extent.
———— 3. Yes, to some extent.
———— 4. No, very little.

C5. Would you like to be the kind of person your cousin is?
———— 1. Not at all.
———— 2. In just a few ways.
———— 3. In several ways.
———— 4. In most ways.
———— 5. Yes, completely.

C6. Within the past two years or so, how often have you seen your cousin?

_____ 1. Every day.   _____ 6. Several times a year.

_____ 2. More than once a   _____ 7. About once a year.
       week.   _____ 8. Less than once a year.

_____ 3. Once a week.   _____ 9. Never.

_____ 4. Several times
       monthly.

_____ 5. About once a
       month.

C7. If you have not seen him (her) at all, how long has it been since you have seen him (her)? (Insert no. of years). _____ (Skip to q. *C22*).

C8. Whose idea is it usually that you get together?

_____ 1. Your idea.

_____ 2. Your spouse's idea.

_____ 3. Your cousin's and/or his (her) spouse's idea.

_____ 4. Sometimes your idea, and sometimes his (hers).

_____ 5. No one's idea; circumstances bring you together.

C9-C21. In the past two years or so, how often have you and your cousin engaged in the following types of activities? (Use 1, 2, 3, or 4).

_____ C9. Commercial rec-   _____ C17. Baby sitting.
       reation.   _____ C18. Happy occasions.

_____ C10. Home recreation.   _____ C19. Attending the same re-

_____ C11. Outdoor recrea-   ligious group.
        tion.   _____ C20. Shopping together.

_____ C12. Brief conversa-   _____ C21. Other (Specify: . . . . .
        tion visits.   . . . .).

_____ C13. Vacation visits.

_____ C14. Large family re-
        unions.

_____ C15. Emergencies of
        any sort.

_____ C16. Working at the
        same location or
        job.

C22. Do you wish you could see your cousin more or less often than you do?

_____ 1. Much less often.   _____ 4. A little more often.

_____ 2. A little less often.   _____ 5. Much more often.

_____ 3. You see him (her)
       just often enough.

C23. How often do you (your spouse) write to your cousin?
     _____ 1. Never.
     _____ 2. Only on special occasions.
     _____ 3. Several times a year.
     _____ 4. About once a month.
     _____ 5. Several times a month.
     _____ 6. Once a week or more.

C24. Do you ever talk with your cousin on the telephone?
     _____ 1. No, never.
     _____ 2. On special occasions, or in emergencies.
     _____ 3. Several times a year.
     _____ 4. About once a month.
     _____ 5. Several times a month.
     _____ 6. Once a week or more.

(If *never*, omit *C25*).

C25. Do you (your spouse) usually call your cousin, or vice versa?
     _____ 1. You almost always call her (him).
     _____ 2. You call a little more often.
     _____ 3. You call each other about equally often.
     _____ 4. He (she) calls a little more often.
     _____ 5. He (she) almost always calls you.

C26-C27. If you have been in touch with your cousin, how important a reason for keeping in touch is the feeling that you *ought* to, or have an obligation to keep in touch? Is this a very important, somewhat important, or unimportant reason to you? (1, 2, or 3). C26. .... How important a reason for keeping in touch is the fact that you simply *enjoy* him (her), and want to keep in touch? C27. ....

C28. Would you say that you feel closer now to your cousin than when you were growing up, or not as close?
     _____ 1. Nowhere near as close.
     _____ 2. Not quite as close.
     _____ 3. About the same.
     _____ 4. A little closer.
     _____ 5. Very much closer.

C29-C31. Are there any of your grandparents, aunts, uncles, or cousins with whom you are in touch more often, or to whom you feel closer, than with the cousin we have been talking about? (If not, put 0 in each space. If so, insert number).
     _____ C29. Grandparents.
     _____ C30. Aunts and uncles.
     _____ C31. Other cousins.

C74. One final question: we have been talking about all sorts of different relatives. Now, *you* know what is really important, or really matters, to you in life. What I want to know is this. Are your relatives one of the most important aspects of your life (excluding your spouse and children), or are they somewhat important, or are they relatively unimportant in your total scheme of things? (Insert 1 for most important, 2 for somewhat, or 3 for unimportant). ———.

Also included, as A19-A32 and C32-C73, were q's regarding spouse, friends, and in-laws. These questions were not utilized in the present analysis and are thus omitted from Appendix A.

GLOSSARY OF KEY TERMS

Affines: Those individuals related to one by marriage, e.g., an aunt's husband or a cousin's wife. In the present study they are included in the enumeration of the respondent's kin network.

Age-near sibling: An abbreviated designation of the sibling who is closest to the respondent in age. He or she is the focus of the greater part of the sibling discussion in the Greensboro study.

Ascending and lateral kin: Ascending kin are those of generations previous to that of *ego,* including aunts, uncles, grandparents, and parents. Lateral kin are those of *ego's* own generation, especially siblings and cousins.

Communication, interaction, and contact: Communication consists of letter writing and telephoning, i.e., the forms of indirect or non-face-to-face contact. Interaction signifies face-to-face contact, or actually being together. Contact is used to refer to communication and/or interaction, with a synonymous term being "keeping in touch." Thus, communication + interaction = contact.

Contact Patterns: This term means contact of any of the various sorts delineated in the study, including social activities, attendance of the same organization, home visits, and so on, with a specified frequency of recurrence. Though somewhat arbitrary, a contact pattern is considered to be present if a given type of activity has occurred three or more times a year for the past two years.

Kin Acquaintances: Kin whom the individual would recognize if he passed them on the street. This includes Firth's intimate and effective kin, and possibly a few of his nominal kin who are recognizable but with whom contact is no longer maintained.

Kin Network or Kindred: Phrases utilized almost interchangeably to signify the total numbers of the individual's kin acquaintances. We have used network in preference to "kin group," due to its non-localized nature. Furthermore, the term "extended family" has been avoided except when quoting. Though extremely prevalent in the sociological literature on kinship, Raymond Firth has rightly noted in an essay on urban-industrial kinship (see Halmos volume in bibliography) that the term

211

"extended family" has anthropological connotations involving a corporate lineal character, i.e., three generations or more with cooperative productivity, common ownership of assets, and frequently a shared dwelling location.

Nominal, effective, and intimate kin: Nominal kin are those known to exist, but with whom the individual maintains no contact. Effective kin are those with whom contact is maintained, but with whom relationships are relatively shallow. Intimate kin are those closest to the individual, with whom he would be considered to have a primary relationship.

Occupational mobility, stability, and disparity: In the present study occupational mobility refers to an intergenerational move from a blue-collar household (based on father's occupation) into a white-collar occupation, or from a white-collar household into a blue-collar occupation. Occupational stability means holding an occupation within the same dichotomous category in which the father's occupation is found, whether blue-collar or white collar. Occupational disparity indicates a present difference between occupational positions, e.g., two brothers, one of whom holds a white-collar position and the other a blue-collar position.

Secondary kin and kin of orientation: These mutually exclusive categories are used to distinguish between degrees of kinship among young adults. The kin of orientation includes one's parents and siblings, or those from the same family of orientation. Secondary kin are all others: grandparents, aunts, uncles, cousins, and others.

BIBLIOGRAPHY

A. Annotated

ADAMS, BERT N. "Interaction Theory and the Social Network," *Sociometry*, 30 (1967), 64-78. A discussion of consensus and positive concern as attributes of social relations, differentially characteristic of friends and kin, and of different kin.

BOTT, ELIZABETH. *Family and Social Network*. London: Tavistock Publications, Ltd., 1957. An insightful look at the kin and social networks of twenty London families. Introduces notions of comparative use of kin, of certain kin being intimate regardless of distance, and of occupational mobility having little direct relation to kin interaction.

CUMMING, ELAINE, and DAVID M. SCHNEIDER. "Sibling Solidarity: a Property of American Kinship," *American Anthropologist*, 63 (1961), 498-507. One of the few analyses of adult sibling relations, including the idea of cousins as sibling surrogates.

FIRTH, RAYMOND. "Family and Kinship in Industrial Society," *The Development of Industrial Societies*, Paul Halmos, editor. The Sociological Review Monograph No. 8, Keele: University of Keele, 1964, 65-87. A recent discussion of urban kinship, which indicates both the dimensions of kin networks and the functionality of kin obligations.

GARIGUE, PHILIP. "French Canadian Kinship and Urban Life," *American Anthropologist*, 58 (1956), 1090-1101. An excellent article on a subgroup in urban Canada. It includes many testable generalizations regarding kin relations in an urban setting.

KOMAROVSKY, MIRRA. *Blue-Collar Marriage*. New York: Random House, Inc., 1964. A recent study of working-class family relations which is especially useful in understanding relations with aging parents.

LEMASTERS, E. E. "Social Class Mobility and Family Integration," *Marriage and Family Living*, 16 (1954), 226-232. An early study noting the disruptive effects upon family relations of differential sibling mobility.

LITWAK, EUGENE. "Geographic Mobility and Extended Family Cohesion," *American Sociological Review*, 25 (1960), 385-394.

———. "Occupational Mobility and Extended Family Cohesion," *American Sociological Review*, 25 (1960), 9-21.

213

————. "The Use of Extended Family Groups in the Achievement of Family Goals," *Social Problems,* 7 (1959-1960), 177-187. The three Litwak articles postulate the manner in which kindred can and sometimes do function to aid the individual in his adjustment to urban-industrial life.

PARSONS, TALCOTT. "The Kinship System of the Contemporary United States," *American Anthropologist,* 45 (1943), 22-38. The classic statement of the isolation of the urban nuclear family and functional insignificance of kin in urban-industrial society.

REISS, PAUL J. "The Extended Kinship System: Correlates of and Attitudes on Frequency of Interaction," *Marriage and Family Living,* 24 (1962), 333-339. A statement, drawn from his dissertation, on frequency of interaction and certain accompanying attitudes. Brief and readable.

ROBINS, LEE N., and MIRODA TOMANEC. "Closeness to Blood Relatives Outside the Immediate Family," *Marriage and Family Living,* 24 (1962), 340-346. A study of kin interaction, which deals with sex and stratum differences in kin involvement.

SCHNEIDER, DAVID M., and GEORGE C. HOMANS. "Kinship Terminology and the American Kinship System," *American Anthropologist,* 57 (1955), 1194-1208. Discusses terminology and states the deleterious effect of social mobility upon kin ties.

SUSSMAN, MARVIN. "The Isolated Nuclear Family: Fact or Fiction?," *Social Problems,* 6 (1959), 333-340.

————, and LEE BURCHINAL. "Kin Family Network: Unheralded Structure in Current Conceptualizations of Family Functioning," *Marriage and Family Living,* 24 (1962), 231-240. These are two examples of Sussman's work showing the manner in which kin relations function in the urban United States.

WILLMOTT, PETER, and MICHAEL YOUNG. *Family and Class in a London Suburb.* London: Routledge and Kegan Paul, 1960.

YOUNG, MICHAEL, and PETER WILLMOTT. *Family and Kinship in East London.* Baltimore, Md.: Penguin Books, 1964. These two volumes are the best books to date on kinship in an urban setting. Both focus primarily upon parent—adult offspring relations, and the latter deals exclusively with a working-class London borough, but they are nevertheless an excellent introduction to kin of orientation functioning.

B. Other Sources

ABU-LUGHOD, JANET. "Migrant Adjustment to City Life: The Egyptian Case," *American Journal of Sociology*, 67 (1961), 22-32.

ADAMS, BERT N. "Occupational Position, Mobility, and the Kin of Orientation," *American Sociological Review*, 32 (1967), 364-377.

————. "The Middle-Class Adult and His Widowed or Still-Married Mother," forthcoming in *Social Problems*.

ALBRECHT, RUTH. "The Parental Responsibilities of Grandparents," *Marriage and Family Living*, 16 (1954), 201-204.

ALDOUS, JOAN. "Urbanization, the Extended Family, and Kinship Ties in West Africa," *Social Forces*, 41 (1962), 6-12.

AXELROD, MORRIS. "Urban Structure and Social Participation," *American Sociological Review*, 21 (1956), 13-18.

BELL, WENDELL, and MARION D. BOAT. "Urban Neighborhoods and Informal Social Relations," *American Journal of Sociology*, 62 (1957), 391-398.

BENDIX, REINHARD, and BENNETT BERGER. "Images of Society and Problems of Concept Formation in Sociology," *Symposium on Sociological Theory*, Llewellyn Gross, editor. Evanston, Ill.: Row, Peterson, and Company, 1959, 95-113.

BENNETT, JOHN W., and LEO A. DESPRES. "Kinship and Instrumental Activities," *American Anthropologist*, 62 (1960), 254-267.

BERGER, BENNETT. *Working-Class Suburb*. Berkeley and Los Angeles: University of California Press, 1960.

BERKOWITZ, LEONARD, and LOUISE R. DANIELS. "Affecting the Salience of the Social Responsibility Norm: Effects of Past Help on the Response to Dependency Relationships," *Journal of Abnormal and Social Psychology*, 68 (1964), 275-281.

BLALOCK, HUBERT M., JR. *Social Statistics*. New York: McGraw-Hill Book Company, Inc., 1960.

BLITSTEN, DOROTHY. *The World of the Family*. New York: Random House, Inc., 1963.

BLUMBERG, LEONARD, and ROBERT R. BELL. "Urban Migration and Kinship Ties," *Social Problems*, 6 (1959), 328-333.

BLUMER, HERBERT. "Attitudes and the Social Act," *Social Problems*, 3 (1955), 59-65.

BOSSARD, JAMES H. S. and ELEANOR STOKER BOLL. *The Large Family System*. Philadelphia, Pa.: University of Pennsylvania Press, 1956.

BRONFENBRENNER, URIE. "The Changing American Child—A Speculative Analysis," *The Journal of Social Issues*, 17 (1961), 6-18.

216 / KINSHIP IN AN URBAN SETTING

BROWN, JAMES S., HARRY K. SCHWARZWELLER, and JOSEPH J. MANGALAM. "Kentucky Mountain Migration and the Stem-Family: An American Variation on a Theme by Le Play," *Rural Sociology*, 28 (1963), 48-69.

CAPLOW, THEODORE. "Further Development of a Theory of Coalitions in the Triad," *American Journal of Sociology*, 64 (1959), 488-493.

CODERE, HELEN. "A Genealogical Study of Kinship in the United States," *Psychiatry*, 18 (1955), 65-79.

COULT, ALAN D., and ROBERT W. HABENSTEIN. "The Study of Extended Kinship in Urban Society," *Sociological Quarterly*, 3 (1962), 141-145.

CUMMING, ELAINE, and WILLIAM E. HENRY. *Growing Old: The Process of Disengagement*. New York: Basic Books, Inc., 1961.

CURTIS, RICHARD F. "Differential Association and the Stratification of the Urban Community," *Social Forces*, 42 (1963), 68-77.

DINKEL, ROBERT M. "Attitudes of Children Toward Supporting Aged Parents," *American Sociological Review*, 9 (1944), 370-379.

———. "Parent-Child Conflict in Minnesota Families," *American Sociological Review*, 8 (1943), 412-419.

DOTSON, FLOYD. "Patterns of Voluntary Association Among Urban Working-Class Families," *American Sociological Review*, 16 (1951), 687-693.

DYNES, RUSSELL R., ALFRED C. CLARKE, and SIMON DINITZ. "Levels of Occupational Aspiration: Some Aspects of Family Experience as a Variable," *American Sociological Review*, 21 (1956), 212-215.

ELDER, GLEN H., JR., and CHARLES E. BOWERMAN. "Family Size, Sex Composition, and Child Rearing," *American Sociological Review*, 28 (1963), 891-905.

ELLIS, ROBERT A., and W. CLAYTON LANE. "Structural Supports for Upward Mobility," *American Sociological Review*, 28 (1963), 743-756.

FARBER, BERNARD. *Family: Organization and Interaction*. San Francisco: Chandler Publishing Company, 1964.

FESTINGER, LEON, STANLEY SCHACHTER, and KURT W. BACK. *Social Pressures in Informal Groups*. New York: Harper and Brothers, Publishers, 1950.

FIRTH, RAYMOND, and J. DJAMOUR. "Kinship in South Borough," *Two Studies of Kinship in London*, Raymond Firth, editor. London: London School of Economics Monographs on Social Anthropology, Number 15, 1956.

FORM, WILLIAM H., and JAMES A. GESCHWENDER. "Social Reference Basis of Job Satisfaction: The Case of Manual Workers," *American Sociological Review*, 27 (1962), 228-237.

GERSTL, JOEL. "Leisure, Taste, and Occupational Milieu," *Social Problems*, 9 (1961), 56-68.

GLASSER, PAUL H., and LOIS N. GLASSER. "Role Reversal and Conflict Between Aged Parents and Their Children," *Marriage and Family Living*, 24 (1962), 46-51.

GLICK, PAUL C. *American Families.* New York: John Wiley and Sons, Inc., 1957.

GOODE, WILLIAM JOSIAH. *World Revolution and Family Patterns.* Glencoe, Ill.: The Free Press, 1963.

GOULDNER, ALVIN W. "The Norm of Reciprocity: a Preliminary Statement," *American Sociological Review,* 25 (1960), 161-178.

GRAY, ROBERT M., and TED C. SMITH. "Effect of Employment on Sex Differences in Attitudes Toward the Parental Family," *Marriage and Family Living,* 22 (1960), 36-38.

GREENFIELD, SIDNEY M. "Industrialization and the Family in Sociological Theory," *American Journal of Sociology,* 67 (1961), 312-322.

GREER, SCOTT. "Urbanism Reconsidered: a Comparative Study of Local Areas in a Metropolis," *American Sociological Review,* 21 (1956), 19-25.

———, and ELLA KUBE. "Urbanism and Social Structure: A Los Angeles Study," *Community Structure and Analysis,* Marvin B. Sussman, editor. New York: Thomas Y. Crowell Company, 1959.

GULICK, JOHN, and CHARLES E. BOWERMAN. *Adaptation of Newcomers in the Piedmont Industrial Crescent.* Chapel Hill, No. Carolina: Institute for Research in Social Science, University of North Carolina, 1961.

HALLER, A. O. "The Urban Family," *American Journal of Sociology,* 66 (1961), 621-622.

HILL, REUBEN, J. JOEL MOSS, and CLAUDINE G. WIRTHS. *Eddyville's Families.* Chapel Hill, No. Carolina: Institute for Research in Social Science, University of North Carolina, 1953.

HOLLINGSHEAD, AUGUST B. "Class Differences in Family Stability," *The Annals,* 272 (1950), 39-46.

HOMANS, GEORGE C. *The Human Group.* New York: Harcourt, Brace, and World, Inc., 1950.

———. *Social Behavior: Its Elementary Forms.* New York: Harcourt, Brace, and World, Inc., 1961.

IRISH, DONALD P. "Sibling Interaction: a Neglected Aspect in Family Life Research," *Social Forces,* 42 (1964), 279-288.

KAHL, JOSEPH A. "Educational and Occupational Aspirations of 'Common Man' Boys," *Harvard Educational Review,* 23 (1953), 186-203.

KEPHART, WILLIAM M. "Occupational Level and Marital Disruption," *American Sociological Review,* 20 (1955), 456-465.

KEY, WILLIAM H. "Rural-Urban Differences and the Family," *Sociological Quarterly,* 2 (1961), 49-56.

KOHN, MELVIN L., and ELEANOR E. CARROLL. "Social Class and the Allocation of Parental Responsibilities," *Sociometry,* 23 (1960), 372-392.

KOLLER, MARVIN R. "Studies of Three-Generation Households," *Marriage and Family Living,* 16 (1954), 205-206.

KOMAROVSKY, MIRRA. "Continuities in Family Research: a Case Study," *American Journal of Sociology*, 62 (1956), 42-47.

———. "Functional Analysis of Sex Roles," *American Sociological Review*, 15 (1950), 508-516.

LENSKI, GERHARD. *The Religious Factor*. Garden City, N.Y.: Doubleday and Co., Inc., 1961.

LINTON, RALPH. "The Natural History of the Family," *The Family: Its Function and Destiny*, Ruth Nanda Anshen, editor. New York: Harper and Brothers Publishers, 1949.

LIPSET, SEYMOUR MARTIN and REINHARD BENDIX. *Social Mobility in Industrial Society*, Berkeley: University of California Press, 1964.

———, MARTIN TROW, and JAMES COLEMAN. *Union Democracy*. Garden City, N.Y.: Doubleday Anchor Books, 1962.

MARRIS, PETER. *Widows and Their Families*. London: Routledge and Kegan Paul, 1958.

McGUIRE, CARSON. "Conforming, Mobile, and Divergent Families," *Marriage and Family Living*, 14 (1952), 109-115.

McKINLEY, DONALD GILBERT. *Social Class and Family Life*. New York: The Free Press of Glencoe, 1964.

MOGEY, JOHN. "Family and Community in Urban-Industrial Societies," *Handbook of Marriage and the Family*, Harold T. Christensen, editor. Chicago: Rand McNally and Company, 1964, 501-529.

MONAHAN, THOMAS P. "Divorce by Occupational Level," *Marriage and Family Living*, 17 (1955), 322-324.

MOORE, BARRINGTON, JR. *Political Power and Social Theory*. Cambridge, Mass.: Harvard University Press, 1958.

MUIR, DONAL E., and EUGENE A. WEINSTEIN. "The Social Debt: an Investigation of Lower-Class and Middle-Class Norms of Social Obligation," *American Sociological Review*, 27 (1962), 532-539.

NEWCOMB, THEODORE M. "The Prediction of Interpersonal Attraction," *The American Psychologist*, 11 (1956), 575-586.

———. *The Acquaintanceship Process*. New York: Holt, Rinehart, and Winston, 1961.

———, and GEORGE SVEHLA. "Intra-Family Relationships in Attitude," *Sociometry*, 1 (1937), 180-205.

PARSONS, TALCOTT. "The Social Structure of the Family," *The Family: Its Function and Destiny*, Ruth Nanda Anshen, editor. New York: Harper and Brothers, Publishers, 1949.

PRECKER, JOSEPH A. "Similarity of Valuings as a Factor in the Selection of Peers and Near-Authority Figures," *Journal of Abnormal and Social Psychology*, 47 (1952), 406-414.

QUARANTELLI, ENRICO L. "A Note on the Protective Function of the Family in Disasters," *Marriage and Family Living*, 22 (1960), 263-264.

RAINWATER, LEE, RICHARD P. COLEMAN, and GERALD HANDEL. *Workingman's Wife.* New York: Oceana Publications, Inc., 1959.

REDFIELD, ROBERT. "The Folk Society," *American Journal of Sociology,* 52 (1947), 293-308.

ROGERS, EVERETT, and HANS SEBALD. "A Distinction Between Familism, Family Integration, and Kinship Orientation," *Marriage and Family Living,* 24 (1962), 25-30.

ROGERS, MARIA. "The Human Group: a Critical Review with Suggestions for Some Alternative Hypotheses," *Sociometry,* 14 (1951), 20-31.

SCHORR, ALVIN L. *Filial Responsibility in the Modern American Family.* Washington, D.C.: Social Security Administration, United States Department of Health, Education, and Welfare, 1960.

SCHUSKY, ERNEST L. *Manual for Kinship Analysis.* New York: Holt, Rinehart, and Winston, Inc., 1965.

SECORD, PAUL F., and CARL W. BACKMAN. "Interpersonal Congruency, Perceived Similarity, and Friendship," *Sociometry,* 27 (1964), 115-127.

SHANAS, ETHEL. *Family Relationships of Older People.* Health Information Foundation, 1961.

SHARP, HARRY, and MORRIS AXELROD. "Mutual Aid Among Relatives in an Urban Population," *Principles of Sociology,* Ronald Freedman *et al,* editors. New York: Henry Holt and Company, 1956.

SHERIF, MUZAFER, and CAROLYN W. SHERIF. *Groups in Harmony and Tension.* New York: Harper and Brothers, Publishers, 1953.

SHIBUTANI, TAMOTSU. "Reference Groups as Perspectives," *American Journal of Sociology,* 60 (1955), 562-569.

SJOBERG, GIDEON. "Familial Organization in the Pre-Industrial City," *Marriage and Family Living,* 18 (1956), 30-36.

———. *The Pre-industrial City.* New York: The Free Press of Glencoe, 1960.

SMITH, JOEL, WILLIAM H. FORM, and GREGORY P. STONE. "Local Intimacy in a Middle-Sized City," *American Journal of Sociology,* 60 (1954), 276-284.

SMITH, WILLIAM M., JR. "Family Plans for Later Years," *Marriage and Family Living,* 16 (1954), 36-40.

STREIB, GORDON F. "Family Patterns in Retirement," *The Journal of Social Issues,* 14 (1958), 46-60.

STUCKERT, ROBERT P. "Occupational Mobility and Family Relationships," *Social Forces,* 41 (1963), 301-307.

SUSSMAN, MARVIN. "The Help Pattern in the Middle Class Family," *American Sociological Review,* 18 (1953), 22-28.

———, and LEE BURCHINAL. "Parental Aid to Married Children: Implications for Family Functioning," *Marriage and Family Living,* 24 (1962), 320-332.

SUTCLIFFE, J. P., and B. D. CRABBE. "Incidence and Degrees of Friendship in Urban and Rural Areas," *Social Forces,* 42 (1963), 60-67.

SWEETSER, DORRIAN APPLE. "Asymmetry in Intergenerational Family Relationships," *Social Forces,* 41 (1963), 346-352.

TOWNSEND, PETER. *The Family Life of Old People.* London: Routledge and Kegan Paul, 1957.

TURNER, RALPH H. "Some Family Determinants of Ambition," *Sociology and Social Research,* 46 (1962), 397-411.

United States Department of Commerce, Bureau of the Census. *United State Census of Population: 1960.* Washington, D.C.: U.S. Government Printing Office, 1961, North Carolina.

WEEKS, H. ASHLEY. "Differential Divorce Rate by Occupations," *Social Forces,* 21 (1943), 334-337.

WINCH, ROBERT F. *The Modern Family,* revised edition. New York: Holt, Rinehart, and Winston, 1963.

WIRTH, LOUIS. "Urbanism as a Way of Life," *American Journal of Sociology,* 44 (1938), 1-24.

YOUMANS, E. GRANT. *Aging Patterns in a Rural and an Urban Area of Kentucky.* Lexington, Ky.: University of Kentucky Agricultural Experiment Station, Bulletin 681, 1963.

INDEX

Achievement orientation, *see* Economic motives and values
Affection between kin, 5
  measurement of, 14
  See also Cousins; Parents; Siblings
Affines, 18, 211
Age-near siblings, *see* Siblings, age-near
Aiken, Michael T., viii
Albrecht, Ruth, 50
Anthropology, *see* Kinship, in anthropology
Anticipatory socialization, 59
Articulation, *see* Kinship and other societal systems
Ascending kin, 103, 134, 152, 160, 211
Aspirations
  role of parents in, 29, 41, 185n
  studies of, 41, 185n
  See also Socialization
Aunts and uncles, 13, 156-157
  as socializers of nephew or niece, 136
  compared to other secondary kin, 134, 150, 152, 166
Axelrod, Morris, 50, 51, 177

Baby sitting, 14
Bendix, Reinhard, 25, 64, 76, 80
Berger, Bennett, 64, 76, 80
Bilaterality, 2, 4, 135, 179n
  predominance among middle-class males, 139
Blitsten, Dorothy, 103, 133
Blumer, Herbert, 64, 83
Boot-strap hypothesis of occupational mobility, 90
Bott, Elizabeth, 8, 28, 34, 42, 97, 116, 120, 124, 146, 150, 157
Bowerman, Charles E., viii, 116

Bronfenbrenner, Urie, 58
Burchinal, Lee, 46, 50, 79, 98, 133

Campbell, Don, viii
Caplow, Theodore, 95
Carroll, Eleanor E., 66, 67
Chicago school of sociology, 2, 177
Choice in kinship, 2, 103
  cousins, 137-138, 155
  parents, 39, 71, 74, 76
  secondary kin, 136
  siblings, 110, 112
Classical urban theory, 2, 179n
  comparative and historical character of, 3, 177
Codere, Helen, 133, 142, 156, 157, 159
Combination opportunities, 129-131, 145
Communication, 1, 2, 8, 211
  by letter, 7, 14, 45-47, 98, 100, 185-186n
  by telephone, 7, 14, 45-47, 98, 100
  measurement of, 13
  See also Contact; Cousins; Parents; Siblings
Comparative reference group
  kin as, 5, 21, 123
  siblings as, 116-119, 164
  See also Status gain and deference
Computer Center, University of Wisconsin, viii
Consanguineal kin, 18, 26
Contact, 183n, 211
  between cousins, 142-153
  between kin, 2
  kinds of, 2, 4, 8, 181n
    comparative importance of, 50
  measurement of, 14, 52
  occasions for, 4-5

221